# 100 HIKES in™

# NEW MEXICO

## SECOND EDITION

# 100 HIKES in™

# NEW MEXICO
## SECOND EDITON

## Craig Martin

THE MOUNTAINEERS BOOKS

*For June, still my favorite hiking companion*

Published by
The Mountaineers Books
1001 SW Klickitat Way, Suite 201
Seattle, WA 98134

© 2001 by Craig Martin

First edition, 1995. Second edition, 2001.
Previously published as 75 *Hikes in New Mexico*

Published simultaneously in Great Britain by Cordee, 3a DeMontfort Street, Leicester, England, LE1 7HD

Manufactured in the United States of America

Project Editor: Julie Van Pelt
Editor: Erin Moore
Cover and Book Design: The Mountaineers Books
Layout: Mayumi Thompson
Mapmaker: Craig Martin
Photographer: Craig Martin unless otherwise noted

Cover photograph: *Chimney Rock*
Frontispiece: *Volcanic cliffs along the Middle Fork of the Gila River*

*Library of Congress Cataloging-in-Publication Data*
Martin, Craig, 1952-
  100 hikes in New Mexico / by Craig Martin.— 2nd ed.
    p. cm.
Rev. ed. of: 75 hikes in New Mexico. c1995.
Includes bibliographical references and index.
  ISBN 0-89886-790-8 (pbk.)
  1. Hiking—New Mexico—Guidebooks. 2. New Mexico—Guidebooks. I.
Title: One hundred hikes in New Mexico. II. Martin, Craig, 1952-
75 hikes in New Mexico. III. Title.
  GV199.42.N6 M37 2001
  917.8904'54—dc21
                              2001005253

 Printed on recycled paper

# CONTENTS

## NORTHWEST PLATEAU AND ZUNI MOUNTAINS

## CENTRAL MOUNTAINS

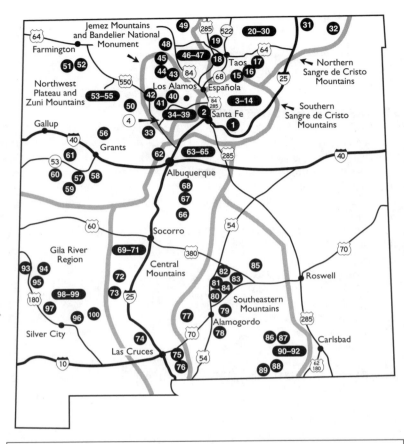

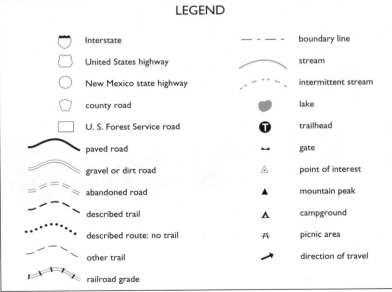

## LEGEND

| | |
|---|---|
| Interstate | boundary line |
| United States highway | stream |
| New Mexico state highway | intermittent stream |
| county road | lake |
| U. S. Forest Service road | trailhead |
| paved road | gate |
| gravel or dirt road | point of interest |
| abandoned road | mountain peak |
| described trail | campground |
| described route: no trail | picnic area |
| other trail | direction of travel |
| railroad grade | |

# INTRODUCTION

Like a richly colorful Navajo rug, New Mexico is a blend of vibrant, dissimilar peoples woven into a unique cultural fabric. Native Americans have lived in large, permanent villages in the high desert for 1,200 years and continue to live in traditional pueblos. The Spanish were the first Europeans to settle the high deserts along the Rio Grande, and Spanish and Mexican cultures still play a dominant role in the state. Anglo-Americans arrived in the mid-nineteenth century, and in many places in the state they remain the minority.

New Mexico's landscape is similarly diverse and contrasting in geology and biogeography. The southern half of the state meets most tourists' expectations of the Southwest: broad desert valleys separating rock-pile mountains. Many are surprised to find that the Rocky Mountains extend into New Mexico, such that the north-central region is dominated by snow-covered peaks. Strangely eroded badlands, recent lava flows, shimmering dune fields, and rugged river gorges are all part of the natural tapestry of the state.

The rolling hills of the Great Plains extend into the eastern third of New Mexico. Covered with a sea of grass, this part of the state is home to extensive, private ranches. Little public land and thus few hiking opportunities are afforded by this pattern of land ownership. Public lands—national

*Red columbines bloom in the northern mountains from late May through June.*

forests, Bureau of Land Management holdings, national parks, and national monuments—are concentrated in the mountainous central and western thirds of the state. This book focuses on the wide diversity of trails found on public lands within New Mexico's mountains.

Alpenglow—sunset's pink wash over the snowcapped peaks of the high mountains—has given a morbid but appropriately spiritual name to the southernmost range of the Rocky Mountains, the Sangre de Cristo. The flanks of the range were settled by Spaniards around the start of the seventeenth century, years before the better-known colonies on the shores of the Atlantic Ocean at Jamestown and Plymouth. Driven by religious zealotry—and not a small dose of gold lust—the Spaniards came to the foothills of the Rockies and settled Santa Fe as their capital. On crisp, sparkling winter evenings, the setting sun turned the nearby mountains a pastel red, a regular phenomenon that over the years influenced a switch in the name of the range from the generic Sierra Madre to Sangre de Cristo—the Blood of Christ.

The highest peaks of the Sangre de Cristo Mountains in New Mexico dominate the north-central part of the state. Alpine scenery surrounds Wheeler and the Truchas (trout) Peaks, both above 13,000 feet. The high country extends from the Colorado border to just south of Santa Fe. Much of the range is within the Carson and Santa Fe National Forests, and the high peaks are protected by the Wheeler Peak, Pecos, and Latir Wilderness Areas. Scattered high lakes and tumbling mountain streams are an added attraction, and fishing is excellent in most waters. The scenery may not be as dramatic as the more popular outdoor playgrounds in neighboring Colorado, but New Mexico's alpine terrain is far less crowded.

To the south, the Sandia Mountains leap from the eastern edge of Albuquerque, rising to over 10,000 feet within only 2 horizontal miles from the foothills. The rugged granite cliffs of the Sandia Wilderness create challenging hiking opportunities on the doorstep of the state's largest city.

West of the main chain of the Rockies lie the Jemez Mountains, the remains of a huge volcano that blew out 50 cubic miles of ash in a Mount St. Helens–style explosion. Here one can have the unique experience of hiking for miles inside a long-dormant volcano. The western flank of the Jemez range is broken by deep canyons carved into soft rock. About 700 years ago, the well-watered canyons attracted farmers from the Ancestral Pueblo culture. On the canyon floors and in the juniper woodlands on the mesas, the Ancestral Pueblos built thousands of living quarters, ranging from summer farming huts to five-hundred-room pueblos. Bandelier National Monument protects a large number of these ancient pueblos.

The northwest corner of New Mexico sits atop the Colorado Plateau, home of horizontal sedimentary rocks, striped mesas and buttes, and long vistas. The rock layers here are the same as in better-known localities such as Canyonlands, Arches, and Mesa Verde National Parks. This colorful landscape was also home to the Ancestral Pueblo people, and their abandoned homes are scattered throughout the region, reaching a glorious

*Most cacti have large, waxy flowers like this hedgehog cactus.*

pinnacle in the huge pueblos at Chaco Canyon. On the southern edge of the plateau, recent volcanic activity has created El Malpais—the Badlands—where hikers can roam lava flows, explore lava tubes, and climb small volcanoes.

Below Interstate 40, which cuts east to west across the upper third of the state, the character of New Mexico changes to island mountains surrounded by seas of grasslands and desert plains. In the central region, the Manzano, Magdalena, and San Mateo Mountains rise over 10,000 feet, providing a haven for cool-weather tree species, such as alpine fir, amid the desert. The scattered units of the Lincoln and Cibola National Forests offer miles of hiking within these ranges.

Southern New Mexico is a land of lonesome mountain ranges separated by more than neighborly distances. Between the ranges lie dry desert plains, long fingers of the Chihuahuan Desert reaching up from Mexico. Tough-leaved creosote bush characterizes the monotonous basins, and the foothills of each mountain are adorned with desert rock gardens. Here plants take on strange and wonderful shapes, such as Mickey Mouse–eared prickly pears, dagger agaves, grass-skirted yucca, and spider-legged ocotillo.

Each of the wrinkled mountains rising from the basins has its own unique characteristics. The high peaks of the Sierra Blanca in the southeast part of the state are northern in character, with summits clothed in fir and spruce forest. Indeed, the name Sierra Blanca—White Mountains—comes from the range's annual snowcap, a rare sight in desert latitudes. Along the Rio Grande, the Organ Mountains barely reach 8,000 feet, but their jagged ramparts of granite lend an attractive backdrop to the desert near Las Cruces. To the east, the massive limestone pile of the Guadalupe Mountains is best known for its plentiful and extensive caverns, but on the outside the range is no less interesting. Pygmy forests—stunted by severe and frequent wildfires—cover the range; canyon walls and mountain fronts are composed of repeating layers of gray limestone, thick with the fossil remains of ancient sea life.

In the southwest quarter of New Mexico, high desert mountain ranges are drained by the Gila River, a major tributary of the Colorado River. These dry mountains are part of the state's largest concentration of wilderness. Best known is the Gila Wilderness, the first area in the country to receive such a designation. Nearby, the long Black Range is protected in the Aldo Leopold Wilderness, named in honor of the man who originated the wilderness concept in the Southwest. Good-sized streams flow through the region, and their canyons are ideal for hikers.

## HIKING SAFETY IN THE LAND OF ENCHANTMENT

Hiking in New Mexico is eminently enjoyable if you are well prepared and ready for the unexpected.

### Hike Preparation

Before venturing into the backcountry of New Mexico, consider the possible hazards that may be encountered on the trip. Using a map, become familiar with the terrain. Carefully study the main route and determine quick escape routes for use in an emergency. Obtain a weather forecast for the time of the hike and adjust plans to avoid potentially dangerous storms; always pack adequate foul-weather gear and warm clothing. Before heading out, leave a detailed itinerary with a trusted friend. It is best not to hike alone, but experienced hikers, who plan carefully, do and can enjoy complete solitude in the wilderness.

### Keeping an Eye on the Weather

New Mexico's diversity of landscape and range of elevation creates a climate noted for its extreme variations. Temperatures range from summer highs of over 100 degrees Fahrenheit in the southern desert to winter lows of minus 40 degrees Fahrenheit in the northern mountains. Even within a single day, hikers often find temperature swings exceeding 35 degrees. These conditions make it important for hikers to enter the backcountry prepared for extremes, always carrying an extra layer of warm clothing and raingear.

In general, spring is characterized by a mixed assortment of weather conditions throughout the state, with the one constant being high winds. Mornings are cold and afternoons warm to hot, such that dressing in easily removed layers is advised to ensure a comfortable trip. Cold fronts frequently sweep across the state, dumping wet snow to push spring back into winter. Before starting out on springtime mountain hikes, plan carefully and keep an eye on the weather forecast. In the southern half of the state, spring hiking conditions are usually delightful, but winds and even snow are possible through late April.

In the summer, high temperatures in southern New Mexico preclude comfortable hiking at low elevations, but the southern mountains are pleasant to hike in during the warm months. Summer conditions are often ideal in the northern part of the state, with warm days and cool nights through June. Early to mid-July brings a change as moisture moves in from the south, generating almost daily thunderstorms. The storms are often violent, with high winds, hail, and frequent lightning.

September and October can bring ideal hiking conditions. Blue skies and windless days prevail along with cool days and chilly nights. In the south, these conditions can last until early November. Fall hikers should always ascertain the current weather forecast before starting on a trip. Blustery, fast-moving cold fronts can bring heavy snow to the northern mountains as early as mid-September, although these storms usually wait until mid-October. Each fall, search-and-rescue teams are kept busy by hikers who head unprepared into the backcountry regardless of the forecast.

Mountain trails in the north are closed by snow by late October or mid-November. In the south, mountain trails are often open until December but desert hikes are possible throughout the winter, except when surprisingly cold storms bring wind and snowy conditions for a day or two at a time. Always know the latest weather forecast before any winter trip.

*In the fall, bugling bull elk can be heard in the northern mountains.*

### Lightning, Flash Floods, and Wildfire

Open spaces are no place in which to be caught during a summer thunderstorm: New Mexico ranks second in the nation in number of lightning-caused deaths per year. Plan to be off ridges and peaks before noon. Storms build rapidly, and hikers need to be constantly vigilant of the weather. When caught by an unexpected storm, stay off ridgelines and open mesa tops, and keep out of meadows and away from lone trees or rocks. Seek safety in low ground, in extensive forested areas, or in large caves. When no shelter is available, avoid small caves and shallow depressions. Stow backpacks and other metal objects at least 30 feet away, and use clothing to insulate yourself from the ground. Squat on two feet and keep as low a profile as possible.

A great paradox of hiking in the dry Southwest is the serious threat posed by running water. Precipitation may be rare in the desert, but summer storms can nonetheless produce inordinate amounts of rain in a short time. Water quickly collects in drainages, turning a dry streambed into a raging torrent within minutes. Stay out of dry washes and arroyos during storms, and never set up camp in a dry watercourse. Be aware that a storm in the upper portion of a drainage can send a wall of water down to a sunny, lower portion, so keep an eye on the surrounding weather. Do not

*The Dome Fire scorched 17,000 acres of forest in the Jemez Mountains in 1996.*

try to ford streams filled with flood water. Be patient—high flow rates usually subside in a few hours.

An increasing threat to the landscape and to hikers is wildfire. Records indicate that the past two decades have been unusually wet in the Southwest and that the region is apparently entering the drought portion of its climatic cycle. In addition, grazing, fire suppression, and other factors have created unnaturally dense forests. The result is conditions ripe for uncontrollable fires that jump into the crowns of trees and burn thousands of acres of pine and mixed conifer forest. Thus, hikers need to be extremely careful with fire. Always use a stove to heat water or cook food. Except in emergencies, don't build campfires.

For their own safety, hikers should be aware of prevailing fire conditions during the fire season, which extends from mid-April to at least the onset of the summer rainy season in July. Keep abreast of existing fires that may be near the area of an intended hike by checking fire agency sites on the Internet. When hiking, be aware of smoke and the prevailing wind direction and speed. Fires can spread 10 or more miles in a day under hot, dry, and windy conditions.

## Importance of Water

Along with sunny skies comes a dry climate where water is precious to all living things. Hikers will lose water to temperature regulation, increased respiration, and increased metabolic rates. By the time a hiker feels thirsty, he or she is already a quart low on fluids. Maintaining body fluid balance is a critical part of hiking in New Mexico.

Excessive fluid loss can lead to heat exhaustion, a potentially serious condition; symptoms include reduced perspiration, rapid pulse, dizziness, and general weakness. Hikers with any of these signs should immediately get out of the sun and drink large quantities of water. Without careful attention, heat exhaustion can lead to heat stroke, a much more dangerous condition characterized by no perspiration, hot skin, and a high body temperature. These signs indicate a medical emergency requiring urgent attention. First aid is an immediate reduction of body temperature by moving to a cool location, increasing fluid intake, and applying cool compresses to the skin.

Heat-related medical problems can be avoided by drinking plenty of water before starting out on a hike and then drinking regularly during the trip. Plan on at least a half-gallon of fluid per person per day for day hikes and a gallon per person per day for overnight trips. For day trips, a hydration system with a 100-ounce bladder is ideal.

## Protection from the Sun

The near-constant blue skies of the high desert are no myth, but there is a price to pay. Skin cancer rates are high in the Southwest, and visitors and natives alike must take precautions against too much of a good thing.

Summer and winter, hikers must protect themselves from the sun. The best protection is a long-sleeved shirt and long pants, even in summer. Light colors will help reflect the intense summer sun, and a loose fit will help keep hikers cool. Wide-brimmed hats are standard equipment all year long. Additional protection for the eyes is provided by high-quality sunglasses that screen at least 95 percent of the ultraviolet radiation.

In addition to protective clothing, hikers should use copious sunscreen. Apply an SPF 15 or higher formula at least every 4 hours. Sweatproof types of sunscreen now available stay on well during exercise. For full protection, coat hands, neck, face, and ears.

### Elevation Factors

Many mountain trails in New Mexico lead to elevations above 8,000 feet. Out-of-state hikers unaccustomed to altitude can often avoid problems with high elevations by allowing at least 2 days to acclimate at a mid-range elevation before attempting a hike above 9,000 feet. Thin air increases exertion and visitors should slow down to a comfortable pace, which may be considerably slower than their normal hiking speed. Quick ascents above 10,000 feet can lead to a variety of medical problems, such as mountain sickness. Symptoms include headache, nausea, weakness, and general achiness. Problems usually disappear with a return to lower elevations, but if symptoms persist, medical attention is required.

### Critter Complications

Eight species of rattlesnake reside within the borders of New Mexico, and at least one type is found in all habitats ranging from lowland deserts to conifer forest. In the north, most rattlesnakes are found below 7,000 feet, but they are occasionally spotted up to 9,000 feet. In the southern part of the state, rattlesnakes are common at all elevations up to 10,000 feet.

Rattlers hibernate during the winter months and into May in the north. In summer, they avoid hot sunshine and are generally encountered at night. Use caution and a flashlight when hiking at dusk or at night. Rattlers are most active in the daytime during spring and fall. Snakes will be found sunning on ledges or in the partial shade of trees. Hikers can avoid rattlesnakes by staying on the trail and always watching their footing. Most bites occur below the knee, and high-top boots and long pants afford some protection from snakes. Off the trail, never place your hand on a ledge above your head. The buzzing rattle of the snakes is an effective warning of their presence, although many a hiker has unknowingly stepped directly over rattlers, hidden behind rocks or logs in the trail.

Although the once-common grizzly bear is no longer found here, black bears are common inhabitants of all forested mountain ranges in New Mexico. Bear encounters are infrequent, but increase during dry summers. A bear spotted along a trail will usually turn tail and be quickly gone. Hikers who encounter a bear should make the bear aware of their presence by

*Like this gopher snake, most wildlife encountered on New Mexico trails are harmless, but hikers should remain on the lookout for rattlesnakes.*

talking in conversational tones, and make certain not to get between a mother and her cubs. In camp, it is good practice to tie food or items that smell like food such as toothpaste in a tree at least 10 feet off the ground and 4 feet from the trunk. This will also protect your camp from other wild critters. If a bear does get food or equipment, do not attempt to take it away.

Scorpions range throughout New Mexico and are most common in the southern half of the state. New Mexican species are not deadly and have stings similar to that of bees. Scorpions hide under rocks and tree bark during the day, coming out at night to prey on insects. Their secretive habits make them easy to avoid; most hikers will never see one. Because scorpions seek damp, dark places, it is, however, a good idea for backpackers to shake out clothing and check shoes and boots before putting them on in the morning.

Bothersome insects are pleasantly absent from most parts of New Mexico, but two kinds of arthropods found here carry serious diseases and should be avoided. Tall grasses are home to ticks, which are most abundant in spring and early summer. Although Lyme disease has not yet been found to originate in New Mexico, it may arrive soon. Ticks do carry Rocky Mountain spotted fever and Colorado tick fever. Symptoms for both are flu-like. Check for ticks after each trip. Check your animals, too. If any are found, remove them with tweezers, and for several weeks, watch for signs of illness.

More serious in nature is the presence of bubonic plague. This life-threatening disease is carried by fleas living on host animals. Thus, it is important to avoid contact with wild animals, particularly members of the rodent family, dead or alive. Camp away from animal burrows. After an outdoor trip in New Mexico, anyone with high fever and swelling in the armpits and groin—particularly visitors who have returned home where plague is not known to occur—should alert physicians to the possibility of plague.

Hantavirus is another life-threatening disease found not only in New Mexico but throughout the world. Carried by the deer mouse, hantavirus is a serious respiratory illness. Humans primarily contract this disease by inhaling dried mouse urine or saliva that is carried on particles in the air when the rodent's habitat is disturbed; but it can also be transmitted through ingestion of contaminated food or water. Flu-like symptoms—fever, headache, rapid breathing, and cough—are followed by a rapid increase of fluid in the lungs. Half of all cases end in death. Avoid hantavirus by avoiding rodent-infested areas and by taking a few simple precautions. Backpackers should use a tent with a floor and pitch it on a campsite away from rodent burrows. Store food in sealed containers and off the ground. Be particularly vigilant during years following a large piñon nut crop, because rodent populations will also be high at this time.

## WHAT TO BRING ALONG

Preparation is often the difference between an enjoyable outdoor excursion and a disaster. Careful planning for all hikes, no matter what distance, is important for the safety of all hikers. An excellent starting place for loading a pack is the list of the Ten Essentials from The Mountaineers:

1. Extra clothing
2. Extra food
3. Sun protection, including sunglasses
4. Pocketknife
5. Firestarter candle or chemical fuel
6. First-aid kit and snakebite kit
7. Matches in a waterproof container
8. Flashlight
9. Map
10. Compass

### Clothing

Hikers in New Mexico are likely to encounter a wide range of temperatures during the course of a day. To meet the challenges of weather, always dress in layers. In cool seasons—spring and fall—begin with a zipper-neck shirt made from a moisture-wicking synthetic material. Synthetic-material tights or nylon pants are also suitable for this time of year. For an insulating layer, a light- or mid-weight fleece jacket or pullover is an excellent choice. When it is colder, fleece pants are warm and offer good protection even when wet.

Proper dress is important in summer, too, when low temperatures and rain or even snow are always possible at high elevations. Wear a long-sleeved shirt and long pants made of light synthetic. For an overnight trip, add a light fleece jacket and pants. Carry extra, warm clothing, even in July and August.

In all seasons, carry raingear. Getting wet is the most serious threat to backcountry hikers, because a drenching from a storm can quickly lead to hypothermia. Anticipate summer showers every afternoon by carrying a rain jacket and pants. Waterproof outer layers are even more important in spring and fall when temperatures can quickly drop to dangerous levels. Breathable, waterproof materials are best, allowing hikers to stay cool even in summer.

Footgear is an important part of hiking equipment. Sturdy, lightweight boots are best for comfort and help reduce erosion to the trail. Because of the dry climate, light-duty boots with fabric and leather uppers are adequate for much of the hiking in New Mexico. These are generally a few ounces lighter and are cooler than other boots, but they often lack good waterproofing. For mountain hiking, especially during the summer rainy season, waterproof boots with full leather or synthetic uppers are recommended. Heavy boots also offer additional protection on rough, rocky trails. Proper socks can also add to comfort. A combination of thin liner socks with thicker synthetic or wool padded outer socks works best.

## Maps and Navigation

A good state map will lead you to the vicinity of the trailhead. Pick one up at one of the tourist information centers around the state, or call the New Mexico Tourism Division (see "Sources of Additional Information" in the back of this book). Maps of the state's five national forests will be helpful in locating most trailheads and are available for a moderate fee from the Forest Supervisor offices, also listed at the end of this book.

The outline maps included with each hike in this book are meant as general guides and, particularly for longer hikes into the backcountry, should not take the place of large-scale maps. Nothing can substitute for the most recent United States Geological Survey (USGS) 7.5-minute quadrangle maps. The maps required for each hike are listed in the summary block at the start of each hike. Topographic maps are available at many retail outdoor outfitters around the state, and directly from the USGS at their Western Distribution Branch (see "Sources of Additional Information").

Digital maps allow for detailed trip planning. They permit accurate determination of distances; the selection of predetermined, low-impact campsites; and an estimate of exertion level based on elevation gain and grade. Mapping software will also allow creation of customized maps for any trip. For cross-country explorations, digital maps are used to feed data to GPS receivers to keep hikers on course. Excellent digital coverage of New Mexico is available from several manufacturers.

The latest generation of GPS receivers offers another dimension of safety for hiking in the backcountry. In conjunction with topographic maps, GPS units help hikers accurately determine their location within a few tens of feet.

## Water

The importance of water to hikers in New Mexico cannot be overstated. Low humidity, high temperatures, and high elevation combine to create conditions that require hikers to carry at least a half gallon of water per person for a day hike and at least a gallon per person per day for an overnight trip. Always keep an emergency supply of water in the support vehicle.

Hikers should bring all the water they need on day trips, but carrying sufficient water for an extended stay in the mountains is difficult. Plan to camp near water. All water taken from backcountry sources must be treated before use. Cattle often graze in the backcountry and share water sources with hikers. Giardia, a protozoan parasite that causes an unpleasant and potentially serious intestinal disorder, is present throughout the state.

The safest method of treating water is to boil it vigorously for 10 minutes. Because water boils at a lower temperature at high altitude, boiling time must be increased above 7,000 feet. Chemical treatment with chlorine or hyperiodide tablets is an easy method of water treatment. Mechanical filters can treat large volumes of water in a short time, but they vary in efficiency. For the safest results, use a filter with a 0.02-micron screen.

## RESPONSIBLE HIKING

As in most states, visiting New Mexico's backcountry comes with certain responsibilities that, when carried out, assure continued protection of and access to the state's wild areas.

### Private Land

Complicated land ownership laws dating back to the days of Spanish rule and the abundance of mining claims have left New Mexico checkered with pockets of private land within public use areas. As a result, eleven of the hikes in this book pass through private land and many other trips pass close to private property. To avoid problems with landowners, note the boundaries of public land on the hike maps and obey all No Trespassing signs.

Five hikes cross private land on public easements negotiated by the Forest Service or the Bureau of Land Management: Atalaya Mountain (Hike 1), Lobo Peak (Hike 20), Broad Canyon (Hike 74), Willie White Canyon (Hike 79), and Devils Den Canyon (Hike 89). In addition, four hikes require crossing private land to access the trailhead: Glorieta Baldy (Hike 9), Williams Lake (Hike 21), Petroglyph National Monument (Hike 62), and South Sandia Peak (Hike 65). In each case, hikers are permitted to cross private land on the trail or road. Do not stray from the designated pathway, though, and leave all gates as they are found. These easements are the result of the landowners' generosity, and their continuance is dependent upon courteous and respectful use by hikers. Landowners can close access through their property at any time. Before starting out on one of these hikes, check with the managing agency on the current status of the easement.

For the Kitchen Mesa (Hike 46), and Box Canyon and Mesa Montosa (Hike 47) trips, permission to hike must be obtained at the Ghost Ranch Office, as detailed in the hike descriptions.

## Minimum Impact Use

Before the explosion of wilderness use over the last 30 years, hikers gave little thought to what they did or left behind in the backcountry. But with increasing numbers of wilderness users, it has become necessary for each hiker to consider the impact that his or her trip has on the trail, the environment, and other trail users. Current thinking is best expressed by the phrase, "leave no trace." All hikers should carefully plan how they can minimize their impact on the outdoors while still enjoying the wilderness experience.

Minimum impact use goes far beyond common sense. All hikers should carefully study the ways they can become clean users of the backcountry and develop an attitude that every user shares responsibility to leave the wilderness in its pristine condition. The following suggestions are based on Leave No Trace materials developed by the National Outdoor Leadership School, the Bureau of Land Management, the National Park Service, and the United States Forest Service:

**At home.** Minimum impact hiking begins at home with careful planning. A well-thought-out trip reduces the potential for a damaging and costly search-and-rescue operation. Carry a map and compass, and know how to use them to stay on the planned route as well as to determine location when lost. Before starting a trip, hikers should leave a detailed itinerary of their trip with a knowledgeable friend. Also, reduce waste before hiking by repacking food in reusable containers that will not be inadvertently left behind.

**On the trail.** When hiking, be considerate of other trail users. Hike quietly, and rest off the trail on rocks or other durable surfaces that will not show signs of trampling.

Trails and the surrounding terrain can be easily damaged. On established trails, hike single file to avoid widening the tread. On muddy stretches of trail, hike in the established tread to avoid creating new tracks. Do not shortcut switchbacks, a practice that leads quickly to severe trail erosion. When hiking on routes with no established trail, hike abreast to avoid repetitive trampling of vegetation, and step on rock or sand whenever possible.

**In camp.** Select a campsite that already has distinct signs of use or one in an area that will not be damaged. Locate sites at least 200 feet from water and trails, with the distance increased to a minimum of 300 feet in deserts. In river canyons, camp on sandy beaches or gravel bars below the high-water line. The best campsites are also away from and out of view of other campers.

Most packaging material will not burn completely, so pack out all trash and all uneaten food. Buried food will soon be discovered and excavated by animals, increasing their dependence on unnatural food sources.

Minimize the impact of campfires by cooking with a backpacking stove. When building a campfire, use existing fire rings or a metal firepan and burn only small-diameter dead and down wood. Before leaving, make certain the fire is out, then remove the cold ashes from the ring and scatter them away from camp. Dry washes and sand or gravel stream banks below the high-water line make good locations for pit fires. To remove signs of a pit fire, scatter the remains, then fill in the hole. In desert areas, the small amounts of dead wood available are important to the ecosystem and should not be used for fires. Carry in all firewood or go without.

Human waste is best disposed in a "cat" hole at least 6 inches deep, placed at least 200 feet from camp and the nearest water. After use, cover the hole with natural materials. Do *not* bury toilet paper with the waste; pack it out. When cleaning cooking utensils, use only a small amount of biodegradable soap. Remove and pack out food particles. Dishwater should be broadcast over a wide area away from camp and water sources. In desert areas, hikers should increase the distance of all waste from water sources to 300 feet.

In narrow river canyons, special precautions must be taken. In silty rivers with large flow volumes, urine and waste water can be dumped into the flow; the large volume will dilute the waste. In mountain canyons with low flows, urinate on the banks below the high-water line to allow some filtration before the waste reaches the clear stream. Human waste should be packed out of narrow canyons or left in holes well away from the main or side streams.

For more detailed information on how to reduce user impacts on the wilderness, contact Leave No Trace (see "Sources of Additional Information").

## SELECTING A HIKE

This book holds an eclectic collection of hikes. Trips in several categories were selected. Hikes judged to be New Mexico classics—ones that most resident hikers as well as hikers who visit the state will want take—are of course included. The climb to the summit of Wheeler Peak is one such classic; hikes through the blazing reds of autumn in Fourth of July Canyon and across the shimmering dunes at White Sands are other examples. Also included are a large number of hikes in out-of-the-way places that see few visitors. Trips to Valle Vidal, Sawmill Park, Navajo Peak, Three Rivers Canyon, Vicks Peak, and many others fall into this category. Other locations are little known and deserve recognition, such as the Three Rivers Petroglyph Site, the Rim Vista Trail, and the Cruces Basin Wilderness. Personal favorites of mine are hikes with a special historic or natural history focus. Hikers on Barranca Hill, in Chaco Canyon, on the Catwalk, and on Cerro Americano will find a wealth of historic or geologic features that make these true explorations rather than simple hikes.

In most instances, hikers will find clusters of three or more hikes listed for a given mountain range or canyon. The clusters were designed to provide a full weekend of hiking opportunities with a minimal amount of driving.

Throughout this book, five abbreviations are used in connection with roads. Interstate highways are designated with I, United States highways with US, New Mexico state highways with NM, county roads with CR, and Forest Service roads with FR.

Use the summary table at the beginning of each hike description to select a hike honestly suited to your skills. Hikers unaccustomed to walking at elevation should look carefully at the hike distance and elevation range and gain. Visitors should wait several days before tackling trips over 8 miles long or with more than 2,000 feet of elevation gain.

The summary block for each hike provides the following information:

**Distance.** Unless otherwise noted, the distances given are for round trips. Hike distances were estimated from field data, information provided by the managing agency, and from careful measurement on topographic maps. This method has its shortcomings, and hikers may find stated distances are as much as 20 percent in error.

**Difficulty.** A subjective evaluation of exertion level required for each hike, biased toward casual hikers and those unaccustomed to elevation. Ratings used are easy, moderate, difficult, and strenuous.

Easy hikes have little elevation gain (usually less than 500 feet) on easy-to-follow trails that traverse relatively flat terrain. These trips are suitable for visitors coming from lower elevations, for novice hikers, and for families. Moderate hikes are typically between 4 and 10 miles long, involve climbing between 500 and 1,500 feet, and exhibit some steep sections. Difficult trails include those with long, steep sections that gain more than 1,500 feet, and usually cover more than 10 miles; however, shorter trails that traverse rough surfaces may be rated as difficult. Trips that require sus-

*Petroglyphs on a horizontal surface are unusual.*

tained climbing to gain more than 2,000 feet of elevation, or those that cover long distances above 9,000 feet, are rated as strenuous and should be attempted by strong and experienced hikers only.

**Elevation range.** The highest and lowest points of the hike.

**Elevation gain.** The cumulative elevation gain for the route as described, including all ascents, as determined with a recording altimeter.

**Best time of year.** The best months to take each hike, based on an average year, which rarely occurs. The weather in New Mexico is notoriously variable, and hikers should always consult the latest weather forecast before starting out on a trip.

**Water.** The location of potential drinking water along the route. When possible, hikers should carry enough water for the entire hike and not depend on nature to provide a safe and adequate supply. Remember that all water should be treated before use.

**Maps.** The best available maps for the hike; all USGS maps listed are 7.5-minute quadrangles.

**Managed by.** The landowner or managing agency for each hike, who to contact for more or up-to-date information. A list of addresses and telephone numbers is given in Sources of Additional Information at the end of this book.

**Features.** The attractions that make each hike worthy of the reader's attention.

### A NOTE ABOUT SAFETY

Safety is an important concern in all outdoor activities. No guidebook can alert you to every hazard or anticipate the limitations of every reader. Therefore, the descriptions of roads, trails, routes, and natural features in this book are not representations that a particular place or excursion will be safe for your party. When you follow any of the routes described in this book, you assume responsibility for your own safety. Under normal conditions, such excursions require the usual attention to traffic, road and trail conditions, weather, terrain, the capabilities of your party, and other factors. Because many of the lands in this book are subject to development and/or change of ownership, conditions may have changed since this book was written that make your use of some of these routes unwise. Always check for current conditions, obey posted private property signs, and avoid confrontations with property owners or managers. Keeping informed on current conditions and exercising common sense are the keys to a safe, enjoyable outing.

*The Mountaineers Books*

*Facing page: Winter hiking to a frozen waterfall in the southern Sangre de Cristo Mountains*

# SOUTHERN SANGRE DE CRISTO MOUNTAINS

# 1 ┃ ATALAYA MOUNTAIN

**Distance: 9 miles, day hike**
**Difficulty:** difficult
**Elevation range:** 7,300 to 9,100 feet
**Elevation gain:** 1,800 feet
**Best time of year:** April to November
**Water:** carry water
**Map:** USGS Santa Fe
**Managed by:** Santa Fe National Forest, Española Ranger
   District
**Features:** views of Santa Fe, trailhead close to town

A climb to the top of Atalaya Mountain on the outskirts of Santa Fe provides hikers with a unique view of the old city. The steep but pleasant trail leads through shady conifer forest to the summit. Santa Fe, with its historic plaza and sprawling new growth, spreads out below. A couple hours on this trail can be a welcome relief from the usual tourist fare in Santa Fe. Be watchful on weekends, when this trail may receive moderate use by mountain bikers.

To reach the trailhead from the intersection of Cerrillos Road and St. Francis Drive in Santa Fe, go south on St. Francis 0.2 mile and turn left onto Cordova Road. Continue 1.5 miles, passing Old Pecos Trail where the name of Cordova Road changes to Armenta Street. At a T intersection, turn left onto Camino Corrales. Cross Old Santa Fe Trail, then bear right onto Garcia Street. At another T intersection, turn right onto Camino del Monte Sol. Almost immediately, turn left onto Camino de Cruz Blanca, which is signed for St. Johns College. Turn right (south) at the entrance to St. Johns in 0.6

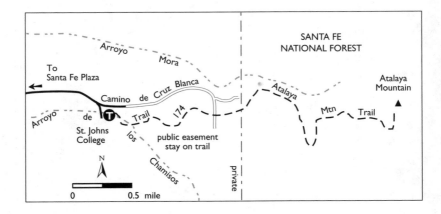

*Mushrooms growing in the lush forests of the Sangre de Cristos*

mile and park in the lot near the entrance at the signs marking the Atalaya Mountain Trailhead.

Walk east as Trail 174 winds through junipers along the edge of the Arroyo de los Chamisos. After dropping into the arroyo, watch for signs marking the trail, which soon exits the east (left) side of the streambed to enter a narrow side canyon. The winding path leads along an easement through private land; stay on the trail in this section. At mile 0.9, cross a road and continue straight. On top of a low ridge at mile 1.4, intersect Trail 170, an alternate branch of the Atalaya Mountain Trail. Bear right onto a wider trail as it contours around the southwest slope of a ridge through tall ponderosa pines.

After reaching the nose of a spur ridge, the trail swings left and begins to climb. Grades are steep from here to the summit of Atalaya Mountain, which is visible to the right. Where an old, deeply eroded route continues steeply straight ahead, turn right onto a more gentle, but still steep, trail. Climb across a steep slope to reach the ridgeline at mile 2.5. Turn left and continue 0.4 mile to the summit where a reward of fine views of the city of Santa Fe and the Jemez Mountains awaits. After enjoying the view, turn around and descend by the same route.

## 2 | CAJA DEL RIO CANYON

**Distance: 6 miles, day hike**
**Difficulty:** easy
**Elevation range:** 5,450 to 5,850 feet
**Elevation gain:** 400 feet
**Best time of year:** September to May
**Water:** carry water
**Map:** USGS White Rock
**Managed by:** Santa Fe National Forest, Española Ranger District
**Features:** spectacular small canyon in a volcano, scenic views, the Rio Grande

The trailless route along Cañada Ancha through Caja del Rio Canyon leads through a small volcano. Locally, this canyon is called Diablo, and the devil had some fun here slicing a narrow cut through six-sided columns of hard basalt. The route follows a wash into the depths of White Rock Canyon and to the Rio Grande, reaching the river near the site of Buckman, a railhead for logging operations on the nearby mesas during the 1920s. Several deep caves are located on the volcanic slopes, but the sheer drops below the entrances dictate that hikers stay out.

From the intersection of Cerrillos Road and St. Francis Drive (US 84/285) in Santa Fe, go north on St. Francis about 2.5 miles to the NM 599 exit. Head west on NM 599, which is also known as the Santa Fe Bypass. In 3.6 miles, turn right onto Camino de la Tierra. In 0.8 mile, continue straight at a stop sign. At 2.3 miles from NM 599, bear left to stay on Camino de la Tierra at the entrance to the Las Campanas Clubhouse. The pavement ends at mile 3.9. This all-weather road is passable to all vehicles when dry. Eight

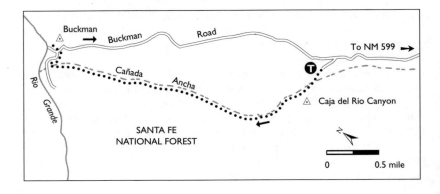

*The Cañada Ancha sliced through a small volcano to form Caja del Rio Canyon.*

miles from NM 599, bear left onto a track heading down to Cañada Ancha and park in the large open area near the wash.

Walk toward the slash in the rock wall by crossing a fence and walking down the bottom of Cañada Ancha. The wash soon enters the narrow canyon below soaring towers of brown basalt. To the right, the walls of the canyon are made of intricate patterns of cooled lava; the left side is a jumble of house-sized boulders that have crashed down from the cliffs above. Farther along, a streak of orange soil on the wall shows where lava scorched the ground as it flowed over the surface about a million years ago. Hikers may be torn by conflicting desires to linger and enjoy this unique spot and to hustle to avoid being caught in a rockfall.

Toward the end of the narrows, a spring adds a trickle of water to the scene. Emerge from the narrow canyon to walk down a broad wash. To the right, views of the cliffs paint a detailed picture of the workings of a small volcano, with tilted and twisted layers of rock and a variety of colors and rock types. Continue downstream and enjoy the expanding view, which soon encompasses Otowi Peak, another small volcano straight ahead, and the airfall volcanic deposits of the Pajarito Plateau across the river. At about mile 1.7, the wash angles toward the northwest.

Cañada Ancha continues to widen. About 3 miles from the start, just before reaching the Rio Grande, intersect a dirt road that crosses the wash. Turn right onto the road and continue another 0.25 mile to intersect a road/ arroyo combination in a thicket of tamarisk. Turn left and walk a few yards to the Rio Grande and the site of Buckman. Nothing remains of the bridge and buildings once found here, but across the river, Buckman Road can be seen winding up the orange cliffs.

To return, either backtrack up Cañada Ancha, or to avoid trudging up the sand, walk up Buckman Road to the trailhead.

# 3 | BIG TESUQUE/BEAR WALLOW LOOP

**Distance: 8 miles, day hike**
**Difficulty:** moderate
**Elevation range:** 8,300 to 9,700 feet
**Elevation gain:** 1,400 feet
**Best time of year:** April to early November
**Water:** Tesuque Creek
**Map:** USGS Aspen Vista
**Managed by:** Santa Fe National Forest, Española Ranger District
**Features:** shady conifer forest, aspen stands, flowing water, wildflowers in summer

The Big Tesuque Trail is the forgotten link in the extensive trail system on the west face of the Sangre de Cristo Mountains near Santa Fe. Hikers flock to nearby trails, but Big Tesuque is usually an excellent choice for a walk in solitude. This loop, which is a variation of the popular Bear Wallow Tri-angle hike, is delightful in midsummer when wildflowers dot the mead-

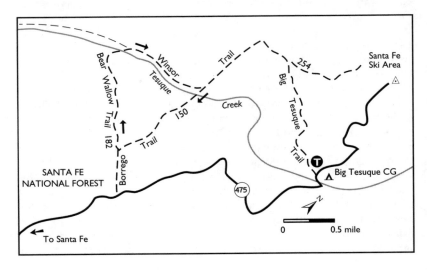

ows or in fall when the canyon slopes become golden with turning aspen leaves. The aspens, colonizers of the forest following fire, are evidence of the crucial role wildfires play in maintaining the forest mosaic in the Sangre de Cristo Mountains. The huge aspens along the trail date from fires in the early decades of the twentieth century.

The trail starts directly across NM 475 from Big Tesuque Campground on the north side of Tesuque Creek. Reach the trailhead from the Santa Fe Plaza by taking Washington Avenue north 0.5 mile to Artist Road, also identified as NM 475. Turn right onto NM 475 and head toward the Santa Fe Ski Area, noting your mileage. Big Tesuque Campground is on the right (east) side of the road in 11.7 miles.

From the parking area, carefully walk across NM 475 and pick up the well-worn path that dives from the road and heads toward Big Tesuque Creek. Reach the creek and angle downstream. Two hundred yards from the trailhead, bear right and climb above the stream as it cuts across an aspen-dotted meadow. The trail is soon out of earshot of the stream and swings along a minor drainage. Pass through a hikers gate and into a second meadow, which reaches a colorful maximum of wildflowers in early July. For the next mile, the trail contours in and out of side canyons under stately Douglas fir and shimmering aspen. The thick canopy occasionally opens to offer views down into the surprisingly deep canyon of Tesuque Creek.

About 1.5 miles from the trail's start, intersect the Winsor Trail 254. Turn left and follow the trail along a saddle, then follow the tread as it descends steeply to the left (south). In a minute, take the left fork that climbs slightly then contours around a hill. When the trail reaches the next major drainage, it heads left and descends toward Tesuque Creek. The trail drops through a second-growth mixed forest with Douglas fir, ponderosa and limber pine, and broad-leafed maple and Gambel oak, with a liberal dash of aspen.

Shortly before reaching Tesuque Creek, angle left onto the Borrego Trail 150. After 100 yards, cross the stream on a log bridge. Continue the easy climb over a low ridge, first along a small drainage, then up two gentle switchbacks. About 4 miles from the start, reach the top of a saddle and drop steeply for about two hundred yards. At the next intersection, angle sharply right and descend the Bear Wallow Trail 182 toward Tesuque Creek. The trail crosses the drainage several times before climbing up the north wall of the deepening canyon. After 0.75 mile on Trail 182, the route goes over a rocky slope. The sound of rushing water rushes up as the trail turns sharply around the nose of a ridge and descends two switchbacks to meet Tesuque Creek.

Cross the small stream on a log bridge and again intersect the Winsor Trail. Turn right and begin the ascent along the creek. Over the next mile, an abundance of delightful lunch spots can be found between the trail and the stream.

The Winsor Trail climbs continually with a few steep, rocky sections. After about a mile of climbing, arrive again at the junction with the Borrego

*Big Tesuque Creek near the trailhead*

Trail. Turn left to retrace the route up the Winsor Trail to the Big Tesuque Trail, and from there back to the trailhead.

# 4  ASPEN RANCH LOOP

**Distance: 8 miles, day hike or backpack**
**Difficulty:** difficult
**Elevation range:** 8,900 to 10,200 feet
**Elevation gain:** 1,600 feet
**Best time of year:** late May to mid-October
**Water:** Rio en Medio
**Map:** USGS Aspen Basin
**Managed by:** Santa Fe National Forest, Española Ranger District
**Features:** high-country scenery, fall aspens, picturesque stream

The Aspen Ranch Loop is a scenic hike through the high country of the Sangre de Cristos near Santa Fe. The trip offers miles of pleasant walking on shaded slopes, views of large aspen stands, and a steep climb along a cascading stream. On a smaller scale, hikers will find thousands of summer wildflowers along the route as well as intricate swirling patterns in the banded gneiss at trailside. Take along a fishing rod and try for some of the small trout found in the deep pools of the Rio en Medio. These trails are uncrowded, but on weekends, watch out for mountain bikers on the Winsor Trail.

From Santa Fe, take Washington Avenue north from Paseo de Peralta 0.1 mile to Artist Road, NM 475. Turn right and head toward the Santa Fe Ski Area. Continue about 14 miles to the parking area at the ski basin. Park at the Winsor Trailhead at the northwest corner of the lot near an information kiosk.

Begin walking south on the Winsor Trail 254. Immediately cross a bridge and turn left to parallel a small stream. In 0.2 mile, pass through a fence into an impressive blowdown of huge trees and continue to descend to the intersection with the Rio en Medio Trail 163. Turn left to stay on the Winsor Trail; the loop returns to this point at the end of the hike via the Rio en Medio Trail. The Winsor Trail crosses the Rio en Medio, then crosses several smaller, usually dry drainages as it heads southwest.

About a mile from the start, the Winsor Trail reaches a parking area and cross-country ski trail along NM 475. Cross the parking area and pick up the Winsor Trail at a small sign near the road, then descend a series of switchbacks. After crossing a small drainage, begin a long, pleasant stroll as the trail contours along the side of a branch canyon of Tesuque Creek. At mile 2.2, reach the top of eight gentle, descending switchbacks. At the

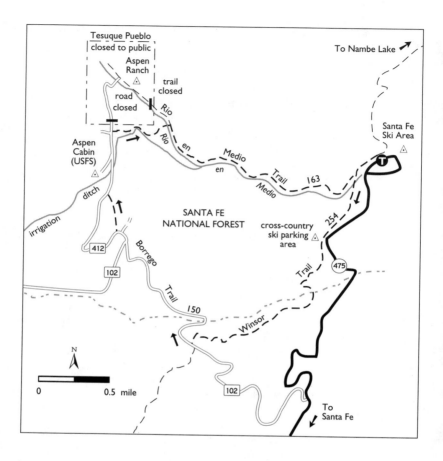

bottom, intersect FR 102, which is designated here as the Borrego Trail 150. Turn right and walk the dirt road, heading downhill. Continue on the road through the conifer forest for 1.3 miles to the intersection with FR 412. Turn right and walk north on FR 412. In 100 yards, pass a dirt double-track heading north. Continue to the next bend on FR 412, then leave the road on the unmarked Borrego Trail 150 as it climbs steeply up the west side of a small dry drainage.

At the top of the hill at mile 4.5, rejoin FR 412 and continue north. Cross an irrigation ditch and enter a small meadow. As the road begins to descend toward a gate at the boundary of Tesuque Pueblo land, pass a parking area in a small meadow. Pick up the Rio en Medio Trail 163 at the information board behind the parking area. Climb steeply up a hill, parallel to a fence, heading east. The trail follows an irrigation ditch to the north and east, crossing over to the slopes above the Rio en Medio. At mile 5.2, the trail cuts away from the ditch and drops steeply down the slope

*Intricate folds in banded gneiss along the Rio en Medio*

through a wonderful open stand of aspen. At the bottom of the hill, the trail crosses the Rio en Medio and a few small campsites are found nearby. Turn right and climb on the wide trail parallel to the stream. The trail soon enters a narrow stretch of canyon where the trail, perched above the delightful stream, is steep and rocky.

At mile 6, the climb moderates. In another mile, enter a large, wet meadow. The trace of the trail disappears in the wet grasses. Head uphill, bearing slightly away from the stream. At the far end of the meadow, the trail leaves the Rio en Medio, enters the forest, and briefly follows a small side stream. After crossing the stream, the trail rejoins the Rio en Medio and briefly becomes very steep. At the top of the hill, again meet the Winsor Trail. Turn left and backtrack 0.3 mile to the trailhead.

## 5 | NAMBE LAKE

**Distance: 6 miles, day hike**
**Difficulty:** strenuous
**Elevation range:** 10,200 to 11,400 feet
**Elevation gain:** 1,900 feet
**Best time of year:** mid-June to mid-October
**Water:** Rio Nambe
**Map:** USGS Aspen Basin
**Managed by:** Santa Fe National Forest, Pecos Wilderness, Española Ranger District
**Features:** high-country scenery, fall aspens, picturesque stream, alpine lake

Nambe Lake is a crystal-clear gem tucked in a glacial valley between Lake Peak and Santa Fe Baldy. It lies barely a half mile from the lifts at the

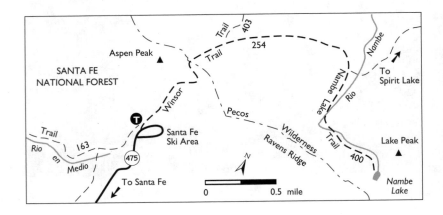

Santa Fe Ski Area, but the rock bowl that holds the lake is like another world. That such spectacular scenery is found so close to Santa Fe surprises more than a few hikers who venture up the mountain to gaze into the waters.

From Santa Fe, take Washington Avenue north from Paseo de Peralta 0.1 mile to Artist Road, NM 475. Turn right and head toward the Santa Fe Ski Area. Continue about 14 miles to the parking area at the ski basin. Park at the Winsor Trailhead at the northwest corner of the lot near an information kiosk.

The Winsor Trail 254 begins behind the information board and immediately passes over a footbridge. Turn right, following the arrows on the signs pointing to Lake Katherine. Several switchbacks lead up the slopes of Aspen Peak and to a saddle at the Pecos Wilderness boundary 0.5 mile from the start. Pass through the fence and walk downhill on a north slope shaded by alternating groves of spruce and aspen. Continue straight at the intersection with Trail 403 to the left. After a mile of gentle descent, listen for the cascades of the Rio Nambe in the steep canyon to the north. In a few minutes, just before reaching a narrow meadow that holds the stream, angle right (south) on a distinct trail marked for Nambe Lake.

Although the beginning of the trail is distinct, the rest of Trail 400 is difficult to follow; but hikers can simply head up the drainage on any one of several routes that climb steeply parallel to the Rio Nambe. Each of the interwoven trails leads upcanyon, but when in doubt, stay close to the stream. The best trail leads back and forth across the stream on a steady climb. Two level bowl-shaped meadows break up the ascent and make acceptable turnaround points for weary hikers. After the second meadow, make the final pitch to the basin where Lake Peak looms directly above. Still, fishless Nambe Lake reflects like a mirror the surrounding rugged circle of rock, and it is worth the effort to walk around the lake. After enjoying the views, return to the trailhead via the same route.

*The headwaters of the Rio Nambe below Nambe Lake*

# 6 | LA VEGA LOOP

**Distance: 8 miles, day hike or backpack**
**Difficulty:** strenuous
**Elevation range:** 10,200 to 10,800 feet
**Elevation gain:** 2,500 feet
**Best time of year:** late May to mid-October
**Water:** Rio Nambe
**Map:** USGS Aspen Basin
**Managed by:** Santa Fe National Forest, Pecos Wilderness,
   Española Ranger District
**Features:** high-country scenery, fall aspens, picturesque
   streams

New Mexico's mountains offer high-country wildflower displays from mid-June through the end of August. Any trail can put hikers in the thick of the show, but the La Vega Loop has an advantage over others because it offers a wide variety of habitats, some spectacular scenery, and a pretty good workout. The destination, La Vega, is one of the loveliest meadows on the west flanks of the southern Sangre de Cristo Mountains (*vega* means fertile plain in Spanish). The meadow's lush grasses and colorful flowers are rimmed with forested peaks. Along the way is the humid canyon of the Rio Nambe, which in July turns lavender with mountain bluebells.

This loop uses Trail 403, nicknamed "The Elevator Shaft" by locals. The very steep drop on Trail 403 dictates that this loop be walked in the direction described. This trail is a downhill workout and not always easy to find or follow. Only experienced hikers should attempt this descent.

Like other hikes leading into the eastern Pecos Wilderness, the La Vega

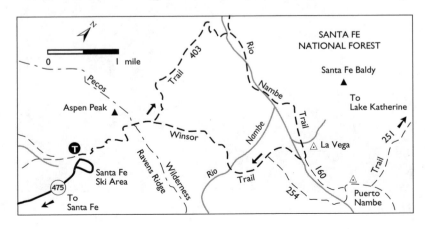

*La Vega is one of the largest meadows in the high country of the Sangre de Cristo Mountains.*

Loop begins at the northwest corner of the parking area at the Santa Fe Ski Area. From Santa Fe, take Washington Avenue north from Paseo de Peralta 0.1 mile to Artist Road, NM 475. Turn right and head toward the Santa Fe Ski Area. Continue about 14 miles to the parking area at the ski basin. Park at the Winsor Trailhead at the northwest corner of the lot near an information kiosk.

Begin hiking behind the information kiosk on the Winsor Trail 254. In a few steps, turn right (north) to follow the signs for Lake Katherine. Climb the flanks of Aspen Peak on switchbacks to reach a saddle at the boundary of the Pecos Wilderness 0.5 mile from the start. In 0.25 mile from the saddle, turn left onto Trail 403 and begin a steep drop into the canyon of the Rio Nambe. The route doesn't provide any niceties like switchbacks, it simply barrels downhill for 2 miles. The trail is faint at times, so hikers must watch for the route carefully.

At the bottom of the south wall of the canyon, cross the Rio Nambe on a log bridge and continue north for a minute to intersect the Rio Nambe Trail 160. Turn right and begin a climb along the cascading stream, fording the little river twice in the next mile. The trail grade increases when the trail swings away from the Rio Nambe, up a side drainage, and into an aspen meadow. At the head of the meadow, the trail doubles back to the right and climbs along a ridge. Once over the top, drop to a small stream, then make another short climb to reach La Vega.

Rock cairns mark the way along the southern edge of the forest-rimmed meadow to a trail sign identifying La Vega. From the trail sign you can pick out a lunch spot, explore the meadow, or head to the far side of La Vega to find a secluded campsite.

To continue on the loop, return to the trail sign and pick up the well-defined trail heading south and downhill into the forest. After descending 0.25 mile, turn right onto the Upper Nambe Trail 101, heading toward the Winsor Trail. In a few steps, cross a stream, then swing right to parallel the stream for a few hundred yards before making the short climb to the Winsor Trail. At the intersection, turn right and follow the trail across the Rio Nambe. The route climbs gradually along the north slope of Ravens Ridge, which is shady and often chilly. Pass the junction with Trail 403, continuing on the Winsor Trail back to the saddle at the wilderness boundary and then down the steep hill to the trailhead.

# 7 | SPIRIT LAKE

**Distance: 12 miles, day hike or backpack**
**Difficulty:** strenuous
**Elevation range:** 10,400 to 11,100 feet
**Elevation gain:** 2,300 feet
**Best time of year:** late June to early October
**Water:** Rio Nambe, Spirit Lake
**Maps:** USGS Aspen Basin and Cowles; USFS Pecos Wilderness
**Managed by:** Santa Fe National Forest, Pecos Wilderness, Española Ranger District
**Features:** high country lake, mountain scenery, fall aspens

The climb to Spirit Lake is a summer getaway from the tourist crowds in Santa Fe, but on weekends the Winsor Trail receives heavy use by hikers. The views from the trail are among the best in the southern Sangre de Cristos and encompass the Jemez Mountains, the Rio Grande Valley, and a close-up look at Santa Fe Baldy. Fall colors are spectacular in this part of

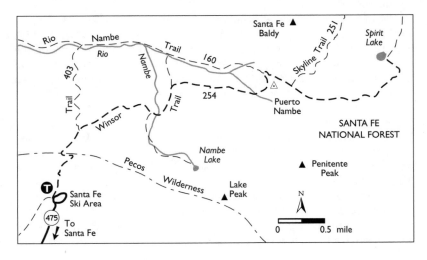

*Bull elephant head*

the range, making this a popular hike in late September. Spirit Lake itself holds rainbow and cutthroat trout, so take along a fishing rod. A few campsites are found in the woods surrounding the lake, but regulations require campsites to be more than 200 feet from the water.

From Santa Fe, take Washington Avenue north from Paseo de Peralta 0.1 mile to Artist Road, NM 475. Turn right and head toward the Santa Fe Ski Area. Continue about 14 miles to the parking area at the ski basin. Park at the Winsor Trailhead at the northwest corner of the lot near an information kiosk.

Begin hiking on the Winsor Trail 254, immediately crossing a bridge and turning right. The first 0.5 mile of trail is the steepest of the trip, climbing 500 feet on several graded switchbacks. At the top of the ridge, cross a fence into the Pecos Wilderness. A stop here for a breather may attract a flock of gray jays tame enough to eat peanuts from an outstretched hand.

A long, pleasant stretch of trail drops gradually on a steep slope high above the Rio Nambe through a deep fir forest dotted with aspen. The deeply shaded north slope can hold snow into late June. At mile 0.75, pass Trail 403 dropping steeply to the left. Cross the headwaters of the Rio Nambe at mile 2.2 and follow the trail as it contours to the northeast. As Santa Fe Baldy comes into view, the trail swings east, passing through small meadows of summer wildflowers. Cross another small stream at mile 3.3, then climb the next ridge on gentle switchbacks to reach Puerto Nambe, a broad saddle between Santa Fe Baldy and Penitente Peak, at mile 4.

Again heading east, walk through the splendid meadows atop the broad saddle, with Santa Fe Baldy to the left and Penitente Peak to the right. Pass the junction with the Skyline Trail 251 to the left and continue straight on the Winsor Trail. Hike single file to prevent further development of parallel tracks across the meadow. The trail drops slowly from the east side of the saddle, traversing a forested south-facing slope. A mile from the saddle, cross a short spur ridge, then drop more sharply to the lake basin. Enjoy the shade of the huge firs surrounding Spirit Lake. The trail's gentle grades make the return trip easier than expected.

# 8 | DECEPTION PEAK

**Distance: 6 miles, day hike**
**Difficulty:** strenuous
**Elevation range:** 10,000 to 12,200 feet
**Elevation gain:** 2,200 feet
**Best time of year:** late June to mid-October
**Water:** carry water
**Map:** USGS Aspen Basin
**Managed by:** Santa Fe National Forest, Española Ranger
  District
**Features:** spectacular summit views

The unmaintained trail to the summit of Deception Peak offers a chance to climb above treeline only a short distance from the Santa Fe Plaza. The weariness brought on by the steep grades of the trail easily melts away amid the grand scenery along the entire second half of the route. From the summit, all of northern New Mexico seems to flow around the base of the mountains. Hikers will want to linger on the ridgeline and drink up

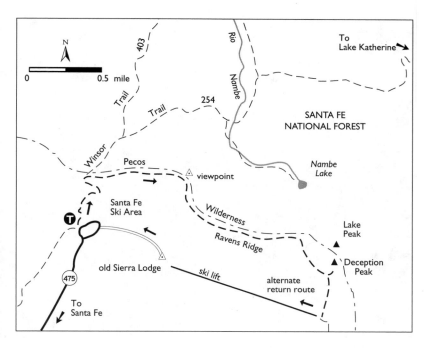

the sights. Be mindful of the weather—particularly in summer—and be prepared to hustle down from the summit if a storm is brewing.

From Santa Fe, take Washington Avenue north from Paseo de Peralta 0.1 mile to Artist Road, NM 475. Turn right and head toward the Santa Fe Ski Area. Continue about 14 miles to the parking area at the ski basin. Park at the Winsor Trailhead at the northwest corner of the lot near an information kiosk.

Begin hiking at the information kiosk for the Winsor Trail 254. In a few steps, cross a footbridge and turn right (north), following the sign that points toward Lake Katherine. Immediately begin climbing several switchbacks to reach a saddle at the Pecos Wilderness boundary about 0.5 mile from the start. The Winsor Trail continues straight ahead, but for this hike take the unmarked but easy-to-follow trail that heads right (east), parallel to a fence. This social (unofficial, well-trodden) trail follows the crest of Ravens Ridge through the conifer forest along the boundary of the Pecos Wilderness. After walking about 1.5 miles from the start, cross a meadow and come to a spectacular viewpoint looking down into the meadows below Nambe Lake and at the humpbacked summit of Santa Fe Baldy to the north. Backtrack a few yards from the viewpoint and pick one of several routes heading south and climbing steeply. Pass two rocky outcrops on the south flank of Ravens Ridge that make for a scenic snack stop.

*View of Santa Fe from Deception Peak*

The ridgeline soon narrows and the branches of the trail are squeezed together. A small boulder field confuses the route for a few yards: If you lose the trail, stay to the left of the boulders but don't descend from the ridgeline. In a few minutes, gain a summit and follow the northern edge of the ridgeline to another rounded summit before dropping 100 feet and crossing a saddle. After the crest of Lake Peak comes into view through the trees, reach a third summit and drop across another saddle.

Climbing from the second saddle, suddenly break out above tree line. Angle up to the top of the ridge on a faint trail, then turn left to reach the summit of Deception Peak, which is about 0.2 mile to the north. The view from the summit stretches from Colorado to central New Mexico. The ridgeline connects to the north with the 200-foot-higher Lake Peak. Most hikers choose to enjoy the view from Deception rather than risk the rugged and exposed trail to the sister summit.

To return, retrace your steps or follow the ridgeline down in the direction of the electronics towers on Tesuque Peak to the south. A well-worn trail starts at the edge of the forest at tree line. A half mile of walking leads to the top of the Tesuque Lift at the Santa Fe Ski Basin. It's a knee-stressing descent under the lift to the old Sierra Lodge. From the lodge, pick up a service road to the right or the left to return to the trailhead.

# 9 GLORIETA BALDY

**Distance: 14 miles, day hike**
**Difficulty:** strenuous
**Elevation range:** 7,800 to 10,199 feet
**Elevation gain:** 3,500 feet
**Best time of year:** late May to mid-October
**Water:** carry water
**Maps:** USGS McClure Reservoir and Glorieta
**Managed by:** Santa Fe National Forest, Pecos Ranger
   District
**Features:** outstanding views, solitude

Apache Canyon at the foot of Glorieta Baldy is a seemingly remote area just a few miles from Santa Fe. A series of old trails and logging roads create a short loop through just the canyon, or the trip can be extended on a new route up steep ridges to the peak itself. While the Apache Canyon loop route is 5.5 miles and an ideal mid-winter walk, the full trip up Glorieta Baldy is a strenuous climb for spring or fall. The summit view stretches from the level plains to the south to the heart of the Sangre de Cristo Mountains to the north. Note that none of these trails are shown accurately on the USGS 7.5-minute quadrangle map.

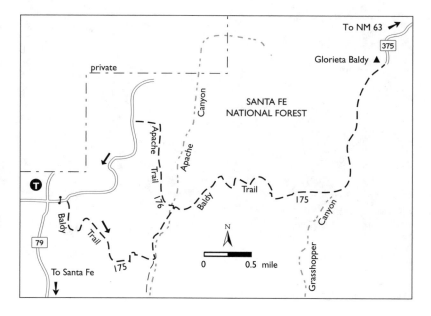

Reach the trailhead from Santa Fe by taking the Old Pecos Trail south to the Old Las Vegas Highway. Turn left and go 3 miles, then turn left onto CR 67C. At a T intersection in 1 mile, turn right onto CR 67. Immediately after the pavement ends in 2.2 miles, bear left onto CR 67A. Drive slowly through the village of Cañada de Los Alamos. Climb steeply out of a small valley, and at the top of the hill, cross a cattle guard and bear left. In 0.7 mile, enter Santa Fe National Forest and again bear left. Now on FR 79, continue 2.8 miles to a four-way intersection and park your vehicle.

Begin walking on the signed "Dead End Road" to the east. In 0.25 mile, pass around a gate, and in 100 yards, turn right onto the Baldy Trail 175. The trail follows a ridgeline, then dives off to the left (east). Several switchbacks lead to a double-track road. Turn left onto the logging road and continue eastward as it winds through a cluster of drainages and ridges, with the aptly-named Shaggy Peak to the east. After almost 1 mile on the double-track, another sign points the way to the trail that leads steeply down into Apache Canyon.

Under the tall Douglas firs of the canyon bottom, turn left onto the trail heading upstream. Enjoy the running water and open meadows in the canyon for about a half mile. Just after the second stream crossing near a tall, dead cottonwood, stay to the left side of the meadow to the junction with the Apache Trail 176. Bear right to continue on the Baldy Trail 175, which soon begins the rigorous ascent of the ridge between Apache and Grass-

*The rounded dome of Glorieta Baldy forms a portion of the eastern skyline from the Jemez Mountains across the Rio Grande.*

hopper Canyons on sharp-angled switchbacks. The grade eases once the trail reaches the top of the ridge, but the ridge itself is a steep ramp leading east. Views of Shaggy Peak to the right enliven this stretch of trail.

About 5 miles from the start, the trail is marked with two posts. At this point the trail swings left (north) onto the ridge that culminates in Glorieta Baldy. Enter a meadow where the trail disappears, following the signs to the forest on the other side where the trail is again easy to follow. Several more meadows follow in the last mile to the summit, all offering outstanding views. Reach the summit, with a lookout tower and accompanying road, about 7 miles from the start.

When it's time to return, retrace your steps down the ridges to the floor of Apache Canyon and the junction with the Apache Trail 176. Turn right and ascend steeply on the Apache Trail, traveling a ridgeline that offers fine views of Glorieta Baldy and Thompson Peak. After 1 mile on the ridge, intersect a graded road. Turn left and follow the winding road across drainages and ridges for 2.5 miles back to the trailhead.

## 10 | CAVE CREEK AND HORSETHIEF MEADOW

**Distance: 5-mile day hike or 11-mile backpack**
**Difficulty:** difficult
**Elevation range:** 8,400 to 10,150 feet
**Elevation gain:** 2,100 feet
**Best time of year:** late June to mid-October
**Water:** Panchuela, Cave, and Horsethief Creeks
**Maps:** USGS Cowles and Truchas Peaks
**Managed by:** Santa Fe National Forest, Pecos Wilderness, Pecos Ranger District
**Features:** stream flowing through a cliff, colorful meadows, fall aspen display

It's a curious twist on the old disappearing stream trick. At The Sinks in Wyoming, the Lost River in Idaho, and a score of other spots, visitors can watch a river suddenly disappear into the gravels of its bed. At Cave Creek in the Sangre de Cristo Mountains, the stream in question makes a detour into a cave to flow a hundred yards inside the bordering mountain, then trickles out into the sunlight again. Limestone is the key here, and water seeping into fractures in the rock gradually formed the surprisingly deep caves. Some of the stream water is perhaps diverted within the caves to travel a system of fissures and contribute flow to springs farther down the creek.

The short, easy stroll to the caves is suitable for all hikers, including families. Those wishing a longer hike can continue up Cave Creek and over

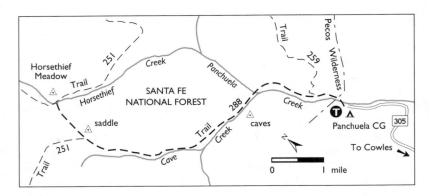

a divide to enter Horsethief Meadow, an extensive grassland with plenty of campsites. A fault determines the trend of the picturesque valley, which reputedly served as a secluded hideaway for holding horses stolen from ranches on the plains to the east of the Sangre de Cristos.

Reach the trailhead by taking I-25 east from Santa Fe to the Glorieta/Pecos exit 299. Turn left, pass over the interstate, then immediately turn right onto NM 50. Drive 6 miles to the village of Pecos. At a T intersection, turn left onto NM 63 and continue about 20 miles to the site of Cowles. Turn left (west) onto FR 121 and, just across the Pecos River, make a sharp right onto the single-lane FR 305, which leads in 1 mile to Panchuela Campground and the trailhead. A $2 per day parking fee is required.

Begin walking at the west end of Panchuela Campground, heading upstream along Panchuela Creek on Trail 288. Cross a bridge and follow the trail as it continues a gentle climb along the slopes above the valley floor. Pass the intersection with the Dockwiller Trail 259. In 1.5 miles, the trail crosses Panchuela Creek and begins to follow the smaller Cave Creek. In about 10 minutes, watch and listen carefully. When the sound of the stream suddenly quiets, look for the caves on the opposite side of the creek.

About half of Cave Creek's flow is diverted into the tunnels. The stream itself widened the fractures in the limestone wall, dissolving away the rock and creating dark passages. Enter the caves with caution due to the slippery rocks and the dark passage.

Hikers going only as far as the caves should turn around and return by the same route. To continue to Horsethief Meadow, resume the climb up Trail 288. The trail climbs high above the creek for the next mile. Bear slightly right at the junction with Trail 251 to continue on the trail now identified as No. 251. About 4.3 miles from the start, the trail angles away from Cave Creek and begins to climb a side drainage on steep switchbacks. Almost at the divide, pass through a small meadow that is loaded with wildflowers in July. Once over the low saddle, drop quickly down into Horsethief Meadow, which stretches north and east. After enjoying the peaceful meadow, return by the same route.

The flow of Cave Creek disappears into two caves along the way to Horsethief Meadow.

## 11 STEWART LAKE

**Distance: 13-mile loop, day hike or backpack**
**Difficulty:** strenuous
**Elevation range:** 8,200 to 10,300 feet
**Elevation gain:** 2,800 feet
**Best time of year:** mid-June to early October
**Water:** Stewart Lake
**Map:** USGS Cowles
**Managed by:** Santa Fe National Forest, Pecos Wilderness,
  Pecos Ranger District
**Features:** high lake, fishing, good base camp

The ramble to Stewart Lake is an exhilarating trip along canyons and ridges of the main crest of the Sangre de Cristo Mountains. The destination is a high lake held gingerly in the cupped hands of the surrounding forest. The trail leading to this picturesque spot offers one of the gentlest climbs to a glacial lake in the range. The emerald green pool of Stewart Lake invites a quiet respite and the local trout may tempt hikers into a bit of angling, so take a fishing pole. The timber stands surrounding the lake provide many inviting campsites and make this an excellent base camp for exploring the surrounding high country.

The trailhead is located near Cowles Campground. From Santa Fe, take I-25 east to the Glorieta/Pecos exit 299. Turn left, pass over the interstate, then immediately turn right onto NM 50. Drive 6 miles to the village of Pecos. At a T intersection, turn left onto NM 63 and continue about 20 miles to the site of Cowles. Turn left (west) onto FR 121 and in a few yards park at the Cowles Campground.

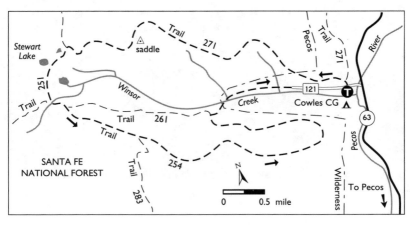

Look for a sign on the north side of the road pointing to Trail 271. Begin walking on the trail, then in a few yards turn left, away from Cowles Campground, and begin climbing on the flanks of a long ridge. A series of switchbacks ease the steady grade as the trail continues to travel high above Winsor Creek through conifer stands and aspen groves. Around 3 miles from the start, cross over a saddle and enjoy views to the south and west. At mile 4.3, drop down a hill to intersect Trail 251. Bear left and complete the trip to the lake in 0.5 mile.

*Shooting stars*

Enjoy the lake, then continue south on Trail 251 for 0.5 mile to the inter-section with Trail 254. Turn left and follow Trail 254 as it descends a long ridge. At mile 5.6, pass the junction with Trail 261 on the left. Continue down the ridge on Trail 254. Near mile 7, the trail enters a meadow and is joined by Trail 283 from the south. On a faint trail, swing around the left side of the meadow and stay on the ridgeline trail (don't drop into the head of Holy Ghost Canyon). After re-entering the forest, the trail is again easy to follow as it continues the descent.

About 3 miles past Trail 283, watch carefully for a poorly marked, sharp left turn. Drop on the north slope of the ridge to mile 11 and the intersec-tion with Trail 261 near the bottom of Winsor Canyon. Turn right and walk 1.0 mile to the end of the trail, then walk FR 121 another mile back to the trailhead.

## 12 | MORA FLATS

**Distance: 8 miles, day hike or backpack**
**Difficulty:** moderate
**Elevation range:** 9,200 to 9,500 feet
**Elevation gain:** 800 feet
**Best time of year:** late May through late October
**Water:** Rio Mora
**Maps:** USGS Elk Mountain; USFS Pecos Wilderness
**Managed by:** Santa Fe National Forest, Pecos Wilderness, Pecos Ranger District
**Features:** huge wildflower-studded meadow, trout fishing, easy access to camping spots

Mora Flats is a huge valley split by several picturesque mountain streams. It makes an easy destination for an overnight trip into the Pecos Wilder-ness and is suitable for beginning backpackers or families. The grades are gentle, the views spectacular, the fishing excellent, and the camp spots plentiful in the flats. From a base camp at the flats, one can day-hike sev-eral trails to high divides or fly-fish for small trout in the Rio Mora or the Rio Valdez. Hikers must camp at least 200 feet from all streams.

From Santa Fe, take I-25 east to the Glorieta/Pecos exit 299. Turn left to cross over the interstate, then turn right on NM 50 for 6 miles to the intersection with NM 63. Turn left and travel up the canyon of the Pecos River. Beyond the Terrero Store, the winding road passes piles of mine tail-ings. About 18 miles from NM 50, bear right onto FR 223, which is signed for Iron Gate Campground. Go 4.3 bumpy and winding miles (which seem like ten) to Iron Gate Campground and park at the designated trailhead. A $2 per day fee is charged for parking.

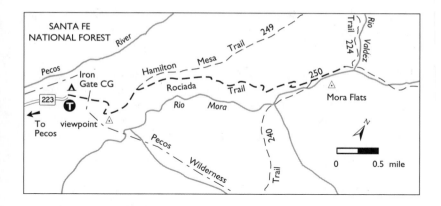

Begin hiking on the Hamilton Mesa Trail 249, immediately passing through a gate and entering the Pecos Wilderness. Begin a gentle climb through the fir forest to the top of a ridge. At the top, take a short spur trail to the right to an overlook into the deep Rio Mora Canyon. Here the main trail swings left (north) along the crest of the ridge, with several more viewpoints along the way.

After crossing a small aspen meadow 1 mile from the start, reach a junction and bear right onto the Rociada Trail 250. The trail traverses a long, winding ridge high above the Rio Mora, passing through open stands of aspen along the way. In early summer, the ridge is covered with large

*Mora Flats as seen from the Rociada Trail*

yellow false pine lupines, wild iris, Richardson's geranium, wild strawberries, and more—as many as fifty wildflower species may be found in bloom. At mile 3.1, pass through a fence and enjoy a view of Mora Flats from above.

The trail now drops to Mora Flats through a series of switchbacks, reaching the meadow at mile 3.8. From the meadow edge, Trail 240 crosses the stream and leads southward to the main portion of the flats, while Trail 250 turns north to parallel the stream. Excellent campsites are found here and in another 0.5 mile near the junction with the Rio Valdez. Return to the trailhead by the same route.

A leisurely two-day trip can be made by joining this hike with the trip to Beattys Flat (Hike 13). Hike to Mora Flats, then, at the junction with the Rio Valdez Trail 224, bear left and travel 2.1 miles upstream, passing several nice campsites along the way. At the junction with Trail 270, turn left (west) and climb over Hamilton Mesa, passing Trail 249 and continuing downhill on Trail 270 to the junction with Trail 260. Turn right to find a campsite above Beattys Flat, then follow Trail 260 back to the Iron Gate Campground.

# 13 | BEATTYS FLAT

**Distance: 11 miles, day hike or backpack**
**Difficulty:** difficult
**Elevation range:** 9,200 to 10,150 feet
**Elevation gain:** 1,600 feet
**Best time of year:** mid-June to early October
**Water:** Pecos River
**Maps:** USGS Elk Mountain and Pecos Falls
**Managed by:** Santa Fe National Forest, Pecos Wilderness,
Pecos Ranger District
**Features:** wildflowers, trout fishing, outstanding views of
Sangre de Cristo peaks

The high meadows of the Pecos Wilderness make for scenic midsummer walks with few peers—one such classic trip is the hike to Beattys Flat. The journey takes hikers through long grasslands painted with extraordinary wildflowers and leads to the Pecos River where hungry trout willingly sip flies on the fast currents. Views along the route are unmatched in the Pecos Wilderness, and the quiet canyon of the Pecos River invites lingering for a few hours or days.

The extensive open area along the river is named Beattys Flat in honor of a former resident who built a cabin in the meadow in the early part of the twentieth century. An account of the way things used to be is colorfully

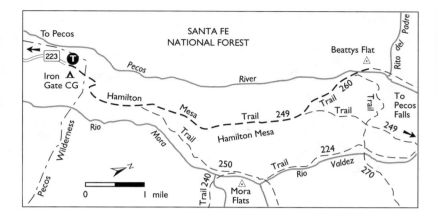

told in the long out-of-print *Beatty's Cabin* by Elliott Barker. Look for a copy of this gem before heading out on the hike.

To reach the trailhead from Santa Fe, take I-25 east to the Glorieta/Pecos exit 299. Turn left, pass over the interstate, then turn right to travel on NM 50 for 6 miles to a T intersection with NM 63 in Pecos. Turn left and continue about 18 miles to FR 223. Bear right onto this bumpy road that requires a high-clearance vehicle or a carefully driven car. Park at the trailhead at Iron Gate Campground in 4.3 miles. A $2 per day parking fee is required.

Head through the gate at the trailhead and begin a gentle climb on the Hamilton Mesa Trail 249. A single switchback takes you up to the ridgeline where the trail swings left. Enjoy viewpoints into the canyon of the Rio Mora as you continue along the rocky ridge and through an aspen stand. In 1.5 miles, bear left to stay on the Hamilton Mesa Trail and begin a moderate climb that stays on the east side of the ridgeline except for a brief stretch along the forested summit. Another few minutes under tall Douglas firs will bring you to a gate and into a huge meadow where wild iris, sunflowers, and dozens of other wildflowers bloom. Continue across the meadow for a few minutes. Close to the top of the ascent, near a stand of aspen, ignore a side trail right and bear left.

The next mile is among the prettiest stretches of trail in all of New Mexico. The huge open meadow offers never-ending views of the surrounding high peaks of the Sangre de Cristos. Finding twenty-five species of wildflowers—including star-eyed grass, three types of wild onion, tall sunflowers, and the uncommon orange skyflower—wouldn't be unusual in midsummer. Pass through several wooded patches before reaching a trail junction at mile 3.5. The trail straight ahead goes to Pecos Falls; to go to Beattys Flat, take the left fork. Descend into the forest as the trail begins the drop to the Pecos River through steep pitches and level aspen stands. After another mile, with the river in earshot, bear left at the junction with

*The meadows along Hamilton Mesa provide one of the prettiest views in all of New Mexico.*

the Rio Valdez Trail, pass through a gate and drop the final half mile to Beattys Flat.

Cross the Pecos River on a stout bridge and enter the flat. Explore upstream to the limestone cliffs at the confluence with the Rito del Padre, or spend some time fishing for brown trout. No camping is permitted in the flat, but ample sites can be found upstream. When it's time to head back, return by the same route.

## 14 | PECOS BALDY LAKE

**Distance: 15 miles, backpack**
**Difficulty:** strenuous
**Elevation range:** 8,800 to 11,400 feet
**Elevation gain:** 2,800 feet
**Best time of year:** mid-June to early October
**Water:** Jacks Creek, Pecos Baldy Lake
**Maps:** USGS Cowles and Truchas Peak
**Managed by:** Santa Fe National Forest, Pecos Wilderness, Pecos Ranger District
**Features:** views of highest peaks in the southern Sangre de Cristo range

Late summer is the ideal time to enjoy a glorious trip to one of New Mexico's premier alpine areas, the high country surrounding Pecos Baldy Lake. The long, strenuous trip to the lake puts hikers at the foot of the humpbacked Pecos Baldy Peaks. In July and August the trail is lined with wildflowers, and in September golden aspens are on stage. Bighorn sheep are found in this area, too, but the lake and the surrounding mountain scen-

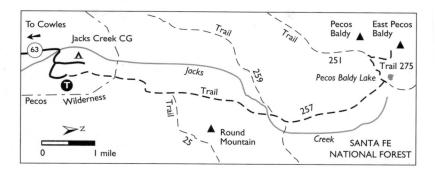

ery are the highlights of this trip. Be prepared to share the trail with plenty of other hikers. Also, be sure to watch the weather and be ready to seek shelter during sudden thunderstorms in this exposed terrain.

Reach the trailhead by taking I-25 east from Santa Fe about 15 miles to exit 299 at Glorieta/Pecos. Turn left, cross the overpass, then turn right onto NM 50. In 6 miles, turn left onto NM 63 and drive 20 miles to Cowles. Continue straight on NM 63 for 3 miles to parking for the Pecos Wilderness Area near Jacks Creek Campground. A fee of $2 per day is charged for the parking area.

Trail 257, the route to the lake, begins at the north end of the parking area. The first mile gains 700 feet of elevation, so be prepared for an early workout. After steep switchbacks the grade eases a bit along a ridgeline. At mile 2.6, take the left fork and pass through grasslands and aspen stands on the west flank of Round Mountain. Follow posts north across the meadow. The views north along this stretch are superb.

At the end of the meadow, Trail 257 again enters conifer forest and makes a gentle drop to Jacks Creek. Hop across the stream and head up the canyon for about 0.25 mile before the trail swings away from the creek. At

*Pikas are common on the talus of the highest peaks of the Sangre de Cristos.*

mile 4.7, Trail 259 angles right toward Beattys Flat. Take the left fork to stay on Trail 257. Resume the steep climb through shady forest and enjoy peeks of East Pecos Baldy around mile 6. One last steep section brings hikers within view of Pecos Baldy Lake. It's a short drop to the lakeshore, but camping is not permitted in the lake basin. Look for campsites in the trees to the north of the lake.

From the lake, consider climbing the 12,528-foot East Pecos Baldy. Take Trail 251 southwest from the lake. The trail climbs steeply up the south flank of the mountain before intersecting Trail 275. This route angles right from the main trail and makes quick work of the remaining 700 feet to the summit.

When it's time to head back, return to the trailhead by the same route.

*Facing page: New Mexico's highest terrain is found in the northern Sangre de Cristo Mountains.*

# NORTHERN SANGRE DE CRISTO MOUNTAINS

# 15 | TRAMPAS LAKES

**Distance: 12 miles, day hike or backpack**
**Difficulty:** difficult
**Elevation range:** 9,100 to 11,400 feet
**Elevation gain:** 2,600 feet
**Best time of year:** mid-June to early October
**Water:** Rio de las Trampas
**Maps:** USGS El Valle and Truchas Peak
**Managed by:** Carson National Forest, Pecos Wilderness, Camino Real Ranger District
**Features:** picturesque canyon, high lakes

As it climbs 6 miles up the canyon of the Rio de las Trampas, the Trampas Lake Trail 31 stays within shouting distance of the cascading stream. The well-worn trail provides a long but reasonably gentle route to the lakes, which are nestled in a rock-lined bowl between Jicarilla and the Truchas Peaks. Around the lakes, the entire horseshoe ridgeline stands above 12,400 feet. As late as 12,000 years ago, the high peaks of the Pecos Wilderness supported small glaciers and the upper canyon of the Rio de las Trampas exhibits the distinctive U shape of glacial valleys. The small stream—the River of the Traps in Spanish—takes its name from the days of the mountain men who came from Taos to trap beaver in the canyon. It is likely that Kit Carson trapped this stream early in his Western career.

Reach the trailhead from Santa Fe by taking US 84/285 north to Española. When US 84/285 turns left, continue straight on NM 68 north. In 14 miles, turn right at the intersection with NM 75 near the town of Dixon. In another 14 miles, turn right onto NM 76. Continue 4.4 miles through the village of Chamisal and turn left onto FR 207 (before reaching the village of

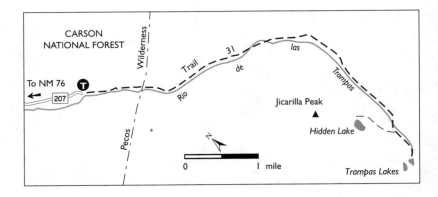

*Streamside trail in the Sangre de Cristo Mountains*

Trampas). Drive through El Valle to the end of FR 207, about 9 miles, and park at the primitive campground.

From the small campground at the trailhead, look for a trail sign on the left near the only structure in camp. Immediately head uphill and begin the steady ascent. In a few minutes, pass through a gate and continue climbing on the heavily forested slope above the canyon floor. This stretch is particularly lovely in July when the wildflowers are at their peak. Enter the Pecos Wilderness after 1 mile, then enjoy expanding views as the trail passes impressive piles of talus. Near mile 2.5, cross the stream on a log bridge and continue about 0.25 mile before another log leads back to the east bank.

Near an open hillside, hikers may have to negotiate a few downed trees within a huge blowdown before again finding a clear path. Pass a prominent avalanche chute on your right before the grade increases. Broad switchbacks help make the climb a bit easier on this last 1.5 miles of trail.

After making another stream crossing, enter a sloping meadow where the trail is often muddy. Near mile 5, a spur trail to Hidden Lake goes right. Bear left on the now faint main trail and follow the small outflow stream to the lakes.

Explore around the basin and enjoy the view from both lakes; then head downhill and return to the trailhead by the same route.

# 16 | SANTA BARBARA DIVIDE

**Distance: 20 miles, 1- or 2-night backpack**
**Difficulty:** strenuous
**Elevation range:** 8,900 to 12,000 feet
**Elevation gain:** 3,500 feet
**Best time of year:** late June to mid-October
**Water:** Rio Santa Barbara, West Fork
**Maps:** USGS Jicarita and Pecos Falls; USFS Pecos Wilderness
**Managed by:** Carson National Forest, Pecos Wilderness, Camino Real Ranger District
**Features:** pristine watershed, high mountain scenery, excellent fishing

Even in the arid mountains of the Southwest, logging has been common for the past one hundred years. Few watersheds have been as fortunate as that of the Rio Santa Barbara. The rugged slopes and remote location of its upper canyon have protected the forests from the ax and chainsaw. The Rio Santa Barbara watershed is the most pristine in New Mexico, remaining much the same as it was in the 1830s when American mountain men out of Taos, just a few miles to the north, trapped beaver in its waters. A walk along the clear, cold waters of the Santa Barbara is like travelling back in time.

The first 2 miles above the campground receive moderate use in summer, but the West Fork Trail beyond sees little traffic. Along the way, the view of the canyon of the West Fork and the humpbacked dome of 12,841-foot Chimayosos Peak is unforgettable. Among fishermen, the Santa Barbara has a reputation as one of the best places in the state to angle for cutthroat trout.

From Española, take NM 68 north 13.5 miles to NM 75 at Dixon. Turn

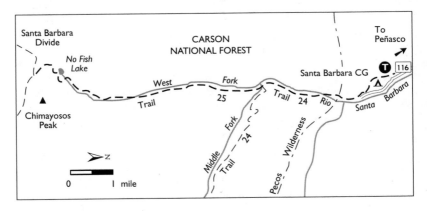

*The humpbacked summit of Chimayosos Peak is visible along the West Fork Trail.*

right and continue to Peñasco, about 15 miles. About one mile past the junction with NM 76, continue straight onto NM 73 as NM 75 turns sharply left. In another 1.5 miles, turn left onto FR 116 and follow the signs 4 miles to the Santa Barbara Campground. Park at the trailhead near the campground entrance.

From the trailhead, begin hiking around the campground on Trail 24. Once past the last campsite, the trail swings close to the river. Soon high cliffs pinch the trail and stream together and, at mile 1.2, the trail enters the Pecos Wilderness. Cross a bridge over the river and begin a gentle climb along the east slope of the canyon. Continue above the river through old Douglas firs in a dense forest.

At a junction 2.2 miles from the start, bear right onto the West Fork Trail 25. Immediately reach a round meadow at the meeting of the Middle and West Forks of the Santa Barbara—a made-to-order rest or lunch spot. The trail continues to the other side of the meadow where it crosses the Middle Fork on a logjam. Use caution at the crossing and do not attempt it during spring runoff or other periods of high water. From the crossing, the trail climbs slowly along the canyon of the West Fork in an open forest away from the stream. This is wild country, and a glimpse of deer, elk, or even a bear would not be unexpected. At mile 4, the trail bears right and emerges into a meadow high above the stream. The river below is puddled into large beaver ponds where big brown trout can be spotted sipping insects from the surface.

After another mile, the trail again enters the forest before crossing to the west side of the stream 6 miles from the start. Begin climbing the west wall of the canyon on a long series of gentle switchbacks. At mile 7.5, cross the West Fork again and pass several nice camping spots, the last ones before the divide. If backpacking, plan to camp here.

The trail now makes wild swings in its attempt to make the final assault on the ridge less difficult, but it is still a tough haul, lightened by stunning views of Chimayosos Peak to the east. Climb a rocky ridge and reach the divide where all the world is below. From the ridge, trails lead east and west along the ridgeline. Enjoy the view, then return by the same route.

## 17 SOUTH BOUNDARY TRAIL

**Distance: 13 miles one-way, day hike or backpack**
**Difficulty:** moderate
**Elevation range:** 7,300 to 10,300 feet
**Elevation gain:** 300 feet; 3,300 foot descent
**Best time of year:** late May to late October
**Water:** American Spring
**Maps:** USGS Shady Brook and Ranchos de Taos
**Managed by:** Carson National Forest, Camino Real Ranger District
**Features:** historic trail, views of Wheeler Peak Wilderness, quiet, solitude

The South Boundary Trail—so named because it runs parallel to the dividing line between the former Taos and Rio Grande del Rancho land grants—travels the length of the Fernando Mountains. The trail was blazed by ranchers in the early 1800s as a route to drive sheep from Taos to grazing areas in the high country. Traversing the north side of the ridge, the route is a long, shady walk through deep Douglas fir and spruce forest. The first 10 miles of the hike descend gently; the last 3 miles are very steep.

To do this hike as a one-way descent, set up a shuttle by leaving a vehicle at the El Nogal Picnic Area 3 miles east of Taos on US 64. Continue east on US 64 for 10 miles beyond the picnic area and turn right onto FR 437. In 0.4 mile, stay on FR 437 by turning right, heading for Garcia Park. Continue 6 miles to the junction with FR 445 to the right and park.

From FR 437, walk west on the wide dirt FR 445 through open stands of aspen, spruce, and fir. At 0.7 mile, come to a four-way intersection. Trail 164 enters from the left and continues into the woods to the right, but it is difficult to follow in this stretch. Turn right to stay on FR 445.

At mile 1, pass a road to the left and begin a gentle climb to skirt around Sierra de don Fernando, passing great views of the Wheeler Peak Wilderness to the right. At mile 1.5, begin descending around the northwest base

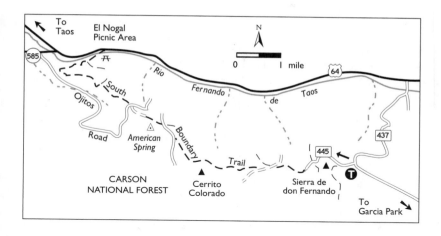

of Sierra de don Fernando. At the bottom of the descent at mile 2.1, leave the road by walking over a berm to the left to pick up a trail heading south. Angle into a small meadow where the trail becomes faint. Look for rock cairns and trail markers in the tall grass. After descending from the top of a small knoll, the trail bears right at a large cairn and is now easier to follow.

Descending through a closed forest, the trail joins an abandoned road. At mile 3.1, bear left. From here the route is often marked with large rock cairns. At a fence in a few hundred yards, bear right off the old road and onto a trail. Begin a long, wonderful, ever-so-gently descending stroll

*Elk tooth marks on aspen*

through thick conifer forest, stands of aspen, and oak scrub.

At mile 6.2, enter a large meadow at the base of Cerrito Colorado, where several scenic campsites are found. At mile 7.2, the trail crosses to the south side of the ridge. Just beyond a small saddle, intersect a road angling back sharply to the left. Bear right as the trail follows the road, passing through drier oak-scrub woodland, then cross away from the road to the north side of the ridgeline. At mile 8.5, walk through a four-way intersection and continue straight on the main trail. Soon pass American (Bear) Spring. Beyond the spring, bear right as a trail enters from the left and continue straight as the trail joins an abandoned road.

At mile 9.3, a sign indicates the trail goes right, but continue straight ahead on the road. In 0.2 mile, meet the Ojitos Road at a four-way intersection and continue straight. From this point, the trail descends steeply on a rocky surface through open woods. At mile 10.5, reach a small saddle on the ridgeline. The trail drops to the south side of the ridge and becomes very steep. When the trail again meets the top of the ridge, turn left at a T intersection. At a Y intersection, bear right off the northwest side of the ridge. At mile 12.2, the trail angles sharply back to the south. Take a sharp switchback to the right, avoiding another branch of the trail straight ahead. Turn through several broad switchbacks descending the north flank of the ridge. At mile 13, reach another trail junction, continue straight, and then make a sharp left. Cross the bridge over the Rio Fernando de Taos and enter the El Nogal Picnic Area.

# 18 | BARRANCA HILL

**Distance: 8.5 miles, day hike**
**Difficulty:** moderate
**Elevation range:** 6,200 to 6,950 feet
**Elevation gain:** 800 feet
**Best time of year:** late March to early May, September to late October
**Water:** carry water
**Maps:** USGS Carson, Taos Junction, and Velarde
**Managed by:** Carson National Forest, Tres Piedras Ranger District; Bureau of Land Management, Taos Field Office
**Features:** historic railroad grade, railroad artifacts, remote canyon scenery

When the Denver and Rio Grande Railroad engineers went looking for a location to drop 1,000 feet from the Taos Plateau to the bottom of the Rio Grande Gorge, they found a suitable place in Comanche Canyon. After the construction of a small station at the top of the grade named Barranca (ra-

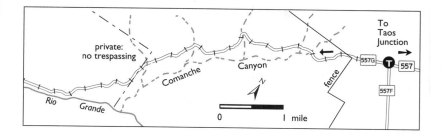

vine), the steep grade below acquired the name Barranca Hill. It was the most infamous stretch on the railroad, requiring special braking procedures on the descent and a double head—two engines—for the climb up.

The railroad folded in 1942. Fifty years of erosion have covered much of the grade in rubble, and short detours are now necessary to get past ravines once spanned by small bridges. Along the way are an abundance of artifacts: rock inscriptions, wooden culverts, old trestle timbers, rail spikes, and more. Hikers should remember to leave all artifacts where they are found.

To reach the trailhead, take US 84/285 north from Española. In about 5 miles, turn right onto US 285 as it splits from US 84. Continue on US 285 through Ojo Caliente and past the junction with NM 111, which is about 25 miles from Española. Nine miles beyond NM 111, at Taos Junction, turn right onto NM 567 and immediately turn right again onto FR 557. This rutted dirt road requires a high-clearance vehicle. Drive on FR 557 for 8 miles, parking at the junction with FR 557G and FR 557F.

Hike down the raised gravel bed of FR 557G, which is directly on top of the railroad grade. At mile 0.8, come to a corral and stock pond. The grade angles through the corral and into the sharp cut in the basalt flows to the southwest. Climb the fence on the west side of the corral and walk the corral

*Trains once passed along this route through Comanche Canyon at Barranca Hill.*

fence to a gap. Turn right past a large juniper tree and angle toward the cut in the rocks ahead where gravel and rotting railroad ties are strewn along the route. Enter the cut and marvel that a railroad once passed this way.

Through the cut, the gravel railbed becomes easier to follow. The route is now in the very head of Comanche Canyon. Walk downcanyon, soon coming to a rockfall blocking the grade. Follow a path to the left. For the next 0.25 mile, walk downhill on the grade through sagebrush, crossing a number of original wooden culverts along the way. The grade swings right through a short cut, then comes to the first major missing trestle. Leave the grade and follow the path to the right. Before climbing up the other side, notice the huge timbers still in place below the grade.

A few hundred feet beyond, another gap in the grade is the site of the second missing trestle. Skirt this obstacle by descending on the rocks to the left and climbing the other side. Once on the grade again, hikers are forced to pick a route through a long rockfall that blocks the grade. From here, the obstacles are easier to pass. Continue downhill on the west wall of Comanche Canyon, enjoying the widening view. Several small missing trestles are easily skirted on well-worn pathways. At mile 3.1, a long detour right takes you around another gap in the grade. Although other small rockfalls stand in the way, the route now is an easy stroll.

Just over 4 miles from the start, the grade reaches a steep arroyo with another missing bridge. This makes a good turnaround point. Note that 0.25 mile beyond the arroyo, the railroad grade enters private land. Do not cross the fence at the boundary. Retrace your steps back up the hill, enjoying the gentle slope carefully designed by the railroad engineers.

# 19 | CEBOLLA MESA/BIG ARSENIC TRAILS

**Distance: 8 miles, day hike or backpack**
**Difficulty:** moderate
**Elevation range:** 6,600 to 7,360 feet
**Elevation gain:** 1,300 feet
**Best time of year:** March to November
**Water:** Red River, Little and Big Arsenic Springs
**Map:** USGS Guadalupe Mountain
**Managed by:** Carson National Forest, Questa Ranger District; Bureau of Land Management, Rio Grande Wild and Scenic River, Taos Field Office
**Features:** deep rugged canyon, large river, fishing

The Rio Grande has carved a gorge 60 miles long and up to 1,000 feet deep through the thick sheets of lava that emanated from the volcanoes of the

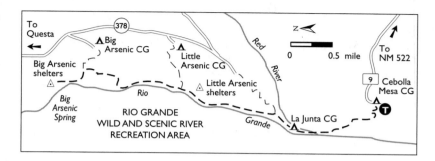

Taos Plateau. The river within the gorge remains wild and free-flowing, fed by snowmelt in Colorado's San Juan Mountains and by thousands of springs within the gorge itself. The basalt walls are steep, and house-sized boulders have tumbled from them to line the river or break the current as in-stream rocks. The polished rocks at streamside are slick, and the water off the banks is often 10 feet deep. Ducks, mergansers, geese, and bald eagles are frequently seen from along the river.

Several trails enter the gorge from the Bureau of Land Management's Rio Grande Wild and Scenic River Recreation Area north and west of Questa, but entering the gorge via Cebolla Mesa requires less driving from Taos. The well-maintained Cebolla Mesa Trail leads to the confluence of the Red River and the Rio Grande and some of the best fishing in the state. Plenty of campsites are available within the gorge; particularly attractive are the shelters and firepits at La Junta, Little Arsenic, and Big Arsenic primitive campgrounds.

To reach the trailhead from Taos, head north on US 64 about 4 miles to the junction with NM 522. Continue straight on NM 522 for about 16 miles to FR 9. Turn left onto this rutted dirt road, which, when dry, is passable to all vehicles. Drive the length of FR 9, bearing left at an intersection 1 mile from the highway, and arrive at the Cebolla Mesa Campground in 3.5 miles.

The Cebolla Mesa Trail quickly drops from the rim on a series of steep switchbacks, passing through mixed vegetation that includes everything from yuccas to Douglas fir. Views of the river and the gorge are spectacular on the entire 1-mile descent. At the Rio Grande, a footbridge crosses the Red River into La Junta Campground; if the bridge is washed out or damaged, wade across the shallow current. Follow the trail as it winds through the shelters and climbs a low ridge that separates the two rivers.

Heading north, the trail stays on the low divide, offering views up the canyon of the Red River. In 0.25 mile from the bridge, the La Junta Trail branches right to climb to the rim. Bear left and immediately drop to the Rio Grande. Continue upcanyon, at times climbing to the bench above the river to avoid large rockfalls. Pass the Little Arsenic shelters, the Little Arsenic Trail leading to the rim and, 0.25 mile beyond the shelters, the spring just to the right of the trail.

At mile 3.5, the trail ascends steeply to avoid a massive rockfall that stretches to the river. From the bench above the river, the climb continues over a low mound of boulders. Just beyond, meet the trail descending from Big Arsenic Campground on the rim. Before the next descent back to river level, more shelters are visible on the flat below. Again along the river, enjoy the shade of the trees and shelters at Big Arsenic. The springs are on the opposite side of the flat. Return to the trailhead by the same route.

*Hiking above the Rio Grande on the Cebolla Mesa Trail*
(Photo by Jessica Martin)

# 20 | LOBO PEAK

**Distance: 11 miles, day hike or backpack**
**Difficulty:** strenuous
**Elevation range:** 8,400 to 12,100 feet
**Elevation gain:** 3,800 feet
**Best time of year:** late June to October
**Water:** Manzanita and Italianos Creeks
**Maps:** USGS Arroyo Seco and Wheeler Peak
**Managed by:** Carson National Forest, Columbine-Hondo
 Wilderness Study Area, Questa Ranger District
**Features:** challenging climb, cool and shady trail, unique
 views

At 12,115 feet, Lobo Peak is the highest point in the small range of mountains that lies between the Rio Hondo and the Red River. The mountains rise abruptly from the bordering canyons, forcing the trail to Lobo Peak to gain almost 4,000 feet in 4.5 miles. Lobo Peak's isolation from other high points makes the views from the top unique, taking in the Taos Plateau and Rio Grande Gorge to the west, the Latir Peaks to the north, and the Wheeler Peak area to the south.

From Taos city center, go north and west on US 64 for 4 miles to the junction with NM 150. Turn right, following the signs for Taos Ski Valley. Continue about 12 miles from US 64 (2 miles from Upper Cuchilla Campground) and park at the trailhead for the Manzanita Trail.

The first section of the Manzanita Trail 58 is on private land, so stay on the trail in this area. Begin on a dirt road, passing through a gate, then bearing left to parallel the creek in Manzanita Canyon and enter Carson

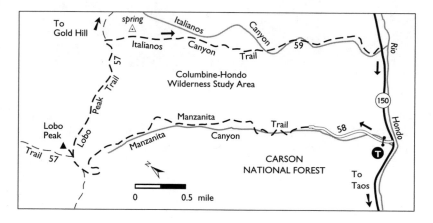

*360-degree view from the top of Lobo Peak*

National Forest. At mile 0.8, where water from a spring drains along the route, the road becomes a true trail. In a few minutes, make the first of many crossings of the creek over the next 0.5 mile.

At mile 1.5, climb two switchbacks and parallel the stream higher on the slope. For the next mile, the grade steepens as the trail becomes almost like a staircase in places. At mile 2.6, the trail bends left to cross a dry drainage, then resumes the steep climb. Cross the base of a small talus slope, then enter a clearing offering views of the ridge to the east. Another clearing is reached at mile 3.7, this one offering views of the high ridgeline to the north. At an unmarked intersection, bear left, then begin walking a series of switchbacks to the top of a narrow ridge. Turn right with the ridgeline and enter a small meadow with great views in all directions. Continue along the ridge, watching carefully for the trail when it crosses open areas. At the junction with Lobo Peak Trail 57 at mile 4.5, go straight to reach the summit of Lobo Peak.

After enjoying the view from the summit, return to the junction of the Lobo Peak and Manzanita Trails. Turn left (northeast) onto the Lobo Peak Trail, following a ridgeline in the direction of Gold Hill. At mile 5.5, skirt the base of a rocky crag before the trail becomes faint as it passes to the left of a small peak. The trail then drops steeply to a saddle.

At the saddle, turn right onto the Italianos Canyon Trail 59. Several quick switchbacks lead to a nice campsite near a small spring. Look carefully for the trail as it leaves the marshy area and climbs the toe of a small ridge. At mile 6.6, reach a meadow where the trail disappears, though a rock cairn visible on the other side of the clearing marks the route. Continue to drop through small meadows and open conifer forest, passing plenty of fine campsites along the way. After a brief flat stretch, descend through switchbacks at mile 8.1 to cross the main stream in Italianos Canyon. The trail remains wet for the next mile, crossing the stream many times. More campsites are found between miles 9 and 10. At mile 10, exit the canyon and reach NM 150. Turn right and walk 1 mile to the Manzanita Trailhead.

# 21 | WILLIAMS LAKE

**Distance: 6 miles, day hike**
**Difficulty:** moderate
**Elevation range:** 10,400 to 11,450 feet
**Elevation gain:** 900 feet
**Best time of year:** mid-June to mid-October
**Water:** carry water
**Map:** USGS Wheeler Peak
**Managed by:** Carson National Forest, Wheeler Peak
    Wilderness, Questa Ranger District
**Features:** views of alpine lake and rugged peaks

Despite the state's relatively southern latitude, New Mexico's highest terrain was covered by glaciers until about 10,000 years ago. Hikers basking in the refreshing air of the alpine world surrounding the shores of Williams Lake will find it easy to picture the thousand-foot-thick sheet of snow

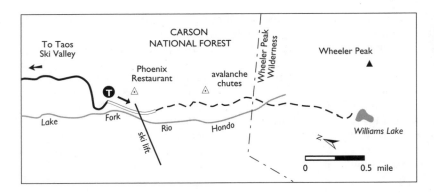

and ice that filled the valley. The lake itself lies in a deep cirque completely surrounded by a jagged ring of peaks. Although the summit is not visible from the lake, Wheeler Peak—the state's highest point—forms the eastern rim of the cirque.

The 900-foot climb to Williams Lake over a gentle pass at 11,400 feet doesn't require a lot of huffing and puffing. The Williams Lake Trail is a popular midsummer stroll that is routinely accomplished by hikers from ages four to eighty.

In some ways, hiking to Williams Lake is easier than finding the trailhead. From Taos, take US 64 north about 4 miles to the intersection with NM 150. Turn right and drive toward Taos Ski Valley. Fifteen miles from US 64, drive to the very eastern end of the parking area for the ski area. Swing to the left and look for the sign for Twining Road. Turn right onto the road and continue 0.5 mile. Turn left onto Phoenix Switchback Road, then make a sharp right onto Kachina Road in another 0.3 mile. Climb past signs for the Bavarian Restaurant, staying on the main road another 1.3 miles to the hikers' parking area.

Follow the wide road heading south from the parking area downhill and past a small pond on the right. At the base of a ski lift and near the Phoenix Restaurant, continue uphill on the road along the Lake Fork of the Rio Hondo. Watch for a sign that points the way to Williams Lake and angle left. In a few minutes, pass a second sign and again bear left. From this point the route is easy to follow.

Walk along the edge of the forest past three impressive avalanche chutes where snapped-off trees tell the tale of recent slides. The climb is gentle but steady as the trail enters the moist spruce-fir forest. Pass through two boulder piles pushed downcanyon by the glaciers. Alpine wildflowers like yellow Indian paintbrush, towering polemonium, and king's crown are found along the trail. At mile 2.8, crest a low pass and suddenly find Williams Lake at the bottom of a huge bowl of rock. Drop to the lake and enjoy the grassy meadows on the south and west edges. After resting, return to the trailhead by the same route.

*Wildflowers are abundant throughout the summer in rocky meadows in the high Sangre de Cristo.*

# 22 | GOLD HILL

**Distance: 9 miles, day hike or backpack**
**Difficulty:** strenuous
**Elevation range:** 9,400 to 12,711 feet
**Elevation gain:** 3,300 feet
**Best time of year:** late June to October
**Water:** Long Canyon
**Maps:** USGS Red River and Wheeler Peak
**Managed by:** Carson National Forest, Columbine-Hondo
    Wilderness Study Area, Questa Ranger District
**Features:** well-graded climb, cool shady trail, superb views

At 12,711 feet, Gold Hill qualifies more as a mountain than a hill, and hikers won't find any precious metal on the summit. And although Gold Hill doesn't quite make it on the list of the state's ten highest named peaks, the view from the summit rivals that of nearby Wheeler Peak. The routes to

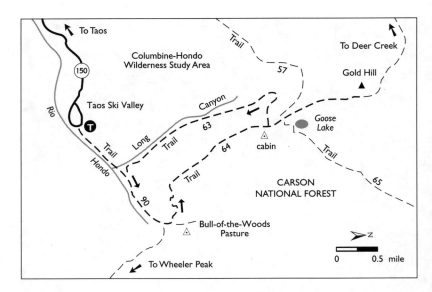

these two high points share the first 2 miles, but at Bull-of-the-Woods Pasture most hikers head right to Wheeler, leaving the left-hand trail to Gold Hill delightfully devoid of people.

The trailhead is located in the upper parking area at Taos Ski Valley. From the center of Taos travel north on US 64. At a traffic signal in 4 miles, turn right onto New Mexico 150. Follow this winding road about 15 miles and reach the parking area at Taos Ski Valley. Bear right and continue past the parking lots about 0.3 mile to the upper parking area.

Look for the Wheeler Peak Trail 90 heading uphill from behind the wilderness information board. The track crosses a road and begins its steep ascent. In the first mile, ignore the winding trail marked for horses and stay on the steeper, wider hiking route. With the Rio Hondo to the right, ascend this steepest portion of the entire hike under a forest canopy.

One mile from the start, the Long Canyon Trail 63—the return route for this trip—heads left. A few yards beyond the intersection, Trail 90 swings left and begins another steep section. Continue straight and uphill and the trail joins an old mining road coming in from the right. The route swings south to again parallel the Rio Hondo, passing through narrow meadows and occasional views back downslope to the ski basin. Much of this section is unshaded, but the trail passes stands of aspen and summer wildflowers, particularly the chartreuse fireweed.

As you approach Bull-of-the-Woods Pasture 1.9 miles from the start, the route splits from Trail 90, which heads to the right. Bear left and in a few yards (before you reach the edge of the soggy pasture) turn left again onto the Gold Hill Trail 64. Begin the moderate, miles-long ascent of the end of the long ridge of which Gold Hill is the summit.

In the course of the next mile, the trail alternates between open meadows and stands of fir, climbing gradually up the quartzite-studded ridge. At mile 4.5, reach timberline and the tundra-clad ridge leading to Gold Hill. Follow the trail through the meadow to the ruins of a cabin near a small mine where the view of Wheeler Peak is superb.

To continue on the now-faint trail, walk a few yards west, back toward the trees, looking for a sign marking the beginning of the Long Canyon Trail 63. A faint track in tall grasses leads to the sign. Once at the signpost, turn right and take the now easy-to-follow Gold Hill Trail 64 up to the ridge. Hikers who miss the route should simply follow the grassy ridgeline heading north.

Passing through scattered bristlecone pines, the trail gains the ridge. Again, the official trail fades, so head to the left of a false summit straight ahead. The trail comes back into view near the junction with the Lobo Peak Trail 57 and skirts left of the false summit. Along the final half mile, the views to the west are especially grand. Goose Lake lies straight down to the right (east) of the ridge. Watch the ground, too, for signs of bighorn sheep.

A small rock shelter marks the summit and provides shelter from the almost constant wind. The view of the rest of the world that stretches from the top reaches into Colorado to the summits of Conejos and Blanca Peaks.

*Old mining cabin on the way to Gold Hill, with an outstanding view of Wheeler Peak*

When it's time to leave, head back down the ridge to the sign, "Columbine-Twining National Recreation Trail," for the Long Canyon Trail 63 located a few hundred feet west of the cabin ruins. The route is easy to follow downhill through grasses surrounded by stands of conifers. As the trail reaches the edge of the Long Canyon, it bears right, enters the forest, and curls toward the canyon's head. After a few minutes of walking across the steep eastern wall of the gorge, reach the canyon floor. Swing left to follow the canyon downhill, ignoring the track that continues straight and goes uphill.

It's a straight shot from here, following Long Canyon for 2 miles. The descent is often steep. The trail stays on the east side of the canyon floor and picks up a stream about halfway down. Springs along the way enliven the spruce-fir forest with splashes of color from wildflowers. Intersect Trail 90, turn right, and drop down, retracing your steps over the last mile back to the parking area.

## 23 | WHEELER PEAK

**Distance: 14 miles, day hike or backpack**
**Difficulty:** strenuous
**Elevation range:** 9,400 to 13,161 feet
**Elevation gain:** 3,700 feet
**Best time of year:** late June to early October
**Water:** Middle Fork of the Red River
**Maps:** USGS Wheeler Peak; USFS Latir and Wheeler Peak
  Wilderness
**Managed by:** Carson National Forest, Wheeler Peak
  Wilderness, Questa Ranger District
**Features:** long walk above tree line, spectacular views

As the highest point in New Mexico, 13,161-foot Wheeler Peak is a popular destination for hikers. A well-worn trail with moderate grades leads to the summit, passing through the state's most extensive area of alpine vegetation. Eye-popping views extend in all directions from the long ridge leading to the peak; a small herd of bighorn sheep and the rare chance to see white-tailed ptarmigan add to the attractions.

A safe hike to Wheeler Peak requires a good deal of common sense. High elevation makes sunscreen mandatory on this trip, even on cloudy days. Snow remains on the upper trail into early or even late July, when the summer thunderstorm season makes it dangerous to be on the ridge. Start your hike early to get off the peak by noon. September is the best time to make the climb, but hikers should know the weather forecast before starting the trip; intense snowstorms can hit the mountains any time after late August.

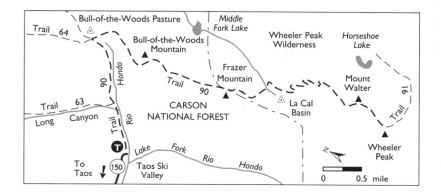

The trip to Wheeler Peak is a long one and hikers should allow 10 to 12 hours for the round trip to the summit.

From Taos, go north and west on US 64 about 4 miles to the junction with NM 150. Turn right, following the signs for Taos Ski Valley. Continue about 15 miles and park in the upper gravel lot at Taos Ski Valley near a wilderness information board.

From the trailhead, follow the signs for Wheeler Peak Trail 90 and begin hiking northeast along the headwaters of the Rio Hondo. Follow the wide hiking route and ignore the winding horse trail. Intersect Long Canyon

*Bull-of-the-Woods Pasture fills a broad saddle at the end of the ridge that culminates in Wheeler Peak.*

Trail 63 at mile 1.0, and stay on Trail 90 by following an old road along the north slope of the canyon, with views back to the ski area. At mile 1.9, reach Bull-of-the-Woods Pasture and the intersection with the Gold Hill Trail 64. Follow the road to the right, staying on Trail 90 and skirting the west side of Bull-of-the-Woods Mountain. The road climbs to the ridgeline and, at mile 2.9, meets an easy-to-follow trail leading up the ridge.

The trail, now above tree line, continues along the ridge, passing the summit of Frazer Mountain at mile 4.1. Descend into the headwaters of the Middle Fork of the Red River, which offers limited campsites and water at mile 5. The trail resumes the climb, passing the La Cal Basin. Another steep mile in thin air leads to the ridgeline. At mile 6.8, reach the summit of Mount Walter. Descend briefly to a saddle, then climb the final 0.25 mile to the summit of Wheeler Peak, where Trail 91 continues along the ridgeline before descending to Horseshoe Lake.

While keeping an eye on the weather, enjoy the view, which takes in the highest peaks of the Sangre de Cristos as well as parts of the Rio Grande Gorge. Return to the trailhead by the same route.

# 24 COLUMBINE CANYON TO HONDO CANYON

**Distance: 13.1 miles one-way, day hike or backpack**
**Difficulty:** strenuous
**Elevation range:** 8,000 to 12,200 feet
**Elevation gain:** 4,400 feet
**Best time of year:** mid-June to mid-October
**Water:** Columbine Creek, Placer Fork, Long Canyon
**Maps:** USGS Questa and Arroyo Seco; USFS Latir and
    Wheeler Peak Wilderness
**Managed by:** Carson National Forest, Columbine-Hondo
    Wilderness Study Area, Questa Ranger District
**Features:** old mining operations, quiet canyon with running
    water, alpine scenery

More than a century ago, miners blasted tunnels in the walls of Columbine Canyon, and the slopes bear the scars of the search for treasure. Throughout the Sangre de Cristo range around Red River, miners combed the canyons for silver and gold deposits. A few found gold in the gravels of Columbine Creek, and the lure of yellow metal still attracts prospectors to the stream. Although hikers can take a gold pan and try their luck, they are more likely to find a bonanza in the form of abundant wildflowers, luscious wild strawberries, or bronze native trout.

Hikers can take either of two approaches to a trip up Columbine Can-

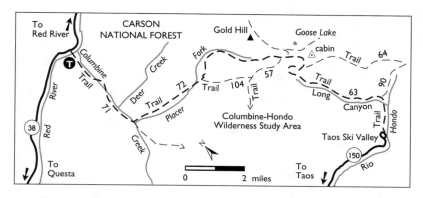

yon. For a leisurely summer stroll, head 3 or 4 miles up the canyon and enjoy its forest and meadows. For a challenging overnight hike, consider the staircase climb over the main ridge and down into the canyon of the Rio Hondo. This route over the crest of the range traverses an old miners trail that connected the camps at Columbine with the ones at Twining, better known now as Taos Ski Valley.

From Taos, set up a shuttle by following the directions to the trailhead in the Taos Ski Valley as described in the Gold Hill Hike 22. Return to the traffic signal at the intersection of US 64, NM 150, and NM 522. Turn right onto NM 522 north and continue 20 miles to Questa. Turn right onto NM 38 and find Columbine Campground in 5 miles on the right.

Begin hiking in Columbine Campground at the signs for the Columbine-Twining National Recreation Trail. The route leads up the canyon bottom along Columbine Creek, which is graced with clear water dancing over a bed of pastel gravel. Along the trail are stately aspens too big for anyone to wrap their arms around. The path frequently swings along the base of talus fields piled against ragged cliffs. Both local species of columbine—the blazing little red and the exquisite blue Colorado—grow along the trail, but in July the sheer numbers of mountain parsley and wild geranium steal the show. Finding more than fifty species in bloom along the trail is not unusual. Wild strawberries are ripe in late July.

Cross two arching bridges before reaching Placer Fork at mile 2.1. Hikers taking the easy route should continue up Columbine Canyon in the direction of Lobo Peak. Just beyond a third bridge, a rocky meadow offers views to the ridgeline to the south and makes a good lunch stop or turnaround point.

To continue on the Columbine-Hondo National Recreation Trail, turn left and head east on the Placer Fork Trail 72. The trail follows the canyon bottom as it gradually gains elevation. Pass the junction with the Willow Fork Trail 104 near mile 3.7. The trail leads to an oval meadow at mile 5.3, dotted with marsh marigolds and shooting stars in July. The forest edges of the meadow offer the best campsites along the way.

From the meadow, continue up the trail and reach a huge bowl. Climb

*Calypso orchid*

the very steep head of the cirque to the grass-covered ridge that connects Gold Hill with the peaks to the west. Intersect the Lobo Peak Trail 57 and bear left. This trail may be difficult to follow as it heads through the meadows below Gold Hill. Near the ruins of a mining cabin, intersect the Long Canyon Trail 63. Follow this trail as it enters Long Canyon, swings south and travels the length of the canyon. At mile 12.1, intersect Trail 90, turn right, and descend to the trailhead at Taos Ski Valley.

# 25 | HEART LAKE AND LATIR MESA

**Distance: 14 miles, day hike or backpack**
**Difficulty:** strenuous
**Elevation range:** 9,200 to 12,600 feet
**Elevation gain:** 3,800 feet
**Best time of year:** mid-June to late September
**Water:** Lake Fork, Bull Creek, Heart Lake
**Maps:** USGS Red River and Latir Peak
**Managed by:** Carson National Forest, Latir Wilderness,
  Questa Ranger District
**Features:** grand views above tree line, alpine lake, running
  water

At the close of the most recent Ice Age, glaciers melted from the highest peaks of the Sangre de Cristo range and left behind a dozen small lakes in cirques at the heads of the valleys and amid the jagged skylines that form their backdrops. Located in the Latir Wilderness, Heart Lake is only 5 miles from the trailhead and is backed by sweeping mesas that reach above 12,000 feet. For casual hikers, it is an easy climb to the lake; strong day hikers and backpackers can make a grand loop past the lake onto the alpine ridges of Latir Mesa, where sweeping views reach from the Latir Lakes below to the summits of distant Colorado.

A few cautions: navigating this route above Heart Lake requires skill with maps, and a compass or GPS. The trails fade in the high meadows,

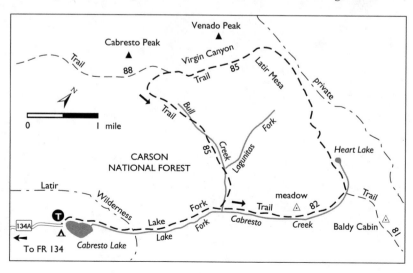

and routefinding is necessary over Latir Mesa and to the Bull Creek Trail. The loop trip traverses more than 4 miles of terrain above timberline, so hikers take care when planning a summer trip into this area. It is a good idea to be down off the ridges by noon, before thunderstorms have the opportunity to build. An alternative is to wait until September, but at that time hikers must be prepared for chilly nights. Camping is not permitted within 300 feet of Heart Lake or in the meadow surrounding Baldy Cabin. Farther along the route, some nice forested sites are found just below the initial steep drop into the Bull Creek drainage.

To get to the trailhead at Cabresto Lake, drive 0.25 mile on NM 38 from the intersection of NM 522 and NM 38 in Questa. Turn left onto NM 563 and travel 2.1 miles, then turn right onto gravel FR 134. Cross into Carson National Forest and drive 3.3 miles to FR 134A. Turn left (north) and continue 2.1 miles to Cabresto Lake and campground. This road is rough in places, so a high-clearance vehicle is recommended, although sedans carefully driven can make the trip.

The Lake Fork Trail 82 starts by skirting to the left (west) of Cabresto Lake, then makes a long, steady climb parallel to Lake Fork of Cabresto Creek. The first 2 miles traverse conifer forest with cork-bark fir dominating the slopes. After passing through several small meadows, meet the Bull Creek Trail 85 about 2.5 miles from the start. Bear right, cross Bull Creek, and continue along Lake Fork on Trail 82.

After climbing the only switchback on the trail, enter a blue spruce forest. At mile 3.5, find a long meadow with excellent campsites on both sides of Lake Fork. In 0.5 mile, the trail re-enters the forest and climbs a low ridge. At mile 4.5, bear left toward Heart Lake at the junction with Baldy Mountain Trail 81. In a few minutes, enter a small meadow and bear right to parallel small streams on both the left and right. As the trail peters out, again pick up the main trail to the left of the streams. From here it is a short distance to Heart Lake.

To reach Latir Mesa, head to the southwest shoreline and find a sign indicating Trail 85 and the way to Latir Mesa. Climb along a ridgeline to get excellent views of Heart Lake, and ascend a steep talus slope to gain the flanks of Latir Mesa. Here the trail fades and hikers must do some routefinding. Head toward the rounded summit of the mesa where the Latir Lakes come into view. Do not cross onto private land on the north side of the ridge.

Skirt the flanks of a summit, indicated as peak 12,692 on the map, then stay close to the ridgeline as it swings around the head of Lagunitas Fork to a saddle at the foot of Venado Peak. From the saddle, stay on the slopes of Virgin Canyon, keeping a row of low rocks on your left. A sign near the valley bottom points toward Cabresto Peak. Ascend this easier-to-follow

*Heart Lake with July snow on Latir Mesa*
**(Photo by June Fabryka-Martin)**

trail up the slopes of Virgin Canyon to the top of the ridge, and to a saddle and the junction with Trail 88. Angle left to follow the arrows to Bull Canyon Trail 85 and walk down the steep head of the canyon. In 0.5 mile, skirt a meadow and watch for campsites along the forest edge. The trail drops steeply for 2 miles to the intersection with the Lake Fork Trail. Turn right and walk downhill to Cabresto Lake and the trailhead.

# 26 | SAWMILL PARK

**Distance: 11 miles, day hike or backpack**
**Difficulty:** moderate
**Elevation range:** 9,600 to 11,000 feet
**Elevation gain:** 1,500 feet
**Best time of year:** late May to late October
**Water:** Sawmill Creek
**Maps:** USGS Wheeler Peak and Eagle Nest
**Managed by:** Carson National Forest, Wheeler Peak
    Wilderness, Questa Ranger District
**Features:** easy hike into a long, high meadow

The 3-mile-long meadow by Sawmill Creek is one of New Mexico's easiest-to-reach high country destinations. The grades of this trail are gentle enough for beginning backpackers. Idyllic campsites are found at the west end of the meadow and in the basins of several side drainages that enter from the west. Most visitors to the Wheeler Peak Wilderness head for the rim country to the west; it is likely that hikers will have Sawmill Park to themselves.

From the east end of the town of Red River on NM 38, take NM 578 south for 6.4 miles to the end of the pavement. Bear left, cross a bridge, and take the gravel FR 58A, the right fork. Continue through private land on the rough road. After about 1 mile, pass through two gates, then bear left at

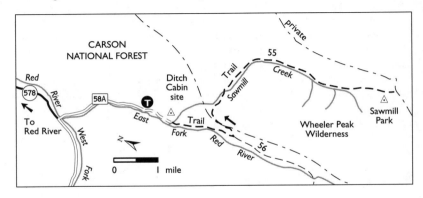

*Wild iris blooms in early summer on the grassy slopes above Sawmill Creek.*

a fork. Park at the East Fork Trailhead 1.4 miles from the pavement.

Begin hiking on a bermed four-wheel-drive road angling uphill into the trees. Climb steadily for 0.4 mile to reach a small meadow, the site of Ditch Cabin. Cross Sawmill Creek on a small bridge, then begin a long, well-graded climb parallel to the East Fork of the Red River.

At a well-marked intersection 1.5 miles from the start, turn sharply left onto Sawmill Park Trail 55. This trail continues the easy climb up the east wall of the East Fork Canyon, crossing into the Wheeler Peak Wilderness. Once over the ridge, the trail again meets Sawmill Creek, following the creek upstream to enter Sawmill Meadow. Pick up the tread of the trail near the trees at the north edge of the meadow. From here, the trail follows the meadow, bursting with wildflowers all summer long and with small but deep Sawmill Creek meandering through the tall grass. Stay on the trail to prevent damage to the meadow. Watch for deer, elk, and snowshoe hare in the forest openings.

About 3 miles from the start, the meadow and trail swing south. The valley narrows and widens several times before reaching Sawmill Park 4.9 miles from the start. The trail is easy to follow to a lone Douglas fir tree standing at the meadow's edge. From the tree, follow the meadow south as it slopes up to a saddle. Here the meadow is always wet and alive with white marsh marigolds. At the saddle, a fence marks the boundary of private property. Return to the trailhead by the same route.

# 27 | HORSESHOE LAKE

**Distance: 13.5 miles, backpack**
**Difficulty:** strenuous
**Elevation range:** 9,400 to 11,950 feet
**Elevation gain:** 2,800 feet
**Best time of year:** late June to mid-October
**Water:** forks of the Red River, Horseshoe and Lost Lakes
**Map:** USGS Wheeler Peak
**Managed by:** Carson National Forest, Wheeler Peak
   Wilderness, Questa Ranger District
**Features:** alpine scenery, high lakes, fishing, wildlife

Horseshoe and Lost Lakes lie in rugged bowls at the foot of the highest ridge in New Mexico. The trail to the lakes is surprisingly gentle, threading through deep conifer forest up and above the canyon of the East Fork of the Red River. Ample campsites are available along the way, and this beautiful area invites more than a day trip. Both lakes host good populations of trout and are popular destinations for anglers. From Horseshoe Lake it is a short trip to the summit of Wheeler Peak, but extending the hike in this manner should be attempted only as part of an overnight trip. Hikers can eliminate the road portion of this hike with a short, 2-mile shuttle by leaving a car or a mountain bike at the Middle Fork Lake Trailhead, then driving to start the hike at the East Fork Trailhead.

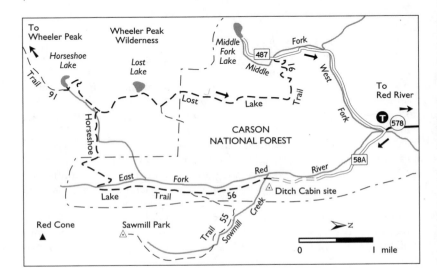

From the east end of the town of Red River on NM 38, take NM 578 south for 6.4 miles to the end of the pavement and park. Begin walking on FR 58A to the east of the parking area and immediately cross the East Fork of the Red River. Bear right and follow the road through the small summer home development 1.4 miles to the East Fork Trailhead. Pick up the Horseshoe Lake Trail 56 over a large dirt berm to the left, which runs parallel to the East Fork to the right. Continue up this abandoned road to the Ditch Cabin site, cross Sawmill Creek on a bridge, and finally begin hiking on a trail at mile 1.7. The trail begins a gentle ascent through mixed conifer forest, rich in wildflowers—calypso orchids, false Solomon's seal, Colorado columbine, monkshood, and cow parsnip—all summer long.

*Horseshoe Lake is backed by the highest ridge in New Mexico.*
(Photo by June Fabryka-Martin)

At mile 2.5, pass the intersection with the Sawmill Park Trail 55 to the left and continue up the canyon of the East Fork. At mile 3.9, drop down to cross the East Fork on a bridge. The trail now climbs several broad switchbacks, wandering through forest, meadow, and talus, with Red Cone often visible on the ridge to the left. As the trail crosses a small ridge, the high ridgeline that includes Wheeler Peak and Mount Walter stretches out in front. After crossing a bridge, reach a trail junction. Turn left to begin the climb to Horseshoe Lake, 0.7 mile from the junction. Camping is not permitted within 300 feet of the lake.

Backtrack down from Horseshoe Lake to the main trail. At the junction, turn left, heading toward Lost Lake. The trail loses elevation and crosses two wide talus slopes. A mile from the trail junction, reach Lost Lake. Many fine campsites are located away from the lake, which holds plenty of cutthroat and rainbow trout.

Continuing down the Lost Lake Trail 91 from the lake, pass an old trail branching to the right, then leave the Wheeler Peak Wilderness. The trail now offers superb views to the north and east as it heads north through forest and talus. At mile 9.2, the trail begins to switchback down from the ridge and enters a dense conifer forest. Over the next 2 miles, the trail drops 1,500 feet to the intersection with Middle Fork Lake Road (FR 487). Bear right and walk down the narrow road, which continues to switchback down the slope. At mile 12, cross a bridge over the West Fork of the Red River. Turn right onto the road parallel to the Middle Fork, soon passing the Middle Fork Lake Trailhead. Continue on the road just over a mile to reach the parking area.

# 28 | COMANCHE CREEK

**Distance: 6 miles, day hike**
**Difficulty:** easy
**Elevation range:** 9,250 to 9,650 feet
**Elevation gain:** 500 feet
**Best time of year:** late May to late October
**Water:** Comanche Creek
**Map:** USGS Comanche Point
**Managed by:** Carson National Forest, Valle Vidal Unit,
  Questa Ranger District
**Features:** rocky-sided valley, mountain vistas, fishing,
  historic trail

The valley of Comanche Creek is quintessential Valle Vidal, a region defined by open and expansive grasslands, shimmering creeks, and islands of conifer forest. This route follows Comanche Creek 2 miles before climb-

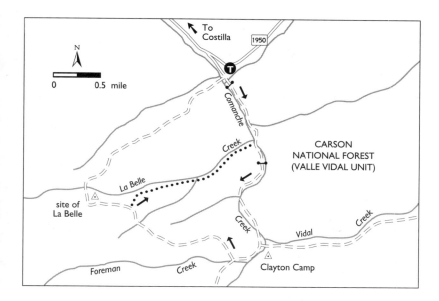

ing to grand views from the mesas above. Near the site of La Belle, a once-thriving gold-mining community near the head of La Belle Creek, the route turns back through a narrows to Comanche Creek. Rumor has it this is the same route taken by Tom Ketchum, one of the last train robbers, when he rode from his hangout in Valle Vidal to Saturday night dances in La Belle, his identity unknown to the local townsfolk. Carrying a map, along with a compass or GPS receiver, will be helpful in navigating this trip.

To reach the trailhead, take NM 522 north of Taos 40 miles to NM 196 at Costilla. Turn right on this paved, then all-weather gravel road. Seventeen miles from NM 522, at the Carson National Forest boundary, the road

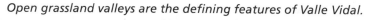

*Open grassland valleys are the defining features of Valle Vidal.*

becomes FR 1950. Six-and-a-half miles beyond the forest boundary, bear right on an unmarked dirt track heading from FR 1950 down toward Comanche Creek. Park at the wide turnout before the gate about 0.5 mile from FR 1950.

From the parking area, walk along the old road that parallels Comanche Creek, immediately passing through a gate. At mile 0.5, at the mouth of La Belle Creek and the return leg of this hike, walk beneath some dramatic outcrops of granite before crossing the stream and climbing to another gate. Two more stream crossings lead to the junction with Vidal Creek at mile 1.8. A branch of the road leads to the sometimes active Clayton Camp, a large ranch building to the left, so stay to the right.

Beyond Clayton Camp, the road rounds a knoll on the right side of Comanche Creek before heading up Foreman Creek at mile 2.3. At the faint junction, the main trail up Comanche Creek bears left across a boggy area; bear slightly right onto a faint road that turns up a small grassy drainage heading northwest. The route follows the traces of the road. Climb to a low ridge, passing a small ruin to the left. On the ridge, the faint road turns left to follow the crest. Look back to the east for a glimpse of a huge, grassy bowl. This valley is Valle Vidal, from which the entire area takes its name.

About 3 miles from the start, the road bears slightly to the right, now heading northwest. Descend through a drainage and climb to another ridge. Once on the other side, look to the head of the valley and the site of La Belle, a once-thriving gold camp from the 1890s. Leave the old road, and drop into the broad valley of La Belle Creek to the right. Near the bottom of the valley, turn right and follow the stream down to Comanche Creek, which is about 1.5 miles away. Cross Comanche Creek and pick up the old road, turning left to return about 0.5 mile to the trailhead.

# 29 | MCCRYSTAL PLACE

**Distance: 7 miles, day hike**
**Difficulty:** easy
**Elevation range:** 8,100 to 8,700 feet
**Elevation gain:** 700 feet
**Best time of year:** late May to late October
**Water:** McCrystal Creek
**Maps:** USGS Van Bremmer Park and Ash Mountain
**Managed by:** Carson National Forest, Valle Vidal Unit,
    Questa Ranger District
**Features:** impressive homestead ruins

In the late nineteenth century, the sprawling Maxwell Land Grant covered more than a million acres of the northern Sangre de Cristo Mountains. That such a huge piece of prime real estate was not in the public domain was too much for some neighbors to accept. Many small ranchers established homesteads on the grant, believing that eventually the land would be rightfully declared open to the public. The grant managers called them squatters.

John McCrystal moved his family to a small valley watered by a small stream draining off Costilla Peak. Despite the knowledge that the land belonged to the Maxwell Grant, he boldly built his house and ranch and soon became a leader among the anti-grant men. As the courts upheld the rights of the grant, pressure on the ranchers increased. In 1890 he was forced to settle with the grant, and purchased 320 acres for $960.

The old road to the McCrystal Place travels 3 miles along McCrystal Creek, offering a solid view of homesteading around the turn of the century. Even in ruins, one can see why the ranch was worth fighting for. Cattle still graze the rich meadows along McCrystal Creek; timber is plentiful in the surrounding hills. The peaceful view from McCrystal's yard extends many miles to the south.

To reach the trailhead, take NM 522 north of Taos 40 miles to NM 196 at Costilla. Turn right on this paved, then all-weather gravel road. Seventeen miles from NM 522, at the Carson National Forest boundary, the road becomes FR 1950. Continue about 20 miles to McCrystal Campground. Park off the road near the campground entrance.

From the campground entrance, walk west along FR 1950 for about 0.25 mile to a dirt road angling to the northwest, and parallel to the campground road, which is just on the other side of a fence. Bear right, pass through a gate, and stroll through the shady pine forest, watching for tassel-eared squirrels and domestic bison run from the nearby Ring Place. After about a mile, the trail meets up with McCrystal Creek to the right. The trail now parallels the creek, passing the large ruins of a sawmill along the way.

At mile 1.5, the road enters a large marshy meadow. A bit farther on, pass a stone foundation to the right and the remains of a wooden structure on the left. At mile 2.6, the road swings to the west to parallel Can Creek. The road heads west for 0.25 mile before bearing right and crossing Can Creek. Descend for several hundred yards before arriving in the meadow surrounding the McCrystal Place.

In a few minutes, reach the large main house and several smaller

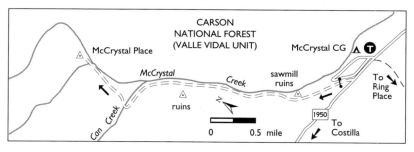

*The main ranch house of the McCrystal Place dates back to around 1900.*

structures of the ranch. The buildings are fragile and dangerous: stay out. Explore around the ranch and enjoy the view down the valley to the mountains beyond, then return to the trailhead by the same route.

# 30 | NORTH PONIL CREEK

**Distance: 8 miles, day hike**
**Difficulty:** easy
**Elevation range:** 7,750 to 8,000 feet
**Elevation gain:** 300 feet
**Best time of year:** late May to late October
**Water:** North Ponil Creek
**Maps:** USGS Van Bremmer Park and Abreu Canyon
**Managed by:** Carson National Forest, Valle Vidal Unit,
   Questa Ranger District
**Features:** scenic meadow, ghost town

Walking the long, flower-laced meadow beside North Ponil Creek is a delightful trip a hundred years back in time. The small valley is much like it was before lumbermen pushed a railroad through its serene grasslands, but the traces of human use are still much in evidence. The Cimarron and Northwestern Railway traveled 22 miles into the mountains from the town of Cimarron to Ponil Park, the broadest part of the meadow, which soon became a bustling railroad and lumber town. The railroad connected Ponil Park, the center of operations in the woods, to a series of lumber camps in the canyon below. Perhaps as many as two hundred people lived there in 1910, working the rails, in the sawmills, or as lumbermen. The surrounding forest never provided as much timber for mine supports and railroad ties as the company had anticipated, so the line was torn up in 1921.

To reach the trailhead, take NM 522 north of Taos 40 miles to NM 196 at Costilla, nearly to the Colorado border. Turn right on this paved, then all-weather gravel road. Seventeen miles from NM 522, at the Carson National Forest boundary, the road becomes FR 1950. Continue about 21 miles to park at an information board 1.5 miles beyond McCrystal Campground.

Begin hiking on the south (right) side of FR 1950 on a double-track behind a "Road Closed" sign. The track leads downcanyon, parallel to the diminutive North Ponil Creek. In several hundred yards, pass around a gate and continue down the wide meadow. Throughout the summer, hikers will be accompanied by the buzz of dozens of broad-tailed hummingbirds as they visit scarlet Southwest penstemon and lavender New Mexico penstemon.

After 1.5 miles, the trail crosses the stream and follows the boundary of the pine forest on the west side of the valley. At mile 2.1, Hart Canyon joins the North Ponil valley from the left. Ruins of the old town are visible across North Ponil Creek. Continue down the west side of the valley, passing a small railroad trestle and then two cabin ruins. Here the trail parallels the railroad. After Seally Canyon enters from the right, the trail runs along the top of the railroad grade and rotting ties are found along the route. Continue to walk on the old railroad for another mile until reaching a standing chimney and fireplace in perfect condition. Just beyond, the trail reaches a fence and private land. Turn around and return on the same trail.

On the return trip, cross to the east side of the valley to the first cabin ruin you saw along the trail. Look for at least a dozen ruins and a small

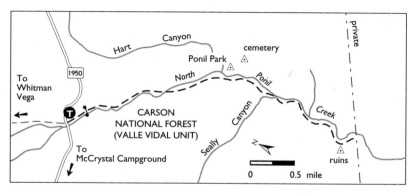

*Raised log railbed at Ponil Park*

cemetery. An interesting raised railbed follows the creek, and a stack of firewood appears ready for the return of people to the park. Please respect these reminders of the past and leave them undisturbed. After enjoying the town, continue back up North Ponil Creek 2 miles to the trailhead.

## 31 | LITTLE HORSE MESA LOOP

**Distance: 6-mile loop, day hike**
**Difficulty:** moderate
**Elevation range:** 7,850 to 8,250 feet
**Elevation gain:** 900 feet
**Best time of year:** May to late October
**Water:** carry water
**Map:** USGS Raton
**Managed by:** Sugarite Canyon State Park
**Features:** scenic meadow, ghost town

One of New Mexico's most scenic state parks, Sugarite is centered on the canyon of the same name. Gambel oak and ponderosa pine paint the canyon walls in a mosaic of green. Turkey and deer are common in the oaks and grasslands, and signs of elk, bobcat, and black bear are common in the forests. As for wildflowers, the park is loaded with unusual species such as the orange-flowered calico bush, Colorado columbine, and Canada anemone.

When ranchers worked the land in the late 1800s, they called the canyon Chicorica, a name that lives on in the creek flowing in the valley today. The name Chicorica may be a corruption of the Spanish *achirocia*, the wild chicory plant, or it may date back to when Comanches lived in the area and named it for the "abundance of birds" on the mesas. Anglo coal miners had trouble twisting their tongues around the word. Before long, Chicorica was corrupted into Sugarite, which is properly pronounced sugar-REET.

The park owes its existence to black and dusty coal. As the most recent sea that covered New Mexico receded about 60 million years ago, thick swamps were left in its wake. The decay of millions of swamp trees accumulated as muck, which was later squeezed by the earth into coal. Nearby deposits were discovered near Raton Pass in 1821 by the Long Expedition, but it wasn't until 1909 that it was economically feasible to begin mining operations in Sugarite Canyon. The Chicorica Coal Company developed the diggings and the accompanying coal camp. Starting with about 500 residents, the town of Sugarite doubled in size over the next 20 years, but faded away as the demand for coal fell.

Sugarite Canyon State Park is located a few miles northeast of Raton.

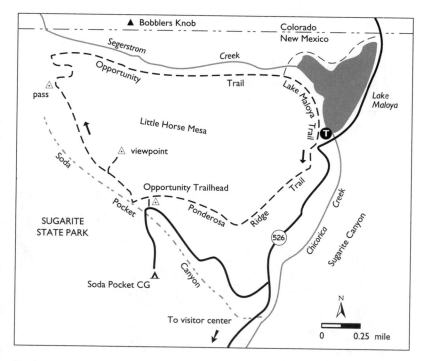

From that city, take exit 452 from I-25 and head east on NM 72. In 3.7 miles, bear left onto NM 526. The park entrance and visitor center are 1.7 miles up NM 526. Stop and pay the small day-use fee before continuing up the canyon. The trailhead is 4 miles beyond the park entrance.

Three trails connect to form a varied 6-mile loop that circles the volcanic ramparts of Little Horse Mesa. The circuit, along with a short spur trip, offers views of the sandstone and coal walls of Sugarite Canyon, the rolling grasslands of the mesa tops, Lake Maloya, and the secluded Segerstrom Creek.

Begin at the small parking area on NM 526 at the west end of the dam that backs up Lake Maloya. (Note that hikers can also begin the loop at the horse corral near the entrance to Soda Pocket Campground.) A sign points the way to the Ponderosa Ridge Trail, the first leg of the journey. Head left on the trail as it winds through pine forest. Steep, eroded switchbacks lead to a level bench that offers views down Sugarite Canyon. A mile from the start, another steep pitch in the trail leads to a second bench. Weaving in and out of meadows, the trail descends to the road to Soda Pocket Campground and the head of the Opportunity Trail at mile 2.

From the Opportunity Trailhead, head northwest on the now rocky trail as it ascends Soda Pocket Canyon on a moderate grade. Gambel oak shades much of the narrow trail. At 2.4 miles from the start, hikers can take the 0.25-mile-long Little Horse Mesa Trail to the right. This trail makes short work of the ascent to the mesa top, where views of the sloping top of Bartlett Mesa and the old volcano or Bobblers Knob sit to the north. Return to the Opportunity Trail and continue upcanyon. The trail soon smoothes out until it reaches a lovely meadow beneath the cliffs of Bartlett and Little Horse Mesas.

About 3 miles from the start, the trail reaches a pass and begins to descend through open forest. Switchbacks lead down the slope to the bottom of Segerstrom Canyon at mile 3.4. Bear right and proceed downcanyon with the sound of the flowing stream nearby. The trail passes through tall-

*Early morning is the best time for a walk on the Opportunity Trail along Segerstrom Creek.*

grass meadows and stands of oak for the next 2 miles. At a broad meadow near the end of the canyon, look to the left for the rounded Bobblers Knob on the cliff above.

At mile 5.2, bear right at the junction with the Lake Maloya Trail. Follow the old road along the lakeshore back to the trailhead.

# 32 | CAPULIN VOLCANO RIM TRAIL

**Distance: 1 mile, short day hike**
**Difficulty:** easy
**Elevation range:** 7,900 to 8,182 feet
**Elevation gain:** 300 feet
**Best time of year:** year round
**Water:** at visitor center
**Map:** USGS Folsom
**Managed by:** Capulin Volcano National Monument
**Features:** huge pile of volcanic cinders, spectacular long-range views

The Great Plains may seem an unusual setting for volcanic activity, but the Raton-Clayton volcanic field covers more than two hundred square miles and holds about one hundred volcanic centers from which lava has flowed during the past 8 million years. These volcanoes mark the easternmost limit of recent volcanic activity in the United States.

Capulin Volcano is the centerpiece of a small national monument located in extreme northeastern New Mexico. The nearly perfect cinder cone was set aside as a classic example of this type of volcanic vent in 1916. The cone—built up by small bits of lava forcibly ejected from the central vent—is surrounded by four lava flows that oozed from cracks at the base. Each of the flows is visible from the crater rim; together they appear as waves of dark green vegetation rippling from the mountain. During the eruptions that occurred from 8,000 to 2,500 years ago, the sticky, chunky lava never flowed far from the volcano. Much of the Raton-Clayton volcanic field can be seen from the trail that travels the crater rim. Most impressive are the

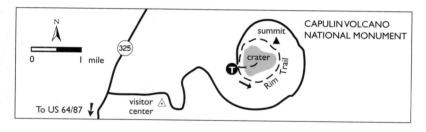

*Lava flows from the base of Capulin Volcano are best seen from the rim of the crater.*

lava-capped mesas to the north and west, and the immense shield volcano called Sierra Grande to the southeast.

Reach Capulin Volcano by taking exit 451 from I-25 at the city of Raton. Go east on US 64/87 about 28 miles to the town of Capulin. Turn left onto NM 325 and follow the signs about 4 miles to the national monument entrance. From the visitor center, take Crater Rim Drive as it corkscrews to the western edge of the crater and a small parking area.

The Rim Trail heads to the right (east) from the southern end of the parking area. The route is paved the entire way, but steep grades make comfortable walking shoes a must. Climb counterclockwise, first south then along the eastern edge of the crater. Just below are the lobes of the second lava flow, delineated by sweeping lines of trees. The view south from the summit takes in the old volcanoes. Watch for the aerial displays of turkey vultures as they play on the air currents within the crater. The trail also provides an opportunity to look at the ways the junipers hold together the cinders of the cone.

Before getting back in your car, take a short spur trail that leads down into the bottom of the crater. The view from the bottom offers an interesting vantage point, providing a measure of understanding about how the surrounding pile of cinders and rocks was formed.

*Facing page: The narrows at Kasha-Katuwe Tent Rocks National Monument*

# JEMEZ MOUNTAINS AND BANDELIER NATIONAL MONUMENT

# 33 | OJITOS WILDERNESS STUDY AREA

**Distance: 5 miles, day hike**
**Difficulty:** easy, but some routefinding required
**Elevation range:** 5,650 to 5,900 feet
**Elevation gain:** 400 feet
**Best time of year:** year round
**Water:** carry water
**Maps:** USGS Collier Draw and Ojitos Spring
**Managed by:** Bureau of Land Management, Albuquerque
   Field Office
**Features:** colorful badlands, unusual rock formations

New Mexico's treasure chest of natural features is so full of gaudy babbles that one can easily overlook the smaller gems. The Ojitos Wilderness Study Area (WSA) is such a place, usually passed over by those heading to the nearby, better-known Jemez Mountains.

At the Ojitos WSA, the soon-to-be-adobe layers of the Morrison formation are eroded into ridges with fantastic shapes. Hikers will find everything from toadstool rocks to banded mud castles. The stone castles are complete with pointed turrets and ramparts studded with shining stones polished smooth by waves on the shore of an ancient sea. Careful observation reveals petroglyphs, geodes, and other special treats.

To get to the area, take I-25 to the NM 44 exit, about 20 miles north of Albuquerque and 40 miles south of Santa Fe. Head west, leaving the

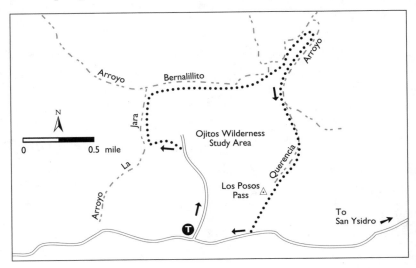

*Hikes in the Ojitos Wilderness Study Area are full of surprises.*

highway about a mile south of the town of San Ysidro. Turn west onto a dirt road and immediately take the left fork. Stay on the road through Zia Pueblo and in 6 miles cross a cattle guard to enter public land. Continue on the all-weather gravel road and park near a closed road heading north, which is located about 12 miles from the highway.

The open vegetation and rolling terrain of the Ojitos WSA invites wandering and that's a good thing: there are no trails in the area. Wander with a map and compass or GPS unit, or try the following suggestion.

From the parking area, walk north on the dirt road heading along a ridge. Follow the road about a half mile as it skirts along the rise. Watch for weird cylinders of rock that look like massive dinosaur bones. Whenever practical, drop into the wide drainage, Arroyo La Jara, to the left. At or near the arroyo bottom, turn right and head downstream. Enjoy the miniature badlands eroded into the soft mudstone of the valley.

After about 0.25 mile in the wash bottom, and about 1 mile from the start of the hike, meet the larger Arroyo Bernalillito. Turn right and continue walking in the sandy wash. Along the way are more badlands, tunnels of mud, and a variety of colorful stones along the gravel bars. Pass an intersection with another arroyo from the north. After about 1.5 miles, Arroyo Bernalillito intersects Querencia Arroyo in a broad plain. Turn sharply right and head up the Querencia drainage. Stay close to the cliffs to the right (west) as the route winds through a confusing maze of washes. Pass through an area of rounded rocks, then over the pass labeled Los Posos on the map. Continue heading south for 0.5 mile to come to the main road. Turn right and return to the parking area.

## 34 | TENT ROCKS CANYON TRAILS

**Distance: 3 miles, day hike**
**Difficulty:** easy
**Elevation range:** 5,800 to 6,200 feet
**Elevation gain:** 400 feet
**Best time of year:** mid-March through November
**Water:** carry water
**Map:** USGS Cañada
**Managed by:** Bureau of Land Management, Albuquerque Field Office; Cochiti Pueblo
**Features:** very narrow canyon, strangely shaped rocks

Tent Rocks Canyon is a narrow slice through tuff ejected from small volcanoes at the edge of the massive Jemez Volcano. In places the walls of the canyon are 200 feet high, yet a child's arms can span the width wall to wall.

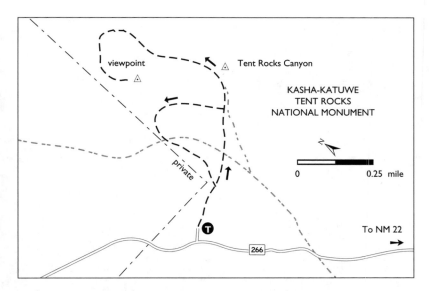

The canyon takes its name from the surrounding weird towers of tuff capped by harder, more erosion-resistant rocks. These cap rocks offer some protection to the crumbly tuff directly beneath, resulting in a hoard of conical spires roughly shaped like tepees.

Tent Rocks Canyon and the surrounding rock spires have spawned New Mexico's newest national monument, Kasha-Katuwe Tent Rocks National Monument. Jointly administered by the Bureau of Land Management and Cochiti Pueblo, the 5,300-acre area has two trails that lead into the wonderland, one along the base of the cliffs, another into the canyon.

Take I-25 south from Santa Fe or north from Albuquerque to the Cochiti exit 264. Go west on NM 16 for about 8 miles to a T intersection. Turn right onto NM 22, heading for Cochiti Dam. Go past the spillway and, at the base of the dam, turn left with NM 22 as it heads toward Cochiti Pueblo. In 1.8 miles, at the end of NM 22, turn right onto FR 266. This dirt road is bumpy but passable to any vehicle. At 4.8 miles, turn right at the sign for Kasha-Katuwe Tent Rocks National Monument. Park in the small lot on the right. Note a small fee is charged for day use of this area. The monument is open from 8 A.M. to 5 P.M. from November 1 to March 31, and from 7 A.M. to 6 P.M. the rest of the year.

Begin hiking the Tent Rocks Canyon Trail at the BLM parking area. Follow the sandy trail, marked with National Recreation Trail signposts, about 100 yards to a junction and bear right. A bit less than 0.5 mile from the start, the trail leads into an arroyo. Bear left and walk up the sandy bottom into a narrowing canyon. Just before reaching the mouth of the canyon, the trail splits at mile 0.6; the left fork is the cliff trail, but for now go right into the canyon.

*New Mexico's newest national monument, Kasha-Katuwe Tent Rocks, was set aside to protect the tepee-shaped rocks found on the flanks of the Jemez Mountains.*

The trail passes between high walls of banded volcanic deposits as the canyon alternates between narrow and open sections. Short stretches are a squeeze for an adult with a day pack. At one point hikers must crawl under a boulder to continue, but this only adds to the fun.

At mile 1.2, a primitive trail continues 0.25 mile to a viewpoint above, climbing the steep slope on loose rock. From the viewpoint, backtrack to the mouth of the canyon. Just outside the canyon at mile 2.1, turn right onto the cliff route and climb steeply out of the arroyo. After 200 yards, drop into a broad amphitheater surrounded by banded cliffs. The trail follows the base of the cliffs, passing a cave that shows signs of use by Ancestral Pueblo people. Just past the cave, descend into a narrow arroyo. At the bottom, turn left and walk down the arroyo. In 100 yards, cross a larger arroyo and continue as the trail skirts the base of the western side of the amphitheater back to the parking area.

# 35 | CERRO PICACHO

**Distance: 8 miles, day hike**
**Difficulty:** difficult
**Elevation range:** 6,400 to 8,113 feet
**Elevation gain:** 2,500 feet
**Best time of year:** March to early June, September to November
**Water:** Sanchez Canyon
**Maps:** USGS Cañada and Cochiti Dam
**Managed by:** Santa Fe National Forest, Dome Wilderness Area, Jemez Ranger District
**Features:** wild canyon scenery, running water, isolated peak

At 5,200 acres, the Dome is the smallest wilderness area in the southwest. The Dome Wilderness sits on the more remote edges of the adjacent Bandelier Wilderness and offers considerable solitude and scenery to adventurous hikers. Named for St. Peters Dome, the highest point in the area, the wilderness encompasses portions of the isolated Sanchez Canyon, a scenic gem with colorful walls, lush vegetation, and a desert waterfall. On the top side, the dome of Cerro Picacho offers outstanding views of the southern portion of the Jemez Mountains as well as of the finger mesas of Bandelier National Monument.

Reach the trailhead by taking I-25 south from Santa Fe or north from Albuquerque to the Cochiti exit 264. Go west on NM 16 for about 8 miles to

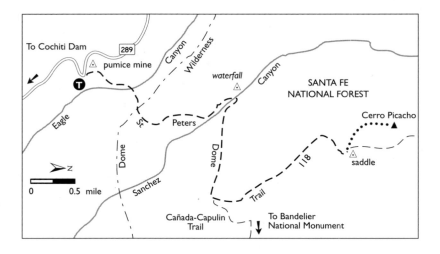

*Much of the Dome Wilderness was burned in the 1996 Dome Fire.*

a T intersection. Turn right onto NM 22, heading for Cochiti Dam. Go past the spillway and, at the base of the dam, continue straight when NM 22 turns left. Head into the village of Cochiti Lake and pass the local shopping plaza. Continue straight for 2.8 miles and turn right onto FR 289. Head up this rough road 3.5 miles to a hairpin turn and a parking area at the abandoned Eagle Pumice mines.

Begin hiking on the St. Peters Dome Trail 118. The trail heads along the cliffs before dropping quickly into the bottom of Eagle Canyon. Don't watch for birds of prey here; the canyon was named for Joseph Eagle, a promoter of early mining operations in the area. After topping a low saddle, pass through an old pumice pit before a second descent, this one into Sanchez Canyon. At mile 1.2, reach the canyon bottom where a permanent stream flows. Just below the trail, the flow drops off a high waterfall that gave the canyon its Pueblo name, "arroyo of the place of the waterfall."

Climb out of the canyon heading east and ascending to a broad bench. Climbing a cliff on what is probably an ancient route, reach the junction with the Cañada-Capulin Trail 2.3 miles from the start. Bear left to stay on Trail 118. Through stands of juniper and piñon, skirt a modest drainage while continuing a gradual but steady climb to the northwest. The grade increases as the trail turns to head northeast and climb out the head of the canyon to a saddle 3.5 miles from the start.

From this point, leave the trail and pick a route up the south ridge of

Cerro Picacho. A 600-foot ascent through open woodlands leads to the summit and a grand view in all directions. After enjoying the view, return to the trailhead by the same route.

## 36 | RED DOT AND BLUE DOT TRAILS

**Distance: 8 miles, day hike**
**Difficulty:** moderate
**Elevation range:** 5,500 to 6,400 feet
**Elevation gain:** 900 feet
**Best time of year:** all year
**Water:** Pajarito Springs
**Map:** USGS White Rock
**Managed by:** Los Alamos County
**Features:** White Rock Canyon, Rio Grande, petroglyphs, springs

White Rock Canyon has been carved by the Rio Grande through thick lava flows emanating from the volcanoes of the Cerros del Rio volcanic field to the east. Two spectacular trails, unimaginatively named for the color of painted circles that mark the routes, lead into the canyon. The trails are stair-step affairs, descending successive blocks of lava that slumped from the cliffs as the Rio Grande wore its way down through the rocks. These are ancient trails that were used by Ancestral Pueblo people to travel from villages on the mesas to agricultural fields within the canyon.

From Santa Fe, go north on US 84/285 for 12 miles to NM 502 and bear left. Continue 8 miles and bear right onto NM 4 to the town of White Rock. At the traffic signal on the north edge of town, turn left onto Rover Boulevard. Make the first left onto Meadow Lane, traveling 0.7 mile to the entrance to Overlook Regional Park. Turn left on Overlook Road and continue past several athletic fields to a gravel road to the right, which leads to two picnic shelters. Park near the shelters. Note that the park closes at 10:00 P.M.

The trailhead is unmarked and difficult to find. From the picnic shelters, climb over a vehicle barrier and walk south (facing the canyon, to the right), picking up the trail nearest the rim of White Rock Canyon. In about 150 yards, the Blue Dot Trail starts at a gap in a fence. Turn left, dropping through a cleft in the rim, and begin the quick descent to the Rio Grande. From here the trail is much easier to follow: look for the blue dots painted on the rocks. Dropping from the topmost lava flow, the trail turns many tight switchbacks and crosses two broad benches. Just above the river, the trail enters a juniper woodland and becomes soggy with water from a few of the many springs that discharge into the river within the canyon.

At a trail junction near the river, the left spur leads in 0.25 mile to a sandy

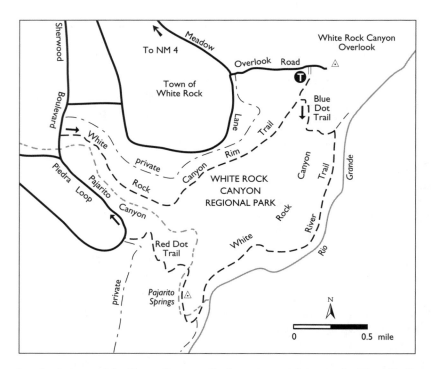

beach at streamside. To continue on the loop, turn right onto the River Trail, which begins with a long, sandy stretch. As the river comes in view again, the trail is squeezed between the river and a long ridge. Follow the trail around the end of the ridge, climbing to a bench covered with river cobbles.

After the trail again drops back to river level, cross the flow from Pajarito Springs using one of the many possible routes at mile 2.7. Pick up the Red Dot Trail on the other side, turn right, and head up the small stream. The trail recrosses the stream within the next couple hundred feet. With the stream to the left, watch to the right for a steep trail and climb over a ridge. In a few minutes, reach the pools of Pajarito Springs. This is a good place to rest before the long climb out of the canyon.

The trail from the springs is very steep. On the way up, take your mind off the hard work by enjoying the expansive view and by watching for elaborate petroglyphs on the rocks. About halfway up, the trail crosses a level bench, then completes the steep route to the rim. Out of the canyon, turn left and follow the trail to the paved Piedra Loop.

To return to Overlook Park, at mile 3.7 turn right on Piedra Loop and walk about 0.5 mile to Sherwood Boulevard. Turn right, then in 200 yards, turn right again at a gate on a dirt road where a small sign to the right marks the beginning of the White Rock Canyon Rim Trail. Follow the Rim Trail as it winds through the juniper woodlands of the mesa top. Many intersecting

*Snow-covered White Rock Canyon from the Blue Dot Trail*

trails lead off in all directions; stay on the main route by heading generally east, keeping Pajarito Canyon on the right and White Rock Canyon ahead. After 1 mile on the Rim Trail, reach the edge of White Rock Canyon and bear left. Follow the trail 1.5 miles along the canyon rim back to Overlook Park.

## 37 | TYUONYI OVERLOOK TRAIL

**Distance: 2 miles, day hike**
**Difficulty:** easy
**Elevation range:** 6,600 to 6,700 feet
**Elevation gain:** 100 feet
**Best time of year:** year round
**Water:** carry water
**Maps:** USGS Frijoles; Trails Illustrated Bandelier National
    Monument
**Managed by:** Bandelier National Monument
**Features:** overhead view of large pueblo

Most visitors to Bandelier National Monument stay on the floor of Frijoles Canyon to tour the main pueblo, Tyuonyi, but the view of the pueblo from above gives a better sense of what the canyon was like during the Ancestral Pueblo occupation 500 years ago. Perched on the peaceful canyon rim 400 feet above the village, one can easily imagine the canyon bustling with the sights and sounds of 600 Ancestral Pueblo occupants. Visit the pueblo first, then take the overlook trail for another perspective.

   The entrance to Bandelier National Monument is located on NM 4, 13 miles west of the intersection of NM 502 and NM 4 near Los Alamos. The trailhead for the Tyuonyi Overlook Trail is at the end of the Juniper Campground road, which is the first right-hand turn after passing through the

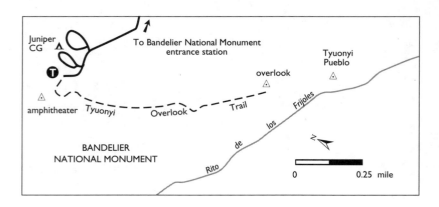

entrance to the monument. Park in the large lot for the amphitheater.

Begin hiking toward the amphitheater at the west end of the parking lot. At the bottom of the stairs, turn left onto the Tyuonyi Overlook Trail. Pass under tall ponderosa pines before entering the juniper woodland beyond. In spring, wildflowers are found growing among the rocks as in a rock garden. Spring is also a good time for bird-watching, with flocks of piñon jays, robins, and evening grosbeaks flitting through the trees. Stay on the wide, main trail.

After 0.5 mile, the trail bears left to parallel the rim of Frijoles Canyon. Views across the canyon take in the sloping walls of Bandelier tuff, or welded

*The circular outline of Tyuonyi Pueblo from the end of the Tyuonyi Overlook Trail*

volcanic ash. To the west, the Jemez Mountains, the remains of the volcano that produced the tuff, make up the skyline. Drop gradually on the now rocky trail to the viewpoint about a mile from the start. Find a quiet spot to enjoy the view of the canyon and the pueblo below, and the play of ravens overhead. Return to the trailhead by the same route.

# 38 | FRIJOLES CANYON

**Distance: 7 miles one-way, day hike**
**Difficulty:** easy
**Elevation range:** 6,100 to 7,600 feet
**Elevation gain:** 1,500-foot descent
**Best time of year:** mid-March through mid-November
**Water:** Rito de los Frijoles
**Maps:** USGS Frijoles; Trails Illustrated Bandelier National
Monument
**Managed by:** National Park Service, Bandelier National
Monument
**Features:** wildlife, cliff dwellings, running water, pictur-
esque canyon

People have used Frijoles Canyon as a route into the Jemez Mountains for centuries, first the Ancestral Pueblo residents in the lower canyon, then their Pueblo descendants. Today the canyon is a quiet, sheltered place with year-round running water, making it a haven for wildlife. Elk are commonly spotted on the plateau above the canyon floor; mule deer are plentiful in the canyon itself. The entire canyon is shady, even in midsummer. The upper canyon supports tall Douglas fir, which gives way to ponderosa pine as the canyon cuts deeper into the rocks. Although the lower end of the Frijoles receives heavy visitation, the upper canyon sees few hikers.

This one-way, downhill hike requires setting up a short shuttle. Park a

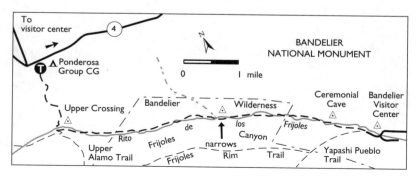

*Tiny Rito de los Frijoles carved the walls of Frijoles Canyon through more than 300 feet of soft volcanic tuff.*

vehicle at the Bandelier Visitor Center, located 10 miles west of White Rock off NM 4. Return to the park entrance and turn left (west) onto NM 4. Continue west 6 miles to the Ponderosa Group Campground and park at the well-marked trailhead for the Upper Crossing.

Begin hiking downhill on a trail that soon joins a fire road entering from the right. Follow the signs to Upper Crossing at a minor intersection at mile 0.4, then enter the Bandelier Wilderness just above the edge of Frijoles Canyon. The trail drops 400 feet on several steep switchbacks to reach the bottom of Frijoles Canyon at mile 1.5. Cross the creek on a log bridge and immediately come to a three-way trail junction with the Yapashi Pueblo Trail. Turn left onto the Frijoles Canyon Trail, heading toward the visitor center and paralleling the Rito de los Frijoles. The trail stays close to the stream with several crossings on log bridges.

About 3.5 miles from the start, an interesting side canyon enters from the left. Just after this junction, walk through the narrows of Frijoles Canyon where the walls are only a dozen feet apart. From this point, the trail crosses the shallow stream more than a dozen times.

The easy, shaded stroll continues until another narrow section of canyon forces the trail up and over a steep ridge. Cliff dwellings appear in the canyon wall to the left, but hikers must stay on the trail. About 6 miles from the start, the trail meets the Ceremonial Cave Trail coming up from the visitor center. Ceremonial Cave sits 140 feet above the canyon floor, and is reached via several long ladders; it is a worthwhile side trip. Continue back on the gravel path to the parking area near the visitor center.

# 39 | YAPASHI PUEBLO

**Distance: 13-mile loop, day hike or backpack**
**Difficulty:** difficult
**Elevation range:** 6,000 to 7,400 feet
**Elevation gain:** 1,800 feet
**Best time of year:** mid-April to October
**Water:** Rito de los Frijoles, Upper Alamo Crossing, Capulin Canyon
**Maps:** USGS Frijoles; Trails Illustrated Bandelier National Monument
**Managed by:** Bandelier National Monument
**Features:** stunning views, large junipers, Ancestral Pueblo village

The best way to see a large portion of the Bandelier backcountry is to set up a short shuttle and hike one-way from Upper Crossing to the Bandelier

Visitor Center via the Upper Alamo Trail. Park a vehicle at the visitor center, return to the park entrance, and turn left (west) onto NM 4. Continue west 6 miles to the Ponderosa Group Campground and park at the well-marked trailhead for Upper Crossing.

In the Bandelier backcountry, canyons are cut between fingerlike mesas radiating from the hand of the Jemez Mountains. This hike drops into and out of three steep canyons, accumulating an elevation gain of almost 2,000 feet. The roughest, steepest climb is at Lower Alamo Crossing near the end of the hike. This trail can be very hot in summer, with little shade available for long stretches.

This long trek invites an overnight stay. No camping is permitted in upper Alamo or Frijoles Canyons, and no fires are allowed in the backcountry: use only gas stoves for cooking.

Yapashi Pueblo is one of the largest pueblos on the Pajarito Plateau. Hikers will find standing walls made of tuff-blocks, kiva depressions, and red and brown pottery scattered throughout the pueblo. To protect this ancient structure, stay off the walls and out of the kivas and leave potsherds where they are found.

Begin hiking on a trail and fire road through the open ponderosa pine forest. Bear right at an intersection about 0.25 mile from the start. About a mile from the start, drop into the head of a small drainage and follow a series of steep switchbacks to the Upper Crossing of Rito de los Frijoles and the cool shady bottom of the Frijoles Canyon.

After crossing the small stream on a log bridge, follow the trail a hundred feet to a junction. Bear left, and in a few yards bear right to follow the trail to Bandelier National Monument, which angles up the south slope of the canyon. (The Frijoles Canyon Trail also goes to the left, but it stays in

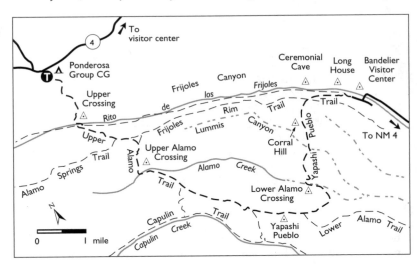

*Alamo Canyon is one of dozens of orange-walled gorges carved into the Pajarito Plateau.*

the canyon bottom.) Climb out of the canyon on several switchbacks, reaching the top at mile 2. The low plant growth and tall standing tree snags on the mesa are evidence this area was hard hit by the 1977 La Mesa fire. After the trail drops into and out of a small drainage, bear left at the junction with the Alamo Springs Trail. At the next intersection at mile 3.1, bear right as the Frijoles Rim Trail goes left, and pass another branch of that trail angling back to the left in a few hundred yards.

The route now drops slowly into Upper Alamo Canyon via a small side drainage. The trail reaches Alamo Canyon directly below several small, colorful tent rocks halfway up the canyon wall. Cross Alamo Creek at a delightful spot about 4 miles from the start. The trail turns downstream in the canyon bottom for 0.25 mile before climbing to the mesa above. Bear left at the junction with a trail marked for Capulin Canyon. From here the trail descends through open pine forest along a small drainage. At mile 6.1, the trail meets the edge of an escarpment, offering more long-range views to the east. Drop down several rocky switchbacks before bearing left at another trail junction at mile 7.3. The trail to the right leads to water and fine campsites in Capulin Canyon.

Continue east on the top of a ridge where at first the trail is confused by a network of side trails. Gradually the main trail becomes easy to follow. About 0.5 mile beyond the side trail leading to Capulin Canyon, reach the low mounds of Yapashi Pueblo. Explore around the perimeter of the pueblo before continuing down the trail.

From Yapashi, follow the ridge top before dropping down into and out of a small canyon. While traveling through open juniper pine woodland, pass the junction with the Lower Alamo Trail to the right. Climb a low ridge, then drop 500 feet to Lower Alamo Crossing. The canyon bottom is shaded by pine and box elder, with flowing water during spring. Make a short hitch west up the canyon bottom under towering orange cliffs. The staircase climb to the next mesa is the hottest, toughest part of the hike, but shady ponderosa pines dot the rim.

Heading north toward Frijoles Canyon, cross a small drainage, then the larger Lummis Canyon. Beyond the foot of Corral Hill, make one last climb to the edge of Frijoles Canyon. About 12 miles from the start, meet the Frijoles Rim Trail and bear right. (For those doing a loop hike, turn left; it is 6.5 miles back to the trailhead.) In a few hundred feet, enjoy views into Frijoles Canyon and look across the canyon for the ladders to Ceremonial Cave. The trail now angles down the south wall of Frijoles Canyon, offering views of Long House along the way, and soon reaches the trailhead near the visitor center.

## 40 | EAST FORK OF THE JEMEZ RIVER

**Distance: 6 miles one-way, day hike**
**Difficulty:** easy
**Elevation range:** 8,000 to 8,600 feet
**Elevation gain:** 600 feet
**Best time of year:** mid-April through November
**Water:** East Fork Jemez River
**Map:** USGS Redondo Peak
**Managed by:** Santa Fe National Forest, Jemez National Recreation Area, Jemez Ranger District
**Features:** dormant volcano, fishing, wildlife, mountain meadows

In contrast to the many rugged hikes found in New Mexico, a stroll along the East Fork of the Jemez River is an easy, relaxing walk. The high-country stream flows within a rocky canyon in a deep conifer forest, yet the river also meanders through a series of open meadows filled in summer with a riot of wildflowers. The canyon is home to mountain wildlife,

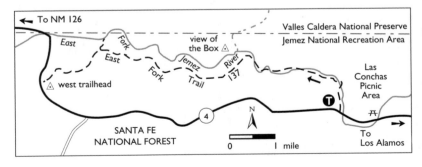

including mule deer, elk, bobcat, raccoon, and porcupine; birdsong fills the air at all times of day. The East Fork is well stocked with rainbow trout, and the most enjoyable hikes along the river include stops at the large pools for a bit of angling.

To set up a shuttle for a one-way hike, leave a car at the U.S. Forest Service East Fork west trailhead. From San Ysidro on NM 44, travel north on NM 4, passing through Jemez Springs and past the intersection with NM 126. The

*The popular East Fork Trail is a good introduction to hiking in New Mexico's high country.*

well-marked western trailhead is about 5 miles from NM 126. From Los Alamos, go west on NM 501 to NM 4. Turn right and continue for 21 miles to the East Fork west trailhead. Once you have parked a car at the western trailhead, drive 3.5 miles east on NM 4 to the Las Conchas Trailhead, which is 0.25 mile west of the Las Conchas Picnic Area.

At the trailhead, the route descends wooden stairs from the parking lot to river level. Follow the trail as it heads downstream past tall cliffs of volcanic rock and through alternating patches of forest and meadow. In the first mile, make five stream crossings on log bridges. Nice campsites are located along the river after the fourth bridge and beyond.

The trail reaches the head of the East Fork Box in 2 miles. Here the main trail turns left and climbs to the canyon rim, but first take the short spur trail that leads along the river to views of the Box, a wild section of canyon. The main trail ascends on gentle switchbacks, then parallels the canyon on the mesa above. Continue west along the rim, parallel to a logging road that stays to the left. Much of this section of trail is a pleasant walk through open ponderosa pine forest.

At mile 4, a spur trail to the right descends again to the river. This trail branches about halfway down, the right fork dropping steeply to the bottom of the Box—a delightful and popular lunch stop—and the left fork leading to a trail along the river. Take both spurs and climb back to the main trail.

The last mile of trail descends slowly through a pine stand over-crowded with small ponderosas. Near the end, the trail merges with a wide logging road, marked as a ski trail with blue diamonds. Reach the west trailhead about 5 miles from Las Conchas, or 6 miles including the side trip to the river.

## 41 | JEMEZ FALLS AND McCAULEY HOT SPRING

**Distance: 5 miles one-way, day hike**
**Difficulty:** easy
**Elevation range:** 6,800 to 7,900 feet
**Elevation gain:** 400 to 500 feet
**Best time of year:** April to November
**Water:** carry water
**Map:** USGS Jemez Springs
**Managed by:** Santa Fe National Forest, Jemez Ranger
District
**Features:** hot springs, tall waterfall, deep canyon

Scattered in New Mexico's national forests are eleven hot springs where hikers can soak in naturally heated water bubbling out of the ground. One

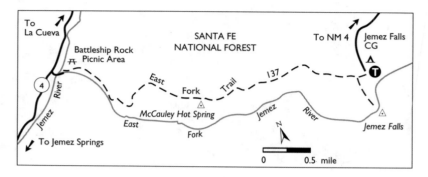

concentration of springs is located in the Jemez Mountains. McCauley Hot Spring is a delightful series of pools that lies in the Jemez backcountry on a bench above the East Fork of the Jemez River. An oval pool as big as a living room is the main attraction, but the warm outflow from the pond collects in three or four smaller rock tubs below. At about 92 degrees Fahrenheit, the water in every pool is delightfully relaxing.

The East Fork Trail 137 leads to the hot spring from two directions. Hikers can start at either trailhead and return via the same route, or set up the shuttle hike described here. The trip from Jemez Falls Campground to the spring and back requires a moderate 400-foot climb on the return. From Battleship Rock Picnic Area, hikers are faced with a steep 500-foot ascent to the springs.

Reach Battleship Rock Picnic Area from Los Alamos by taking NM 501 to NM 4. Turn right onto NM 4 and head toward the town of Jemez Springs. Continue about 30 miles to the village of La Cueva. Bear left to stay on NM 4 and continue 3.2 miles to the picnic area on the left, where a small day-use fee is charged. The area closes at 7 P.M., and no overnight parking is permitted. Leave one vehicle at Battleship Rock, then backtrack to La Cueva and bear right to stay on NM 4. Backtrack another 6 miles on NM 4 to the turnoff for Jemez Falls Campground. Turn right and continue through the campground to the parking area for Jemez Falls.

Start with a short side trip to see the falls. From the parking area, walk down the trail toward Jemez Falls, following the signs pointing left at a trail junction in 200 feet. Descend a minor drainage for 0.3 mile to an overlook of the falls, enjoy the impressive drop of the East Fork over a volcanic cliff, then backtrack to the main trail.

At the East Fork Trail 137, turn left and begin a gradual descent along the slopes above the East Fork. After 0.5 mile, the trail heads down the north wall of the canyon, which exhibits outcrops of colorful tuff—welded volcanic ash—scattered among the pines. An easy walk through the conifers leads to the outflow stream from the hot spring. The trail turns right and leads uphill past small thermal pools and to the main bathing hole.

Forest Service regulations require that bathers keep their clothes on

*A small thermal pool at McCauley Hot Spring*

while enjoying the hot spring. Hikers who want to relax in the thermal water in solitude should arrive early in the day.

From the largest of the pools, the trail continues west. After 0.5 mile of gently rolling terrain beyond the hot spring, the trail begins its 500-foot drop to the East Fork of the Jemez on sweeping switchbacks. Once near the floor of the canyon, ignore a maze of fishing trails that lead left to the East Fork, and follow the main route. Several signposts for Trail 137 help point out the right way. After a few minutes of streamside walking, emerge at an imposing wooden gazebo at the east end of the Battleship Rock Picnic Area and your shuttle car.

## 42 | RITO DE LAS PERCHAS LOOP

**Distance: 13.5-mile loop, backpack**
**Difficulty:** difficult
**Elevation range:** 9,400 to 10,400 feet
**Elevation gain:** 1,800 feet
**Best time of year:** late June through late September
**Water:** Rito de las Perchas, Rio de las Vacas
**Maps:** USGS Nacimiento Peak; USFS San Pedro Parks Wilderness
**Managed by:** Santa Fe National Forest, San Pedro Parks Wilderness, Cuba Ranger District
**Features:** unique plateau scenery, wildlife, solitude, good fishing

The San Pedro Parks Wilderness sits on a high granite plateau at the northwestern edge of the Jemez Mountains. The parks average 9,500 feet in elevation. Damp granitic soils produce extensive meadows interrupted by open stands of fir and spruce, offering an expansive feeling not often found high in the mountains. Although the hiking is easy, this unique landscape is little known and sees few visitors. It is the perfect summer escape from the crowds. The extensive trail network invites a couple days of exploration.

Elk and bear are frequently spotted in the meadows, and native Rio Grande cutthroat trout swim the clear waters of the Rio de las Vacas, Rito de las Perchas, and Clear Creek. Because of the high elevation, snow lingers well into June and trails can be quite soggy until early July. Hikers should bring their best hiking boots and extra socks. Note that the trails often cross open bogs and can be difficult to follow; watch for wooden posts that mark the way.

Reach the San Pedro Parks Wilderness via NM 126 east out of Cuba or north from the village of La Cueva (north of Albuquerque and reached via US 550 and NM 4). Take NM 126 about 30 miles, mostly unpaved, from La Cueva. The road is passable to high-clearance vehicles except in winter and after heavy rains. From Cuba, take NM 126 east about 6 miles; all but the last 0.5 mile is paved. Turn onto FR 70, heading north. In 3 miles, pass the parking for Trail 51 and continue on the winding, but good, gravel road another 10 miles. Park on the left at the large wilderness trailhead.

From the trailhead, walk uphill on the Palomas Trail 50. This climb is the steepest on the hike, with a 500-foot ascent over the first mile. Cross the wilderness boundary shortly before topping out on the ridge, then make a straight drop to the Rito de las Perchas. The trail crosses the creek, then heads upstream 100 feet to intersect the Perchas Trail 418, the return route for this loop. Turn left to stay on Trail 50, heading across a meadow toward the Rio de las Vacas.

Begin another climb up a small drainage. At the top, follow stout trail

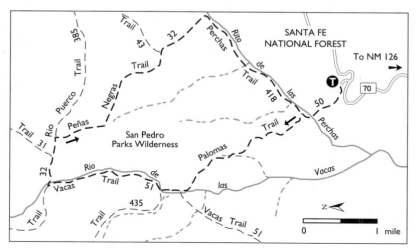

*Most trails in the San Pedro Parks Wilderness parallel streams.*

markers across a small meadow. The trail now bears left and descends to a soupy meadow of tall grasses before dropping into the valley of the Las Vacas. At a prominent intersection, continue straight onto the Vacas Trail 51. In 0.5 mile, cross the Las Vacas and pass the Anastacio Trail 435. At mile 5.8, bear right and continue up the valley, which is now a wide meadow with a small stream meandering through it. Along the edges of the valley are numerous campsites with memorable views.

Near mile 8, at the junction with the Peñas Negras Trail 32, turn right and climb a short drainage to a saddle. On top of the saddle, pass the Rio Capulin Trail 31 to the left. At the junction with the Rio Puerco Trail 385, turn right to continue on the Peñas Negras Trail, which now heads southeast. Walk across a high plateau, then descend along a small meadow. About 3 miles from the Rio de las Vacas (mile 11), pass the Vega Redonda Trail 43 on the left. In another 0.5 mile, come to the Rito de las Perchas and more excellent campsites in wide meadows near the very edge of the plateau.

Near the crossing of the Las Perchas, turn right onto the Perchas Trail 418. Parallel the creek downstream through more wet meadows. In 2.5 miles, intersect the Palomas Trail at the junction noted near the beginning of the hike. Cross the stream on the Palomas Trail, climb the steep hill, then enjoy the descent back to the trailhead.

# 43 | WINDOW ROCK

**Distance: 9 miles, day hike**
**Difficulty:** moderate
**Elevation range:** 5,800 to 6,400 feet
**Elevation gain:** 800 feet
**Best time of year:** March to December
**Water:** carry water
**Maps:** USGS Chili and Mendanales
**Managed by:** Santa Fe National Forest, Española Ranger
    District
**Features:** open spaces, large natural arch

In other parts of the Southwest, even modest natural arches have fanciful names like Backpacker Arch or Hellroaring Bridge. The generic name Window Rock downplays the interest in this attractive hole in rock that might have gone by the name Dragons Mouth. One of northern New Mexico's largest rock spans, Window Rock is punched through a thin ridge of hardened lava. From below, the black, gnarled stone around the opening looks like nasty teeth ready to chomp whoever wanders by.

With a diameter of about 10 feet, Window Rock can be seen from more than 5 miles away, but the arch is much more appealing up close. The view through the window of the surrounding mesas and distant mountains is worth the extra effort required to get behind it.

To reach the trailhead, drive northwest from Española on US 84/285. Continue straight on US 84 when US 285 splits off to the right. About 8 miles from Española, and halfway between mileposts 200 and 201 on US 84, watch for a yellow cattle guard on the left (south) side of the highway. Turn onto the road with the cattle guard and park off the highway near a Forest Service boundary marker.

Begin the hike by walking through a gate, and following the road left

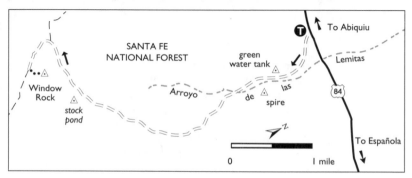

*Window Rock*

and under a power line for 0.25 mile. At a broad, sandy arroyo called Arroyo de las Lemitas, turn right and trudge up the deep, soft sand or along brief stretches of dirt road that appear now and then. Continue up the arroyo toward a lone sandstone spire, passing a green water tank. After 1 mile, the canyon abruptly turns right. At this point, bear left onto a steeply climbing jeep road and climb out of the arroyo. The road pitches slightly uphill for the next mile before descending into a broad valley. At mile 3.4, watch for the arch on the skyline to the left (south).

For a closer look at the window, continue on the road past a stock pond to the shoulder of the ridge that holds Window Rock. Immediately turn left and follow a rocky road on the south side of the ridge for 0.5 mile. Although the arch is hidden from this rocky road, it is easy to find by climbing to the left and searching along the ridge.

After enjoying the view from the arch, return to the trailhead by the same route.

## 44 | RIM VISTA TRAIL

**Distance: 4.5 miles, day hike**
**Difficulty:** moderate
**Elevation range:** 6,700 to 7,900 feet
**Elevation gain:** 1,200 feet
**Best time of year:** March to December
**Water:** carry water
**Map:** USGS Echo Amphitheater
**Managed by:** Carson National Forest, Canjilon Ranger District
**Features:** outstanding view of redrock country

The sedimentary rock layers of the Colorado Plateau create grand scenery from Utah to New Mexico. The rocks tell the story of shallow seas with dinosaurs roaming the shorelines, of shallow freshwater lakes, and a massive sand dune desert rivaling the modern Sahara. Nowhere are these rocks more colorfully displayed than from the edge of the Mesa de los Viejos and an overlook simply called Rim Vista. The hike to the vista climbs from the red mudstones of the Chinle Formation to the top of the Dakota Sandstone, a climb through time of almost 100 million years. Little shade is available on this route, making it ideal in spring, fall, or winter, but to be avoided in summer.

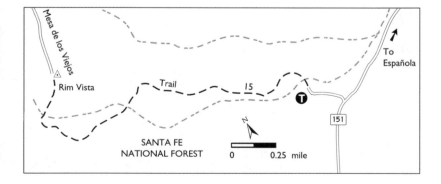

From Española, travel north on US 84 about 37 miles to FR 151, almost 1 mile past the USFS Ghost Ranch Visitor Center. Turn left onto FR 151, a graded gravel road suited for all vehicles in dry weather. Seven-tenths of a mile from the highway, turn right onto a dirt track, which is signed for the Rim Vista Trail. In 0.2 mile, bear right at a Y intersection and park at the trailhead in another 0.1 mile.

Head west on Trail 15, immediately dropping into and out of a small arroyo. Climb around the end of a ridge to the top, passing in 0.2 mile a small knife-edged ridge with views to the right of swirling patterns in the Entrada Sandstone. Continue a steeper climb on the south flank of the ridge. Beyond, blue diamonds mark the wide trail as it climbs a rocky section of slope through juniper-piñon woodland.

As the trail flattens out, climb a broad ridge dotted with sagebrush and large piñon pines. At mile 1.2, the trail swings south, then west again. In another mile, the gradual slope ends as the trail climbs a broad bench, then turns north to parallel the cliff of Dakota Sandstone above. The view becomes grander with each step, culminating at the vista at mile 2.2 where the trail meets the end of a rough road. On the mesa top, pick a rock to sit on and take a well-deserved break to enjoy the long-distance views. From the vista point, the rocks of Ghost Ranch, Abiquiu Lake, the Jemez Mountains, and the Sangre de Cristo Mountains are in view. Return to the trailhead by the same route.

*Mesozoic rocks form colorful bands on the cliff above Ghost Ranch, as seen from Rim Vista.*

# 45 | OJITOS CANYON TRAIL

**Distance: 12 miles, day hike or backpack**
**Difficulty:** difficult
**Elevation range:** 6,350 to 8,100 feet
**Elevation gain:** 1,900 feet
**Best time of year:** mid-March to November
**Water:** intermittent in Ojitos Creek, carry water
**Map:** USGS Laguna Peak
**Managed by:** Santa Fe National Forest, Rio Chama
    Wilderness, Coyote Ranger District
**Features:** colorful cliffs, secluded backcountry camping

A trip into Ojitos Canyon is a hiker's hike, a trip taken more for the sheer joy of walking and being in the backcountry than to reach a destination. The trail is one of northern New Mexico's only completed sections of the Continental Divide Trail. It follows Ojitos Canyon through colorful cliffs of Mesozoic rocks in the little-used Rio Chama Wilderness. The trail is well marked with Continental Divide Trail markers. Backcountry campsites are abundant in the canyon and near the trail's end on Mesa del Camino. A trickle of water will be found in the stream most of the year. Watch for chunks of white quartz, gypsum, and petrified wood, all common in the red Chinle mudstones along the first 2 miles of the trail.

From Española, travel north on US 84 about 37 miles to FR 151, about 1 mile past the USFS Ghost Ranch Visitor Center. Turn left onto FR 151, a dirt road suited for all vehicles in dry weather. Continue about 8.5 miles to Skull Bridge on the Rio Chama and park.

Cross the Rio Chama on the bridge and continue through a gate on

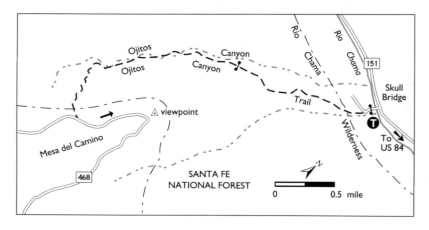

*A Continental Divide Trail marker points the way on the Ojitos Canyon Trail in the Rio Chama Wilderness.*

the dirt road heading south. In 200 yards, the road swings west as the trail continues straight; look for pointed posts inscribed with the Continental Divide Trail symbol. After entering the Rio Chama Wilderness, the trail passes along the wide mouth of Ojitos Canyon through open sagebrush country backed by red, tan, and yellow cliffs. Follow the trail as it turns left, entering a gap; then proceed around a mudstone mesa and over a low saddle before dropping back into the main canyon.

Immediately after passing through another hikers gate at mile 2.1, bear right and watch for the next trail marker. The path now closely follows the canyon bottom, where running water is found most of the year. Much of the trail follows the route of an abandoned *acequia,* and metal flumes from the old ditch appear at several stream crossings.

At mile 4.5, while on the east bank of the stream, the trail leaves the canyon bottom and begins to climb the wall of Mesa del Camino on a long series of steep switchbacks. Here the trail passes through an open forest of ponderosa pine and Gambel oak, offering views of the Ojitos Canyon. About 0.75 mile up the switchbacks, watch for a view through the trees of the canyon country below and of the San Juan Mountains on the distant horizon. Near the top of the climb, the trail leaves the wilderness and reaches a sloping bench at about 8,000 feet. The trail skirts the northwest edge of the bench, ending at a dirt road a couple hundred feet below the flat summit of Mesa del Camino. To the left is a protected campsite. From the end of the trail, hikers can bushwhack straight up to the summit of the mesa, or take the more moderate course of following the road to the north about a mile to a saddle that offers excellent views both to the west and east. Return to the trailhead by the same route.

*Facing page: Sandstone cliffs at El Morro National Monument, covered with inscriptions left by passing travelers*

# NORTHWEST PLATEAU AND ZUNI MOUNTAINS

# 46 | KITCHEN MESA

**Distance: 5 miles, day hike**
**Difficulty:** easy, except for short climb
**Elevation range:** 6,500 to 7,100 feet
**Elevation gain:** 600 feet
**Best time of year:** late April to November
**Water:** carry water
**Map:** USGS Ghost Ranch
**Managed by:** Ghost Ranch Presbyterian Center
**Features:** redrock scenery, wide open vistas

The Ghost Ranch area, with its naked redrock landscape, is more characteristic of northern Arizona or southern Utah than it is of New Mexico. The brick-red mudstones of the Chinle Formation—massive river delta deposits from the age of the early dinosaurs—dominate Ghost Ranch. Above the Chinle are soaring cliffs of yellow-brown Entrada Sandstone capped by gray lake deposits of the Todilto Formation. The trip to the top of Kitchen Mesa takes hikers into the heart of this wilderness of stone, leading to breathtaking views of rocks, cliffs, and Abiquiu Lake to the south.

The Kitchen Mesa Trail traverses private land owned by the Ghost Ranch Presbyterian Center, which is very receptive to use of the trail by responsible hikers. Before hitting the trail, hikers must check in at the office and tell the staff of their plans to visit Kitchen Mesa.

From Española, take US 84/285 north, staying on US 84 when US 285

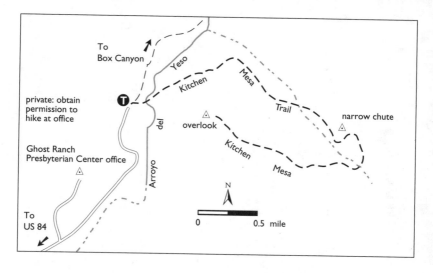

*Hikers must climb this narrow chute to reach the top of Kitchen Mesa.*

splits off about 5 miles from town. Continue about 35 miles from Española, through Abiquiu to the gravel road marked for the Ghost Ranch Presbyterian Center. (This is not the same as the Ghost Ranch Living Museum, which is about 1.5 miles beyond the Presbyterian Center.) Turn right and drive 1 mile to a road fork; follow the signs left to the office and ask for permission to hike the Kitchen Mesa Trail. Drive back to the fork, turn left, and continue slowly through the Center. About 1 mile from the office road turnoff, park in a large area just before a "No Vehicles Beyond This Point" sign.

The Kitchen Mesa Trail is marked with blue coffee cans. Find the first can by walking up the road (north) from the parking area for about 100 yards, then turn right to cross a small stream in Arroyo del Yeso. Climb to the bluff above the stream and walk the easy-to-follow trail across a sagebrush flat. Around a small hill, the trail passes in the shadow of Kitchen Mesa 400 feet overhead. Yes, the end of this trail is only 0.25 mile from the beginning!

The trail suddenly climbs and descends a steep, open slope of red Chinle mudstone, then bears right into a broad canyon. At mile 0.7, the trail crosses the canyon bottom, then climbs up the slope on the north side of the canyon. One mile from the start, the trail crosses a slick stretch of loose rock where caution is required. The route climbs steeply up the rocks; follow the blue cans, painted blue arrows, and the path worn into the rocks. On the last section of the ascent, hikers must climb a narrow chute and boost themselves up through a fissure in the rock to reach the top of the mesa. Fortunately, well-placed hand- and footholds make the short climb easier than it first appears.

Once up the crack, the trail is almost on the mesa top. Bear right and cross the head of an arroyo, then make a final climb. The trail again bears right at the top of the mesa. From the 2-mile point, the trail crosses an eerie, barren white landscape: the gypsum lakebeds of the Todilto Formation. Walk to the end of the mesa and enjoy the expansive view. Bright sun and wind can make the last exposed 0.5 mile of trail unpleasant, so retreat to the edge of the junipers to find some shade for lunch or a rest stop. Return to the trailhead by the same route.

## 47 | BOX CANYON AND MESA MONTOSA

**Distance: 10 miles, day hike**
**Difficulty:** moderate
**Elevation range:** 6,500 to 7,850 feet
**Elevation gain:** 1,800 feet
**Best time of year:** March to November
**Water:** carry water
**Map:** USGS Ghost Ranch
**Managed by:** Ghost Ranch Presbyterian Center; Carson National Forest, Canjilon Ranger District
**Features:** redrock cliffs, fossils, spectacular box canyon and pour off

Mesa Montosa is part of the northern boundary of the basin of Mesozoic rocks surrounding the Rio Chama. On the way to the mesa top, a short side trip leads to Box Canyon. The spur dead-ends at a pour off—a normally dry waterfall—about 200 feet high and with a noticeable overhang.

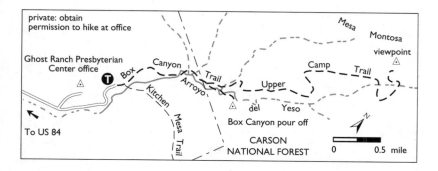

In the Box, hikers are surrounded by yellow rock cliffs on all sides. Throughout late fall to early spring, seeps in the cliff face are frozen, decorating the alcove with pillars of ice. Beyond Box Canyon, the trail climbs through time as well as altitude beginning with Jurassic Entrada Sandstone, which is the cliff-forming rock of the canyon walls. The yellow, green, and purple muds of the Morrison Formation form a broad bench above the cliffs. Finally, the trail climbs the next cliff, the Cretaceous Dakota Sandstone.

This hike begins on the private Ghost Ranch Presbyterian Center at the same trailhead as the Kitchen Mesa Trail (Hike 46). Follow the same directions for access and securing permission to hike.

From the parking area, begin walking on the road marked for Kitchen Mesa and Box Canyon. In a hundred feet, the Kitchen Mesa Trail turns right. Continue straight and follow the road as it skirts the base of a monolith of Entrada Sandstone. Just after crossing an irrigation ditch, take the right fork, dropping down along the bottom of Arroyo del Yeso.

Heading upstream on a wide trail, cross under a flume, which is part of the old irrigation system for the ranch below. The trail now stays close to the stream, crossing it many times in the shade of cottonwoods. At a trail junction at mile 1.2, take the right fork marked for Box Canyon. The primitive trail stays close to the stream, crossing it many times. After several minutes, come to a small oasis where two canyons meet, and enjoy the small pools and waterfalls. Continue up the main canyon for 200 yards to the massive alcove and the high pour off. The last section of trail requires a bit of scrambling over rocks.

After enjoying the alcove, backtrack to the earlier trail junction. Turn right onto the Upper Camp Trail. The trail climbs above the canyon floor before dropping into a side canyon. Next, the trail climbs steeply out of the canyon to a viewpoint overlooking Box Canyon. Crossing a sagebrush flat, the trail levels for 0.5 mile before climbing to another bench. On the bench, the trail swings west before climbing up a small drainage, which is easy to miss. The trail swings back to the east, now paralleling the high cliff of brown Dakota Sandstone to the left.

*In winter, huge columns of ice form at the pour off in Box Canyon.*

At mile 4.4, the trail again crosses the Arroyo del Yeso before climbing around a knoll. This steep section of trail offers great views of the Dakota cliff winding off to the west. Reach a low saddle and begin dropping into the upper Arroyo del Yeso. Before reaching the canyon bottom, bear left on a faint trail that crosses the canyon and climbs the opposite canyon wall on an old road. Several branches of the trail climb the hill: select any one. The old road contours around a point of Mesa Montosa, then climbs to the mesa top. Look for a road to the right that leads to the point of the mesa and long-distance views of the Jemez Mountains, the Rio Chama Canyon, and Abiquiu Lake. After enjoying the view, return by the same route.

# 48 | NAVAJO PEAK

**Distance: 10 miles, day hike or backpack**
**Difficulty:** difficult
**Elevation range:** 6,400 to 7,700 feet
**Elevation gain:** 2,000 feet
**Best time of year:** May to October
**Water:** Rio Cebolla
**Map:** USGS Navajo Peak
**Managed by:** Santa Fe National Forest, Coyote Ranger
    District; Bureau of Land Management, Taos Field Office
**Features:** great canyon scenery, good fishing, solitude

As the highest point on the edge of a broad mesa, Navajo Peak is more accurately described as a summit. Regardless of its label, the point none-theless offers fine views of the canyon of the Rio Chama, the largest tribu-tary to the Rio Grande in New Mexico, and the river that swells the Abiquiu Lake. The canyon walls soar 1,000 feet above the river, banded with yellow

*Above: The ranch house at the McCrystal Place in Valle Vidal. Below: The extensive grasslands of Valle Vidal offer hikers sweeping vistas.*

*Previous page: Orange rocks spewed from the Valles Caldera form the walls of the narrows of Frijoles Canyon.*

Above: The deep violet blossoms of monkshood are found in wet mountain meadows. Below: Ancestral Pueblo farmers frequently adorned rocks with pecked petroglyphs, but few are as elaborate as these twin rattlesnakes.

*Above: The sandstone walls of Box Canyon at El Morro National Monument. Left: Golden aspens add vivid splashes of color to New Mexico's northern mountains in fall.*

*Swirling lines in the dunes at White Sands National Monument*

*The trail paralleling the East Fork of the Jemez River is one of the most popular hiking trips in New Mexico.*

*Right: The Ancestral Pueblo culture is represented along many trails by bold petroglyphs like this decorated shield. Below: Mexican hats*

*Above: Ancient pueblos, like Tsin Kletsin, make attractive hiking destinations. Below: The Sandia Mountains provide challenging trails on the edge of the state's largest city, Albuquerque.*

*Above: Grassy ridgelines are characteristic of the highest ranges in central New Mexico. Right: The alligator juniper is named for its patterned bark.*

*Steep-sided canyons are eroded into the limestone walls of the state's southern mountain ranges.*

*Left: A trickle of water in Devils Den Canyon in the Guadalupe Mountains. Below: Last Chance Canyon holds a lush ribbon of green amid the southern desert.* (Courtesy U.S. Forest Service)

*Above: Sunlight on grass. Below: Sycamores and hackberries shade the canyon bottoms of the tributaries of the Gila River.*

*Above: The Catwalk follows the route of a water pipeline through the narrow gorge of Whitewater Creek. Below left: The West Fork of the Gila River provides access into the depths of the massive Gila Wilderness. (Photo by Bob Julyan). Below right: Hikers on trails along the Gila forks must cross the shallow streams several times in every mile.*

*Above: Red skimmer dragonfly. Right: Trails through meadows in the northern mountains are sometimes difficult to follow.*

*Following page: The ruin of an oven at the abandoned town of Sugarite*

Entrada Sandstone and orange-stained rocks of the Chinle Formation. The river itself flows through the Rio Chama Wilderness Area, which most visitors access by raft. Fishing for brown and rainbow trout is excellent in both the Chama and the Rio Cebolla. The level ground at the confluence of the two streams holds many fine campsites.

To reach the trailhead, take US 84/285 north from Española. Stay on US 84 when US 285 splits off to the north. About 48 miles from Española, and about 8 miles north of the USFS Ghost Ranch Visitor Center, turn left onto FR 145. This dirt road is passable to any vehicle in dry weather but is impassable to all vehicles when wet. In 2.5 miles, pass through private land and continue straight through a gate in the ranch yard. Immediately bear left and continue on FR 145. About 11 miles from the highway, bear right to stay on FR 145 at English Tanks. Continue another 8 miles to the trailhead.

Begin hiking at the mesa edge on the Hart Canyon Trail 293. The trail immediately drops down the canyon wall on a series of steep switchbacks, with grand views of the Rio Chama Canyon and the smaller canyon of the Rio Cebolla. After dropping 400 feet in the first 0.5 mile, the grade moderates as the trail crosses a juniper-covered sloping bench to meet the Rio Cebolla at mile 1.6. At the trail junction, continue straight, following the signs for the Navajo Peak Trail. Immediately begin to climb the north wall of the canyon on a broad switchback. The trail ascends steeply up the Entrada cliff where fine patterns of swirling sand are prominent in the rocks. After crossing a broad bench, the trail swings to the west of Navajo

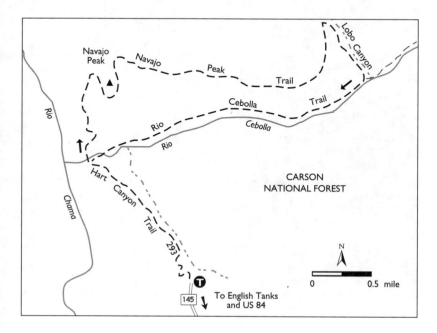

*Chimney Rock*

Peak before reaching the summit and views of the Rio Chama and Rio Cebolla Canyons at mile 2.7.

From the summit, the trail heads generally east along the rim of the canyon of the Rio Cebolla, crossing rolling hills of thick ponderosa pine. Views north to the southern San Juan Mountains occasionally open up through the trees. Continue for more than 2 miles across the mesa to the edge of Lobo Canyon, where the trail descends. Bear right with the trail and head downcanyon, meeting the Rio Cebolla at mile 6. Turn right and follow the Rio Cebolla Trail down through a narrow canyon, clambering over many rocks. After 2.5 miles in the canyon, reach the junction with the Hart Canyon Trail at mile 8.5. Turn left onto the Hart Canyon Trail and make the steep climb back to the trailhead.

## 49  CRUCES BASIN

**Distance: 9 miles, day hike or backpack**
**Difficulty:** moderate
**Elevation range:** 9,250 to 9,900 feet
**Elevation gain:** 1,200 feet
**Best time of year:** late May through November
**Water:** Beaver, Diablo, and Cruces Creeks
**Maps:** USGS Toltec Mesa; USFS Cruces Basin Wilderness
**Managed by:** Carson National Forest, Cruces Basin
   Wilderness Area, Tres Piedras Ranger District
**Features:** rolling mountain scenery, solitude

The Cruces Basin Wilderness is a small gem in Carson National Forest near the Colorado border. Open meadows, clear streams, long vistas, and bold granite outcrops characterize the high plateau. The long, dusty access road discourages most prospective visitors, so hikers are likely to enjoy their trip in relative solitude.

The lack of developed trails helps keep the Cruces Basin Wilderness a lonely place. Hikers must follow unofficial, angler, or game trails. The described loop requires the ability to read a topographic map and find a route through trailless meadows and forest. Plan to spend several days here exploring from a base camp somewhere along the first half of this route. Campsites and water are plentiful in the valleys of all three creeks. Numerous primitive campsites found along FR 572 just outside the wilderness make excellent overnight stops before a trip into the basin.

Entry to the Cruces Basin Wilderness is from Tres Piedras, about 33 miles west of Taos on US 64 and 55 miles north of Española via US 285. From Tres Piedras take US 285 north about 11 miles to FR 87 and turn left. FR 87 is a long gravel and dirt road passable to any vehicle when dry, but sections of

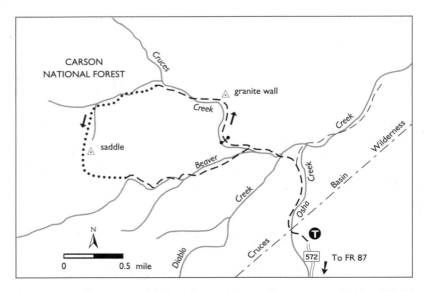

the road can be impassable for days following heavy rains. Follow FR 87 through several junctions, passing FR 87A in 21 miles. A mile beyond FR 87A, turn right onto FR 572, heading uphill. FR 572 is rough and impassable when wet. When the road is dry, a carefully driven car can make the 2 miles to the trailhead.

Begin hiking the well-worn trail heading downhill from behind the wilderness information sign (ignore the fainter trail that follows an old road along the ridge). Drop into the head of Osha Canyon. In a long meadow at mile 1.5, come to a trail junction. Bear left and away from Osha Creek onto the branch leading back into the forest and over a saddle near the end of a ridge.

At the saddle, enjoy wonderful views of the three main streams of the Cruces Basin. To the left is Diablo Creek, and straight ahead are Beaver and Cruces Creeks. The trail drops on loose rock to the junction of Diablo and Beaver Creeks. Make wet crossings of Diablo Creek and then, on the other side of a granite outcrop, Beaver Creek. From here the trail is less distinct, frequently disappearing in the wet meadows surrounding the streams. Head up the right side of Beaver Creek, passing some active beaver lodges along the way.

At mile 2.2, the valley splits with Beaver Creek to the left and Cruces Creek to the right. Follow the faint trail past the stream confluence and up Cruces Creek, soon passing through a gate. Just beyond are several shady sites for a base camp. The stream meanders through the broad meadow, turning west and passing beneath a huge wall of granite. Near the base of the rock wall, the trail crosses the stream and parallels the left bank, climbing more steeply. At mile 3.8, around the west side of the granite wall, the trail enters another extensive meadow. At this point, pick up the small stream that meets Cruces Creek in the meadow and follow the smaller stream as it heads west. Watch for blooms of pink shooting stars and purple bull elephant heads along the banks.

Follow the small stream as it heads uphill and into the forest. In 0.5 mile from Cruces Creek, about 4.3 miles from the trail start, the stream enters a narrow meadow and soon forks. Take the left fork, heading south, staying in the meadow. A faint trail near the edge of the trees leads up the meadow toward a saddle. As the trail reaches the marshy saddle, cross a fence line and look for a small, normally dry drainage heading southeast down the other side. Walk parallel to the drainage, dropping steeply through deep forest into the canyon of Beaver Creek. In 0.25 mile, the drainage enters a large meadow with views of the surrounding canyons and ridges. Drop through the meadow to the bottom and meet Beaver Creek. Pick up a trail on the north slope of the canyon that follows Beaver Creek downstream, rounding a massive granite outcrop that has bent the course of the stream to the north.

After a few minutes walking along Beaver Creek, the canyon opens into a broad meadow. Parallel the stream on faint trails down to the junction with Cruces Creek and pick up the trail used before to ascend the valley. Backtrack past the confluence of Diablo and Beaver Creeks, then make the moderate climb up Osha Creek to return to the trailhead.

*Meadows surrounding Beaver Creek in the Cruces Basin Wilderness*

# 50 | LA LEÑA WILDERNESS STUDY AREA

**Distance: 7 miles, day hike**
**Difficulty:** easy, but requires routefinding skills
**Elevation range:** 6,150 to 6,400 feet
**Elevation gain:** 400 feet
**Best time of year:** March to May, September to November
**Water:** carry water
**Map:** USGS Arroyo Empedrado
**Managed by:** Bureau of Land Management, La Leña
    Wilderness Study Area, Albuquerque Field Office
**Features:** badlands topography, strange rocks

The rangelands of the Rio Puerco watershed are a lonesome landscape that readily displays the paradox of the importance of water in shaping the land in the arid Southwest. Deeply incised arroyos fragment the terrain into thousands of isolated islands of rock. Sheer walls of sandstone border the islands and stretch on for miles. Dark, almost sinister volcanic necks—the throats of dead volcanoes now exposed by erosion of the softer sandstone—punctuate the scene. It is an eerie land that holds many beautiful secrets.

More than 66,000 acres of this inviting landscape have been set aside in a patchwork collection of wilderness study areas known as the Boca del Oso complex. Two units, the La Leña and Empedrado WSAs, sit adjacent to easily driven roads and offer miles of trailless hiking; farther along deteriorating roads lie the Chamisa and Ignacio Chavez WSAs where solitude reigns.

During dry spells that make the access roads passable, winter hiking in the more easily reached sections of the complex is delightful. Summer is

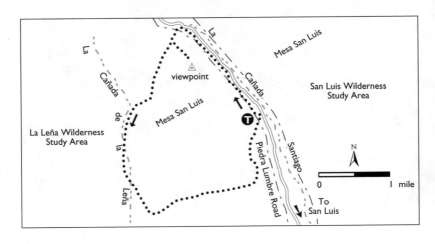

*Dozens of volcanic necks, like the massive Cabazon Peak, lie scattered about the Boca del Oso Complex.*

often unpleasantly hot in this exposed country, so spring and fall are ideal times for a trip to the more remote spots in the Chamisa and Ignacio Chavez WSAs.

As with other WSAs in New Mexico, hikers will not find trails in the Boca del Oso complex. Grab a GPS receiver and wander, or use it to roughly trace the route that follows. The suggested trip circumnavigates an elongated segment of Mesa San Luis, using La Cañada Santiago and La Cañada de la Leña as the route when the terrain gets rough near the mesa. The mesa is rippled with small gullies like claw marks from a monstrous cat, and every gouge invites exploring.

Roads into the Boca del Oso complex are generally good, but become increasingly rough the farther one gets from the highway. The nearest services are at San Ysidro to the south and Cuba to the north. Many roads are intertwined throughout the area, and all are open to public access except those specifically marked as private. Please respect private land.

Entry to all hiking areas is via the gravel CR 39, which is located off US 550 about 19 north of San Ysidro and 22 miles south of Cuba. Head west from the highway on CR 39 and in about 4 miles take the right fork and continue through the town of San Luis. About 12 miles from US 550, take the right fork. In another 1.6 miles, the Piedra Lumbre Road heads right. Bear right (north) onto the road, which is the eastern boundary of the La Leña WSA. Continue 1.3 miles to the crossing of a small arroyo, and park.

Hike up La Cañada Santiago, parallel to the road but as close to the cliffs of the mesa as is comfortable. The attractive rocks will frequently pull hikers close to the mesa, and each of the many fingers is worth exploring. Keep working northwest for about 1.5 miles as the *cañada* slices completely through the mesa. Where La Cañada Santiago breaks out of its confining canyon, swing left around the tip of Mesa San Luis. Now heading south, cross a low saddle where a short side trip to the east leads to the top of Mesa San Luis. Descend any of the shallow drainages leading to the west and, about 3.1 miles from the start, enter the arroyo of La Cañada de la Leña.

The arroyo heads south between rising walls of tan sandstone. Hikers can follow the wash or weave in and out at the base of the cliffs. Four miles from the start, the route leaves the walls of the mesa behind and presents a panorama that includes many volcanic necks to the south. Swing left to stay close to the base of Mesa San Luis, now bearing east. Walk 1.1 miles with the sheer south wall of the mesa to the left, then bear left again to stay between the mesa and La Cañada Santiago. Continue cross-country or ease down the slope to the road and follow it back to the parking area.

# 51 | BISTI SECTION, BISTI–DE-NA-ZIN WILDERNESS

**Distance: 3 to 10 miles, day hike**
**Difficulty:** easy, but requires routefinding skills
**Elevation range:** 5,750 to 6,000 feet
**Elevation gain:** 300 feet
**Best time of year:** March through November
**Water:** carry water
**Map:** USGS Alamo Mesa West
**Managed by:** Bureau of Land Management, Bisti–De-Na-Zin Wilderness, Farmington Field Office
**Features:** badlands topography, strange rocks

In art-rich New Mexico, the Bisti–De-Na-Zin Wilderness is the only gallery dedicated to a mud swamp. The duck-billed dinosaurs who lumbered across the muck 70 million years ago would be flabbergasted to see what's become of their claustrophobic swamp. Gone are the braided streams, giant turtles, and tree ferns; in their stead are rainbow-colored slopes of shale—the erstwhile swamp mud—dotted with living matter turned to stone.

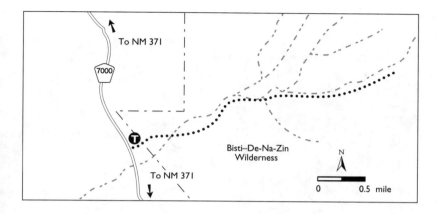

Today's Bisti Wilderness is a haunting pastel landscape of humpbacked mounds, rock-toadstool forests, and goblin stones. Dinosaur bones and petrified wood litter the surface. A maze of miniature canyons holds a variety of hues and erosional sculpturing unmatched in New Mexico. Walking through the wilderness is like strolling through an exotic set from the original *Star Wars* trilogy. (Indeed, the area was almost used as the backdrop of one of the films.)

No trails slice through the wilderness, but the fun here is following the whims of the rocks and exploring places that look interesting. The topographic map will yield a few ideas for locations to check out. Use distinctive mounds of rocks as landmarks for navigation. Precious little shade is available within the rock wonderland, so head to the Bisti when temperatures are cool. Always wear plenty of sun protection and carry at least a quart of water per person.

Easiest access into the badlands is located about 30 miles south of Farmington. Take NM 371 south from Farmington for 28 miles. Turn left onto the gravel Navajo Highway 7000, which is signed for the Bisti Wilderness. In about 5 miles, watch to the left for a large parking area at the main access.

One possible route into the wilderness from this point is to follow the broad, sandy arroyo to the east. Walk on one of the social (unofficial, but well-traveled) trails leading up the canyon, or hike in the bottom of the arroyo. Either route leads into the heart of this amphitheater of clay and sand. After a mile, the terrain turns into a wonderland of interesting-looking crannies to explore. Hikers should wander where their fancy and the whimsy of the rocks take them. Look for narrow passages, crowds of what might be grotesque lawn ornaments, and mazes of rock. Exploring the entire perimeter of the main amphitheater would take more than a day. Use landmarks or the map to return to the trailhead.

*An incredibly convoluted landscape beckons explorers in the Bisti Section of the Bisti–De-Na-Zin Wilderness.*

## 52 | DE-NA-ZIN SECTION, BISTI–DE-NA-ZIN WILDERNESS

**Distance: 4 to 5 miles, day hike**
**Difficulty:** easy, but requires some routefinding skills
**Elevation range:** 6,200 to 6,350 feet
**Elevation gain:** 200 feet
**Best time of year:** March through November
**Water:** carry water
**Map:** USGS Alamo Mesa East
**Managed by:** Bureau of Land Management, Bisti–De-Na-Zin Wilderness, Farmington Field Office
**Features:** badlands topography, strange rocks, isolation

The De-Na-Zin Wilderness is not as well known as its companion wilderness, the Bisti, but it offers six times the land area of similar wild scenery. Rocks deposited in swamps and forests on the edge of an ancient sea have eroded into fascinating shapes. The landscape is filled with lithic mushrooms, chocolate drops, turbans, and goblins. Also abundant within the wilderness are petrified logs, dinosaur bones, and mammalian fossils.

No established trails are found within the wilderness, but cross-country travel is easy. Wandering is encouraged, and the following route is only one of many possibilities for exploring. Hikers should be alert that there are private inholdings within the wilderness, often with unmarked boundaries; fences usually mark the boundaries of grazing allotments. Visitors must stay off fragile formations and are prohibited from collecting rocks and fossils.

Several access points to the wilderness are found along Navajo Highway 7023. Pick up Navajo Highway 7023 at Huerfano Trading Post, about 40 miles south of Farmington on US 550. Turn right (west) onto Navajo Highway 7023 and drive 12 miles to a parking area on the right.

From the parking area, continue straight on a dirt road heading north. Climb a low hill, then drop gradually to reach an arroyo about 0.4 mile from the start. Turn left into the arroyo and walk in the sandy bottom. The arroyo soon drops into a shallow and narrow canyon. At mile 0.9 the canyon opens up into a broader gorge, and at mile 1.2 it intersects the larger De-Na-Zin Wash. Turn left to head down the arroyo. Walking is slow in the sand, but there is plenty of scenery to attract attention. Continue down the

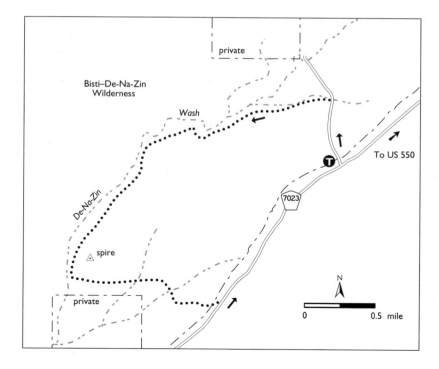

*Eroded badlands in the Bisti–De-Na-Zin Wilderness*

wash, exploring any or all of the interesting side canyons and alcoves found along the way.

After following the convoluted course of the wash for 1.3 miles, watch for a tall spire of rock detached from the cliff to the left. Private land is just downstream, so hikers should turn around here and retrace their steps. An alternative is to exit the arroyo and walk to the east and then southeast, parallel to the low cliff on the left, to reach Navajo Highway 7023 in 1.1 miles, crossing two arroyos along the way. At the road, turn left and walk 1.5 miles back to the trailhead.

## 53 | ALTO MESA LOOP

**Distance: 6 miles, day hike**
**Difficulty:** moderate
**Elevation range:** 6,100 to 6,400 feet
**Elevation gain:** 300 feet
**Best time of year:** year round
**Water:** carry water
**Map:** Chaco Culture National Historical Park brochure
**Managed by:** National Park Service, Chaco Culture National Historical Park
**Features:** best views of large Chaco pueblos and remains of Chaco road system

In a state famous for its abundance of large Native American villages, Chaco Canyon holds the crown jewels. Visitors to the remains of multiple-story towns scattered along 6 miles of canyon floor are soon struck by the magical, mystical nature of the canyon. For whatever reason, the Ancestral Pueblo people, ancestors of the modern Pueblo groups living in New Mexico and Arizona, chose this canyon to build villages with hundreds of rooms.

At present, no paved roads lead to Chaco Canyon. From all approaches, at least 16 miles of rough gravel and dirt road await. When dry, the access roads are passable to any vehicle; they are all treacherous when wet. Tight turns and steep grades at the north entrance may be difficult for long trailers. Visitors who have any doubts about road conditions should call the Chaco Culture National Historical Park (see "Sources of Additional Information" in back) for the latest information.

The easiest access to Chaco Canyon is from the north via US 550. About 3 miles southeast of Nageezi (about 50 miles west of Cuba and 35 miles south of Bloomfield), head south on CR 7900. Follow the signs about 21 miles to the park boundary. The first 5 miles are paved, but after turns onto CR 7950 and 7985, the remaining distance is dirt.

Access from the south is over longer and rougher dirt roads leading from Navajo Highway 9. From Navajo Highway 9 at Seven Lakes Trading Post, NM 57 heads north 21 rough miles to the park. Navajo Highway 46 and CR 7900/7950 lead to the park from Pueblo Pintado over 33 miles of dirt.

Because of its remote location, a trip to Chaco Canyon requires some advance planning. Aside from the campground, no facilities are located in the park. Visitors must fill gas tanks before taking the long dirt roads into the park, and bring all the food and other supplies they will need. Food and gasoline can be purchased during the week at the trading posts along US 550 north of the park.

All trips into the backcountry, including the three described here, require a free permit available at the visitor center. Removing or moving

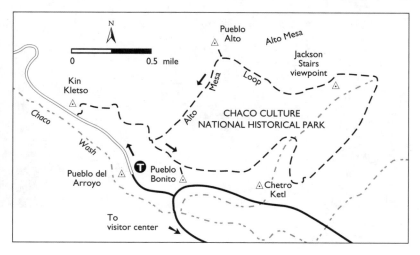

plants, rocks, or artifacts is prohibited. Leave all artifacts where they are found. To prevent damage to the fragile pueblos, stay off the walls. Even in the backcountry, stay on the designated trails. All trails close at sunset, so plan hikes accordingly.

The Alto Mesa Trail is the most popular and diverse backcountry trail at Chaco Canyon. Modern visitors can easily sense the central role that Pueblo Alto played in Ancestral Pueblo commerce. Perched on the very top of the mesa, Pueblo Alto and its attendant smaller villages have a view of many places significant in the Ancestral Pueblo world, such as Mount Taylor to the south and the San Juan Mountains. Ancient roads from towns within the canyon to outlying sites as far as 40 miles away converge at Pueblo Alto.

To reach the trailhead, drive on the paved park road about 4.5 miles from the visitor center to the parking area for Pueblo del Arroyo (do not park along the road). Begin walking west past the gate on the old, dirt park road for 0.4 mile. Directly behind Kin Kletso, a sign marks the beginning of the trail. Follow the well-worn, winding path up the talus along the cliff face, using caution. The trail soon enters and climbs a narrow crack in the rocks. Once on the first bench level of the mesa, follow the copious rock cairns as they lead east along the slickrock.

*A short spur along the Alto Mesa Trail leads to an overhead view of Pueblo Bonito, the largest village at Chaco Canyon.*

The trail parallels the cliff face, winding around the heads of several canyons. A half mile from the start of the trail, the return leg of the loop enters from the direction of Pueblo Alto to the left. Take a short, cairn-marked route to the right to the overlook of Pueblo Bonito almost directly below. Return to the main route and turn right, continuing eastward along the slickrock bench. Climb a short spur of the mesa, then descend along a cliff that offers views of Chetro Ketl.

The trail skirts the head of another box canyon and then follows a short segment of an ancient road alignment. The road is clear of loose rocks and is bordered by a low masonry wall. Round the end of this spur of the mesa and climb steeply northward to the next bench level. In about 200 yards, climb again through a narrow crack to the top of the ridge. After rounding the upper end of the canyon at mile 3, a marked viewpoint provides the best perspective on the Jackson Stairs, a precarious ancient route from canyon bottom to mesa top.

After a few minutes heading west on the slickrock, the trail climbs a sandy hill, leading in 0.5 mile to the remains of the Pueblo Alto complex. From the pueblo, the view encompasses hundreds of square miles to the north, extending from the La Plata Mountains in southern Colorado to Mount Taylor in the south. Line-of-sight connections can be made with pueblos to the north, a signal station in South Gap, Tsin Kletzin on the mesa on the opposite site of Chaco Canyon, and Mount Taylor to the south.

From Pueblo Alto, a sign points the way back to the trailhead. Head south for 0.5 mile, turn right onto the trail taken earlier, and then descend the crack to Kin Kletso and the old park road. Turn left on the road and walk back to the parking area.

# 54 | SOUTH MESA LOOP

**Distance: 5 miles, day hike**
**Difficulty:** moderate
**Elevation range:** 6,100 to 6,650 feet
**Elevation gain:** 550 feet
**Best time of year:** year round
**Water:** carry water
**Map:** Chaco Culture National Historical Park brochure
**Managed by:** National Park Service, Chaco Culture National Historical Park
**Features:** lightly used trail, scenic overlooks, large intact pueblo

South Mesa and South Gap—a wide break in the south wall of Chaco Canyon—played a central role in the Chaco communication system, a complex series of line-of-sight connections between villages. The largest pueblos were probably sited near the South Gap due to the ease of travel through the gap into the canyon. A signal station near this hike's South Gap observation point provided a visual link between Pueblo Alto and Pueblo Bonito. Perhaps no other village demonstrates the importance of the line-of-sight concept as well as Tsin Kletzin. Move the location of the town a hundred yards in any direction and visual connections with other Chaco sites are lost.

Driving directions to Chaco Canyon are found in the Alto Mesa Loop (Hike 53) description. The South Mesa Trail begins at the parking area for Casa Rinconada, about 4 miles west of the visitor center on the eastbound side of the main park road. From the parking area, begin by following the Casa Rinconada interpretive trail. In 50 feet, bear right onto a gravel path heading toward Casa Rinconada. On the back side of the pueblo, find a post marked "South Mesa Loop." Turn right onto a dirt path that heads west, parallel to the base of the cliff. After 0.1 mile, bear left onto a service road, which leads into South Gap.

About 0.75 mile from the start, bear right onto a spur trail heading across the gap to climb to the South Gap observation point. Make the 150-foot climb on a single switchback to the viewpoint. Line-of-sight connections

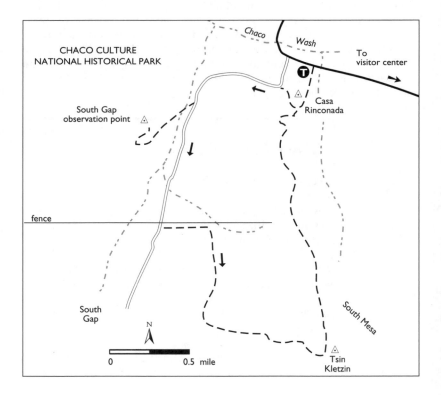

*Round concretions weathered from sandstone along the South
Mesa Trail*

are made with Pueblo Bonito and Pueblo Alto. Do not wander beyond the
protective fence.

Backtrack to the service road. Turn right to continue south on the road.
In about 0.5 mile, follow the signs for the South Mesa Trail as they lead off
the service road and through a fence. At mile 2.7, the trail immediately
turns left to parallel the fence and road, heading east into a broad rincon, a
drainage enclosed on three sides by rock walls. In a few minutes, the trail
bears right into a long side canyon. At the head of the canyon, bear left and
follow a switchback up to the top of a ridge, then climb through white,
orange, and tan layers of sandstone toward the top of South Mesa. Watch
for cairns and lines of rocks that indicate the location of the trail as it climbs.

From the top of the rocks, the trail climbs the final 0.5 mile to Tsin
Kletzin, a pueblo about 3.5 miles from the start. Note the line-of-sight connections with Pueblo Alto to the north and the Chaco outlier, Kin Klizhin,
through South Gap.

A post below the northeast corner of Tsin Kletzin marks the 1.5-mile
return trail back to Casa Rinconada. Descend across a sandy flat, then drop
down steeply over layers of sandstone as the trail approaches the cliff. Just
above Chaco Canyon are fine views of the major pueblos at the foot of the
cliff on both sides of the canyon.

# 55 PEÑASCO BLANCO

**Distance: 7 miles, day hike**
**Difficulty:** easy
**Elevation range:** 6,100 to 6,400 feet
**Elevation gain:** 300
**Best time of year:** year round
**Water:** carry water
**Map:** Chaco Culture National Historical Park brochure
**Managed by:** National Park Service, Chaco Culture
   National Historical Park
**Features:** large collection of petroglyphs, supernova
   pictograph, impressive Ancestral Pueblo village, expan-
   sive views

Near the pueblo of Peñasco Blanco, a short spur trail leads to the most intriguing rock art to be found at Chaco. On a small overhang along the south
wall of the canyon, a red-painted crescent moon, large star, and handprint
adorn the sandstone. Experts speculate the pictograph represents a supernova explosion that occurred in 1064, during the height of the Ancestral
Pueblo culture in Chaco. Chinese astronomers left a written record of the
sudden appearance of a bright new star located near the waxing moon.
Ardent skywatchers, the Ancestral Pueblo people certainly witnessed the
same event, and this unique rock painting may be their own pictorial
record of the explosion.

For driving directions to Chaco Canyon, refer to the Alto Mesa Loop (Hike
53) description. The trailhead to Peñasco Blanco is located along the main
park road at Pueblo del Arroyo, about 4.5 miles from the visitor center.

From the trailhead, walk the wide dirt road heading west and down the
canyon. Pass Kin Kletso and continue to Casa Chiquita at 1 mile from the

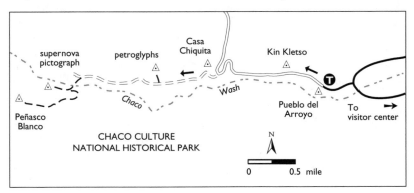

*The supernova pictograph along the trail to Pueblo Peñasco*

start. Follow the trail sign onto a narrow dirt road running parallel to Chaco Wash at the base of the north wall of the canyon. After 1.5 miles of easy walking, look for an arrow pointing to a trail that travels against the very base of the cliff, where many petroglyph panels adorn the smooth faces of sandstone. A particularly striking panel—a tapestry design, bighorn sheep, and a human figure—is pecked high on the canyon wall, about 1.75 miles from the start.

After a large panel of rock art, the trail bears left to rejoin the road, which now angles away from the cliff to the center of the canyon. About 2.7 miles from the start, the trail leaves the road, heading to the left to drop into the wash. Immediately come to a trail junction and bear right on the fork signed for "Pictograph." In a minute, the trail crosses the bottom of the wash. Do not enter the wash when running water is present. At a trail junction 0.2 mile beyond the wash, bear right. Reach the supernova pictograph in a few minutes. The trail is closed beyond this site.

From the pictograph, backtrack to the last trail junction and continue straight on the fork signed "Ruins." Follow the trail along the cliff face, then climb the ledges to reach the main trail about 0.25 mile from the pictograph. Turn right onto the main trail and follow the many rock cairns for another 0.5 mile as they lead up the ledges to bench level, with Peñasco

Blanco in sight most of the way. The pueblo lies high atop the mesa, with outstanding views in all directions.

On the return, bypass the side trail to the pictograph by continuing straight at the junction and dropping down the ledges into Chaco Wash. As the trail swings left, enjoy a walk through the willows for 0.2 mile until the two trails meet near the exit from the wash. Return to the trailhead via the old road.

# 56 | Gooseberry Springs Trail

**Distance: 7 miles, day hike**
**Difficulty:** difficult
**Elevation range:** 9,300 to 11,300 feet
**Elevation gain:** 2,100 feet
**Best time of year:** late May through early November
**Water:** carry water
**Maps:** USGS Mt. Taylor; USFS Cibola National Forest
**Managed by:** Cibola National Forest, Mount Taylor Ranger District
**Features:** huge, open meadows; outstanding views

Mount Taylor is an extinct volcano rising high above the surrounding lava fields near Grants, New Mexico. The mountain is part of a much larger volcanic field extending to Arizona in the west and to jagged volcanic necks, tall spires of hardened magma, to the east. The mountain was built by periodic eruptions occurring from 4 to 2 million years ago. At the end of this period, the peak stood higher than at present. Subsequent eruptions were of the explosive type and the sideways blasts tore the mountain apart, creating a high-rimmed crater draining to the east.

The Gooseberry Springs Trail climbs to the summit of the rim of the ancient volcano, 5,000 feet above the plains below, to take in a command-

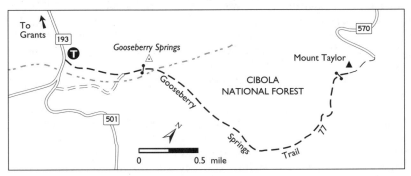

*The Gooseberry Springs Trail crosses the extensive meadows surrounding Mount Taylor.*

ing view. This is a dry hike, with little or no water available at Gooseberry Springs any time of the year. The exposed meadows near and around the summit make this a risky place to hike during the summer thunderstorm season. This trail is best hiked in late May and June, after mid-September, or early on a summer's morning.

From Santa Fe Avenue in Grants, take NM 547 (First Street) north, following the signs for Mount Taylor. Continue about 13 miles to the end of the pavement and turn right onto FR 193. Travel this well-graded gravel road 5 miles to a small sign on the left marking the beginning of Gooseberry Springs Trail 77. (The junction of FR 193 and FR 501 is 0.1 mile beyond the trailhead.)

The first part of the trail climbs along a closed and abandoned portion of forest road through the conifer forest parallel to a small drainage. In 0.6 mile, the trail crosses a grassy area to meet another old road and a new section of trail, which is marked as Trail 77. On the east side of the road, follow the trail and climb through an airy aspen stand on the right (south) side of the drainage. Pass through a gate and rejoin the old road near Gooseberry Springs about 1 mile from the start.

At mile 1.5, the trail leaves the forest and enters the extensive meadows surrounding the summit of Mount Taylor. Here the trail continues to follow an old road as it climbs to cross a ridge about 1.9 miles from the start, with long-range views to the south and east. Swing north (left), climbing toward the summit visible straight ahead. The trail crosses the open meadow with a series of broad switchbacks. At mile 3.2, just below the summit, pass through a gate, then make the final climb to the top. From the summit, the horseshoe-shaped rim of the old volcano is clearly visible to the east. A trail continues to the north, leading down the mountain to FR 570; but, after enjoying the view, retrace your steps to return to the trailhead.

## 57 | BIG TUBES

**Distance:** 2 miles, day hike
**Difficulty:** easy
**Elevation range:** 7,600 to 7,640 feet
**Elevation gain:** 50 feet
**Best time of year:** March to December
**Water:** carry water
**Maps:** USGS Ice Caves; El Malpais Recreation Guide Map
**Managed by:** Bureau of Land Management, El Malpais National Conservation Area; National Park Service, El Malpais National Monument
**Features:** lava tubes, lava flow features

The sprawling El Malpais National Monument and Conservation Area is jointly administered by the National Park Service and the Bureau of Land Management. It features some of the most recent lava flows in North America, perhaps as young as 400 years old.

Lava from the most recent eruption of Bandera Crater flowed more than 20 miles from the base of the cone almost to Grants. Within the flow is a 12-mile-long chain of collapsed and whole lava tubes. The tubes extending from Bandera Crater exhibit large and small holes in their ceilings: big holes are called skylights, smaller ones, windows. Below the openings, in a cool, wet habitat with plenty of sunlight, a unique community of green moss and insects is found. Help protect these biotic habitats by staying off the mosses. Come prepared to explore underground by bringing three sources of light, such as a lantern, flashlight, and candle and matches.

Making the trip to the Big Tubes area requires some careful planning and a bit of luck. The main access road into the area, CR 42, is notoriously impassable when wet, with huge puddles blocking motorized access for weeks after prolonged rains. Make the trip only during dry spells: late May

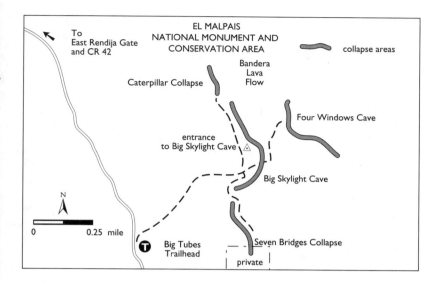

EL MALPAIS
NATIONAL MONUMENT AND
CONSERVATION AREA

To
East Rendija Gate
and CR 42

collapse areas

Bandera
Lava
Flow

Caterpillar Collapse

Four Windows Cave

entrance
to Big Skylight Cave

Big Skylight Cave

N

0          0.25  mile

Big Tubes
Trailhead

Seven Bridges Collapse

private

through early July and mid-September to November are best. Under dry conditions, the road is rough but passable to most vehicles, although high clearance is recommended. For the latest road conditions, contact the Northwest New Mexico Visitor Center in Grants (see "Sources of Additional Information" at back).

From the west side of Grants, take NM 53 south toward El Malpais and El Morro National Monuments for 26 miles (about 1 mile past the entrance to Bandera Crater and Ice Caves) to CR 42. Turn left and continue 4.6 miles on this rough road to East Rendija Gate. Turn left and drive 3.2 miles to the Big Tubes Trailhead. Pick up a brochure and cave map at the trailhead.

The rough trail to the Big Tubes is marked with large cairns. From the information board, find the first cairn and walk to it, then sight the next cairn. Continue in this stepwise manner over the Bandera Lava Flow, watching for the features of recent flows: blocky and jagged a'a; the smooth, ropy surface of pahoehoe; and pressure ridges can all be easily examined at close range along the trail.

Slow walking for 0.5 mile leads to the extensive tube and collapse area. Here the main trail ends at a sign that directs hikers to the three trail branches beyond. Explore all three branches. From the sign, the trail left to the entrance to Big Skylight Cave is not apparent. Take a few steps up, staying on the south side of the collapse, to locate the cairned trail. The entrance to Big Skylight is 100 yards from the sign. The route drops over the wall of the collapse and is not as formidable as it appears from above. However, exploring this tube is made difficult by the huge blocks fallen from the ceiling. Beyond the entrance to Big Skylight Cave, the trail continues along the south rim of the collapse to Caterpillar Collapse.

From the sign at the end of the main trail, cairns along the right fork also lead to a peek into the big skylight of the cave of the same name; cairns then continue several hundred yards to Seven Bridges Collapse. This long, interesting trench is spanned by a series of natural bridges. The trail leads into the collapse, where hikers can follow the trench for a short distance before reaching private property.

Starting again at the sign at the end of the main trail, the trail branch that begins straight and then veers to the left leads to Four Windows Cave, the most easily explored of the lava tubes in the area. This trail leads along the north rim of a collapse for 200 feet before dropping into a small flat and heading north. Follow the cairns a short 0.25 mile to the rim of another collapse. A cairn on the rim marks an easy route into the trench. Enter the cave, but make certain to stay off the moss-covered rocks. Hikers with the proper equipment can follow the cave its entire 1,200-foot length. Having the detailed Park Service brochure and map will minimize the chance of confusion; it is surprisingly easy to become disoriented in the most remote part of the tube.

*Holes in the ceilings of lava tubes are called windows or skylights.*

# 58 | ZUNI-ACOMA TRAIL

**Distance: 7 miles, day hike**
**Difficulty:** difficult
**Elevation range:** 6,600 to 6,900 feet
**Elevation gain:** 400 feet
**Best time of year:** March through November
**Water:** carry water
**Maps:** USGS Arrosa Ranch and Los Pilares
**Managed by:** National Park Service, El Malpais National
    Monument
**Features:** lava structures, ancient trail, isolation

The Zuni-Acoma Trail spans overlapping lava flows from five volcanoes, following an ancient route that connects the two pueblos. Much of the route lies on solid, uneven rock, and the trail twists constantly as it traverses lava ridges and bridges. Make no mistake: despite the relatively short distance, it is a tiring journey. Allow 5 or 6 hours to complete the hike, and take plenty of water and sunscreen.

To walk the entire trail requires setting up a long car shuttle, but it's worth the extra effort. First, head south on NM 117, which is located at exit 89 off I-40, about 65 miles west of Albuquerque and 5 miles east of Grants. A little more than 15 miles from the interstate on NM 117, park in the marked lot along the highway.

Leave a car at this trailhead and return to the interstate. Head west to

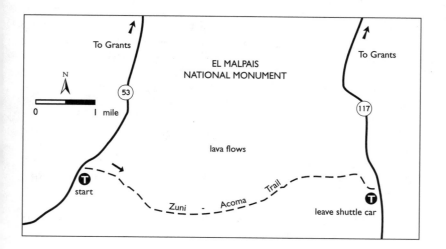

*Rugged terrain and difficult walking awaits hikers along the Zuni-Acoma Trail.*

Grants and, on the west edge of the town, take exit 81 and travel south on NM 53. In 14 miles, park at the marked trailhead on the left.

Begin walking on the dirt road leading east from the parking lot. Watch carefully for a signpost on the right that leads off the road and onto the trail. The trail soon enters the pines, then the first of the lava flows. At this point, forward progress slows considerably. Hikers must divide their attention between looking down at the ankle-twisting terrain and looking up to watch carefully for the hundreds of rock cairns that mark the entire route. If you lose the way and can't find the next cairn, backtrack to the last trail marker and search again.

As the winding trail works across the lava flows, note the distinctive character of each flow. A change in the jaggedness of the rocks is a good indicator of the transitions between flows. Also watch for lava bridges, limestone blocks embedded in the lava, massive sheets of rope-like pahoehoe, and gnarled trees growing in pockets of soil within the lava. Some of these trees are thousands of years old.

The last 0.5 mile of the trail traverses sandy islands between the lava flows. The trail ends at the eastern trailhead on NM 117.

# 59 | CERRO AMERICANO

**Distance: 3 miles, day hike**
**Difficulty:** easy
**Elevation range:** 7,570 to 8,070 feet
**Elevation gain:** 500
**Best time of year:** March through November
**Water:** carry water
**Maps:** USGS Cerro Hueco; El Malpais Recreation Guide Map
**Managed by:** Bureau of Land Management, El Malpais
    National Conservation Area
**Features:** cinder cone, view of volcanic fissure

Cinder cones are huge piles of material spewed from a volcanic vent. Nothing fancy: bits of rock are shot into the air, falling nearby to form a conical mound. Most of the rocks are pebble-sized and called cinders; larger rocks shot higher may cool slightly on the trip down and form volcanic bombs, distinguished by their striated appearance. The resulting piles can rise several hundred feet, forming round hills with small craters in the center. Cerro Americano is one of the highest cinder cones in the Chain of Craters in El Malpais. No trail leads to the summit, but a route that leaves CR 42 circles to the backside of the cone where climbing to the top is easiest.

From the west side of Grants, take NM 53 south toward El Malpais and El Morro National Monuments for 26 miles (about 1 mile past the entrance to Bandera Crater and Ice Caves) to CR 42. This road is notoriously impassable when wet, with huge puddles blocking passage for weeks after prolonged rains. Turn left and continue 7.6 miles, past the East, North, and

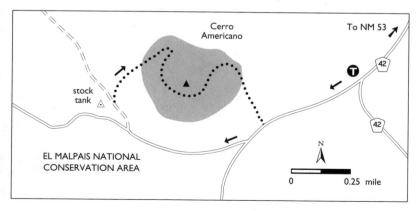

*Climbing a cinder cone at El Malpais Conservation Area*

South Rendija Gates, to an intersection with a double-track road angling to the right. Park off the road.

Begin walking on the double-track, heading southwest with Cerro Americano on the right. The road crosses an open flat, then enters a woodland as it swings by the base of the volcano. At an intersection just short of 0.5 mile from the start, bear right. Views to the left include Cerro Hueco and Cerro Leonides, both along the same rift zone that gave rise to Cerro Americano.

About a mile from the start, just after the road bends gently to the right, look for a double-track angling to the right and take it. In 200 yards, before the track reaches a small stock tank, leave the track and begin the trailless route around to the north side of Cerro Americano. Bear right and climb through the open woodland on the flank of the volcano. Climb gradually at first, picking up any game or cattle trails that might make walking easier. Work around to the north, enjoying views of the Zuni Mountains to the northwest.

At a grassy meadow on the slopes of the volcano, begin climbing more or less straight up, staying on the west side of a fence that crosses the meadow. Near the rim of the crater, follow the fence to the top. Once on the horseshoe-shaped rim, follow the fence south, then east, then north.

From the north side, the views reach beyond the lava flows and cinder cones of El Malpais to Mount Taylor.

From the rim of the crater, visually locate the trailhead below to the east. Get your bearings and drop steeply down the east slope of the volcano, bouncing along through the cinders. At the road, bear left and return to the trailhead.

# 60  RIVERA CANYON

**Distance: 5 miles, day hike**
**Difficulty:** easy, but requires some routefinding skills
**Elevation range:** 7,900 to 8,300 feet
**Elevation gain:** 400
**Best time of year:** April to early November
**Water:** carry water
**Maps:** USGS Valle Largo and Paxton Springs
**Managed by:** Cibola National Forest, Mount Taylor Ranger District
**Features:** old railroad bed, huge trestle, pretty canyon scenery

The Zuni Mountains are composed of tilted blocks of sedimentary rocks with piles of volcanic material scattered on the surface. In the 1920s, the range was the site of intensive logging operations that depended on railroads to move trees from the forest to sawmills in Albuquerque. The southern half of the range was the domain of the George E. Breece Lumber Company. Breece operated a rail line from Grants through Zuni Canyon to spur routes that served as feeders to the main line. When Breece left the Zuni Mountains, he sold his railroad to Grants businessmen Carl Seligman

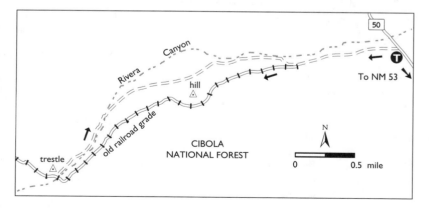

*A square-head nail in an old timber*

and M. R. Prestridge. The new timbermen pushed a route up Rivera Canyon to reach forests on Oso Ridge along the Continental Divide. To span the head of the canyon, the company built a massive log trestle that still stands watch over the canyon.

Following the old railroad up Rivera Canyon is an exercise in the powers of observation. By watching carefully for raised beds and rotting wood, it is possible to trace the entire route from FR 50 to FR 187. A dirt track lies to the north of the railroad and serves as a guide for those who lose the rail bed.

Take NM 53 south from exit 81 off I-40 in Grants. About 27 miles south of Grants, turn right onto the gravel FR 50. Travel north on FR 50 about 6 miles to the unmarked junction with a double-track heading to the left (west), and park.

Begin hiking along the double-track as it parallels a fence line to the right. In 0.25 mile, the track swings right. Search for the bed of the railroad, which stays to the south of the road. Follow the railbed by watching for raised sections of the route, discarded ties, dirt berms, and pathways once cleared of vegetation. The railbed stays above the bottom of Rivera Canyon, which is marked by a band of oak and box elder. About 1 mile from the start, the route swings left, away from the canyon bottom, and skirts the base of a wooded hill. In another mile, the trail approaches the canyon bottom again and enters a logged forest. About 2.5 miles from the start, the route leads to the spectacular Rivera Canyon trestle.

From the trestle, hikers can return by the same route or pick up the old road that heads down Rivera Canyon. The road stays close to the canyon bottom for 0.75 mile before angling off to the right across open country. In another mile, rejoin the canyon bottom and follow the track back to the trailhead.

# 61 | EL MORRO RIM TRAIL

**Distance: 2 miles, day hike**
**Difficulty:** easy
**Elevation range:** 7,200 to 7,400 feet
**Elevation gain:** 200
**Best time of year:** year round
**Water:** carry water
**Map:** El Morro National Monument brochure
**Managed by:** National Park Service, El Morro National
   Monument
**Features:** historic inscriptions, pueblo village, desert
   waterhole

A hike doesn't have to last all day to be a New Mexico classic. The 2-mile trail from the visitor center to the mesa top at El Morro National Monument provides an encompassing look at the history of the state. Along the way are a small pueblo, inscriptions from Spanish colonial times and the early years of American exploration, and some impressive geology—at

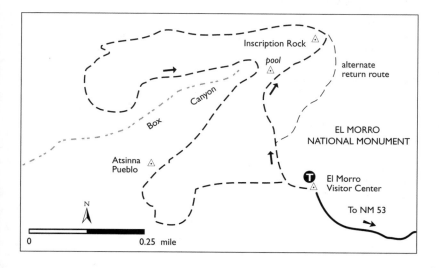

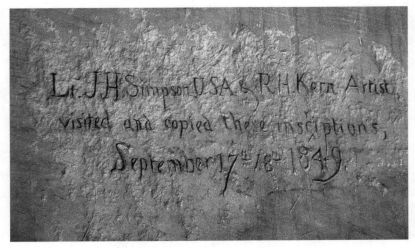

*Lt. James Simpson left his mark on Inscription Rock in 1849 while leading an exploration for the U.S. Army.*

least 10 miles of enjoyment compressed into a leisurely 2-hour walk.

El Morro National Monument is an essential stop for those exploring the wildlands southwest of Grants. Take exit 81 from I-40 on the west side of Grants and head south on NM 53. Continue 41 miles to the El Morro entrance, turn left and park at the visitor center. Pay the fee inside and pick up a copy of the interpretive guide that will add much to your understanding of the inscriptions.

The paved trail begins at the back of the visitor center. Follow the trail right and, at the first two intersections, stay on the Inscription Trail at the foot of the bluff. Pass the deep green pool that attracted travelers to this spot, then walk along the cliff where hundreds of names and messages are carved in the smooth sandstone, dating from Juan Oñate in 1605 to railroad workers in the 1860s.

In 0.5 mile, round the tip of the mesa and climb past more inscriptions. In a few minutes, ascend several switchbacks to gain the mesa top where the view takes in the Zuni Mountains and some of the volcanoes in the nearby El Malpais National Conservation Area. Follow the double lines pecked into the slickrock sandstone around the head of idyllic Box Canyon. About 1.5 miles from the start, pass through the pueblo of Atsinna, an ancient town of more than 800 rooms. Beyond the village, the trail descends through the rocks to return to the visitor center.

*Facing page: Isolated ranges surrounded by desert scrubland in New Mexico's central mountains*

# CENTRAL MOUNTAINS

# 62  PETROGLYPH NATIONAL MONUMENT TRAILS

**Distance: 7 miles for five trails, day hike**
**Difficulty:** easy
**Elevation range:** 5,000 to 5,300 feet
**Elevation gain:** 300 feet
**Best time of year:** May to November
**Water:** at visitor center
**Maps:** National Park Service brochure and pamphlets
**Managed by:** National Park Service, Petroglyph National Monument
**Features:** spectacular petroglyphs

Petroglyph National Monument lies on the very edge of the sprawling western edge of Albuquerque. Along a snaking escarpment of black volcanic boulders, the monument protects an extraordinary collection of more than 15,000 petroglyphs. The artists range from nomadic hunters who visited the site more than two centuries ago to ranchers who chased cows in the area less than 100 years in the past. Most of the drawings, however, are from the Ancestral Pueblo people and are around 500 years old.

Petroglyphs are scattered across the edge of the mesa, but five trails lead hikers past concentrations of these intriguing aspects of Pueblo history. Viewing the rock art is best early in the morning when the sun is not so glaring on east- and south-facing slopes. Plan a visit for the first hours after the park opens at 8 A.M. Take binoculars to spot glyphs high on the cliff, and a pair of polarized sunglasses to make the art easier to see. The trails are sandy, flat, and easy.

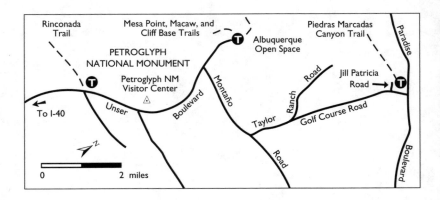

*Thousands of petroglyphs are pecked into the volcanic rocks along the escarpment to the west of Albuquerque.*

Much of the monument lies adjacent to housing developments, and finding the official access points is sometimes an adventure in itself. The easiest way to explore the monument is from the south, starting at the Unser Boulevard exit off I-40. Head north on Unser for 2 miles to the trailhead for the Rinconada Trail on the left.

Head out the trail, which parallels the northern cliff of a huge amphitheater of rock. Clusters of petroglyphs are found along the way, each with a short spur trail leading to it. Follow the Rinconada Trail about 1.5 miles to its indistinct end, then return by the same route. Hikers will undoubtedly be surprised when retracing their steps at how many petroglyphs they missed on the way out.

From the Rinconada Trailhead, drive north on Unser Boulevard and in 0.8 mile stop in at the visitor center. Pick up detailed maps of the trails, then continue north on Unser. At 1.4 miles beyond the visitor center, go straight on Unser at the intersection with Montaño Road. In less than a mile, turn right into the Boca Negra Canyon area where three trails await. The longest, the Mesa Point Trail, is about 0.5 mile long and has the greatest concentration of petroglyphs. The short Macaw and Cliff Base Trails also pass amazing collections of rock art.

To reach the Piedras Marcadas Canyon Trail, return to the intersection of Unser and Montaño. Head east on Montaño 1.3 miles and turn left on Taylor Ranch Road. In 0.5 mile, continue straight onto Golf Course Road as Taylor Ranch Road bears left. At 3.9 miles from Unser, just before a service station at the intersection with Paradise Boulevard, turn left onto Jill Patricia. Park on the right side of the road just before the "Las Marcadas" housing development.

Walk the concrete path to the right along a retaining wall. Swing left and head uphill. At a fork in the trail, take the left branch and pass through a gate. Entering Albuquerque Open Space, follow the wide trail between the base of the cliff and the retaining wall. In less than 0.25 mile, a trail heads right. Take that trail as it winds close to the base of the cliff. The rocks here are decorated with an amazing assortment of masks, snakes, birds, and handprints. You can easily follow the trail for 1.3 miles before turning around.

## 63 | LA LUZ/TRAMWAY LOOP

**Distance: 9 miles, day hike**
**Difficulty:** strenuous
**Elevation range:** 6,600 to 10,300 feet
**Elevation gain:** 3,900 feet
**Best time of year:** May to November
**Water:** at tramway terminals, carry water
**Maps:** USGS Sandia Crest; USFS Sandia Wilderness
**Managed by:** Cibola National Forest, Sandia Wilderness, Sandia Ranger District
**Features:** spectacular, rugged country; one-way hike

The combination of the La Luz Trail and the Sandia Peak Tramway offers hikers a unique opportunity for a challenging one-way hike. The Sandia Mountains are a round-shouldered hump of granite and limestone that dominates the eastern skyline of Albuquerque. The La Luz Trail climbs 3,700 feet from the base of the Sandias to the crest at 10,300 feet. From the summit, hikers can return via the same trail or opt to enjoy a relaxing 15-minute descent back to the base by riding the tram. As an alternative trip, hikers can take the tram to the top of the mountain and walk back down to the base, a trip that is still quite demanding. One-way tram tickets for hikers can be purchased at either terminal. The tram generally runs between 9 A.M. and 5 P.M. Call (505) 298-8518 for the latest information.

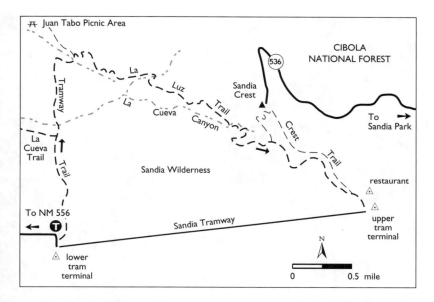

The trailhead for the La Luz Trail is located at the Juan Tabo Picnic Area, but those interested in a loop hike need to begin at the Sandia Peak Tramway parking area and take the Tramway Trail to connect with the La Luz Trail 2 miles above its bottom terminus. This is a popular trail, crowded on weekends with hikers, climbers, and trail runners. The trail has a long history of rerouting and there are many places where old trails may confuse inexperienced hikers. The current trail is well worn its entire length. Note that the steep terrain limits the number of campsites along the trail.

From Albuquerque, take I-25 north to the Tramway Road exit 234, NM 556. Head east on NM 556 for 6 miles, then turn left to stay on Tramway Road. One mile from the turn, enter the Sandia Peak Tramway grounds. After paying the nominal parking fee, park near the base of the tramway.

Begin hiking at the northeast corner of the parking lot at the information kiosk and sign for the Tramway Trail. Head into the granite boulder wonderland, immediately entering the Sandia Wilderness. The trail skirts the foot of the mountains, passing near homes and private property, so stay on the trail. In 1 mile, pass the La Cueva Trail to the left and cross La Cueva Canyon. Climb a narrow ridge directly above some large homes, then cross the ridge and bear right, dropping into another canyon. Here the many switchbacks of the La Luz Trail are visible across the canyon. At mile 2.3, immediately after crossing the bottom of the canyon, intersect the La Luz Trail and turn right.

Begin the long journey through "Switchback City," where the trail builders arguably went overboard to ease the grades of the next 800-foot

*The La Luz Trail crosses a talus slope dozens of times as it winds across the western face of the Sandia Mountains.*

climb. The trail now skirts the north side of a deep canyon on a shadeless slope before reaching a tunnel of vegetation in the canyon bottom. Climb the south wall of that canyon to an open saddle, then continue the ascent on the north slope of La Cueva Canyon. Several broad switchbacks through oak scrub lead to a saddle over a small spur ridge. Drop from the saddle into the conifer forest of upper La Cueva Canyon.

Cross the bottom of La Cueva Canyon at about mile 5, where a sign warns against farther travel in winter. At this point the trail has gained 2,600 feet, with 1,300 feet to go. Take a deep breath and begin the steepest section of trail. The route is a long set of switchbacks that cross and re-cross a talus chute about a dozen times. Views of La Cueva Canyon and a huge granite slab to the right are impressive. One more set of broad me-anders leads to a saddle and trail junction. The trail left goes to Sandia Crest; continue straight across the saddle on the La Luz Trail. Here the trail leaves the granite and travels along the base of a banded limestone cliff. This spectacular section of trail is perched on a wide ledge with nearby views of massive towers of granite. South Sandia Peak dominates the view in the distance.

At mile 8.9, reach the junction with the Crest Trail, which is usually crowded with tourists. To reach the upper tramway terminal, bear right across a wooden deck at the restaurant. The ticket window is in the U.S. Forest Service Visitor Center directly behind the tramway dock.

# 64 | NORTH SANDIA CREST/10K LOOP

**Distance: 7-mile loop, day hike**
**Difficulty:** moderate
**Elevation range:** 9,800 to 10,600 feet
**Elevation gain:** 900 feet
**Best time of year:** May to October
**Water:** Media Spring
**Map:** USGS Sandia Crest
**Managed by:** Cibola National Forest, Sandia Ranger District
**Features:** isolation on the edge of a major city, views

In contrast to the steep western face of the Sandia Mountains, the east side of the range gently slopes from the crest, creating less demanding terrain for hiking and cross-country skiing. The North Crest Trail offers views of both sides of the mountain, traveling along the ridge above vertical granite crags, with a short side trail leading to North Sandia Peak. The 10K Trail, so named because it roughly follows the 10,000-foot contour, drops through the sloping conifer forest of the east side of the range.

To reach the trailhead, go east from Albuquerque on I-40 to the Cedar Crest/Tijeras exit 175 and follow the signs for NM 14 north. In 6 miles, turn left onto NM 536. A day-use fee is charged for entering this area. Continue 14 miles to the Sandia Crest and park in the large lot.

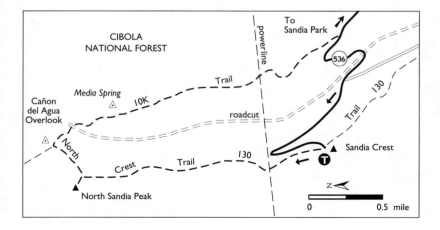

Begin by following the signs for the North Crest Trail 130, heading north. The trail skirts below a forest of radio and TV towers before entering the conifer woods and beginning to descend. Several short side trails lead to views to the west. Watch for Richardson's geranium and larkspur under the fir and spruce, and juncos and mountain chickadees in the trees. Continue through conifer forest along the rim, reaching an unmaintained side trail to North Sandia Peak at mile 1.7. This short trip leads to fantastic views of the granite spires and cliffs to the west. Back on the main trail, make a short descent and reach the Cañon del Agua Overlook at mile 2. Find the often unsigned 10K Trail at the edge of the clearing; watch for the blue diamonds that mark this as a ski trail. Turn right onto the 10K Trail and continue descending.

At mile 2.2, the trail crosses a broad road cut, a scar from a never-completed highway project. In a few minutes, pass a sign for Media Spring, which is misidentified as Osha Spring on some maps. Continue through the deep forest on a rolling trail, passing under a powerline at mile 3.8. Near NM 536, follow the main trail through a confusing stretch and reach the paved road near the road cut. Turn right and walk along the road just over 2 miles back to Sandia Crest.

*Yellow daisies growing beneath rocks on Sandia Crest*

# 65 | SOUTH SANDIA PEAK

**Distance: 12 miles, day hike or backpack**
**Difficulty:** difficult
**Elevation range:** 6,600 to 9,500 feet
**Elevation gain:** 2,300 feet
**Best time of year:** May to October
**Water:** Cañoncito and South Sandia Springs
**Maps:** USGS Sandia Crest and Tijeras; USFS Sandia
   Wilderness
**Managed by:** Cibola National Forest, Sandia Wilderness,
   Sandia Ranger District
**Features:** isolation on the edge of a major city, views

Unlike the developed central section (Hike 64), the southern half of the
Sandia Mountains is isolated and wild, traversed by a half-dozen interesting trails. Hiking up the Cañoncito Trail and then walking the ridge to
South Sandia Peak leads through the heart of this country. Despite the prox-
imity of civilization, be on the watch for black bear, common in the Sandias,
and mountain lion tracks.

The hike requires setting up a short shuttle from the Canyon Estates to
the Cañoncito Trailheads. Hikers looking for a loop trip can hike the described route past South Sandia Spring to the Upper Faulty Trail and then
return to the Cañoncito Trailhead via the Upper or Lower Faulty Trails.

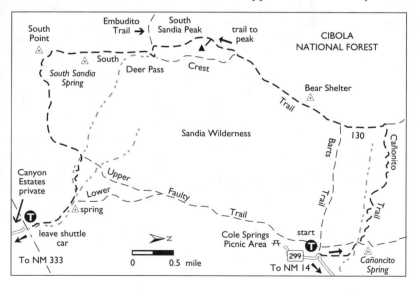

*A windswept fir on the rim of South Sandia Crest*

This variation is a 17-mile loop, a difficult day hike. Hikers attempting the loop should plan on an overnight stay near South Sandia Peak, where water is available at South Sandia Spring.

Set up the shuttle for this hike by driving east from Albuquerque on I-40. Five miles from the foot of Tijeras Pass, exit the highway at Tijeras/NM 337. At the bottom of the exit ramp, turn left, immediately passing under the interstate. Bear right onto a dead-end paved road marked for Canyon Estates. Drive slowly through private land on Arrowhead Road about 0.5 mile to the parking area at the trailhead. Leave a vehicle, then backtrack under the interstate to NM 333. Turn left and in 0.1 mile, follow the signs for NM 14 and Cedar Crest, again bearing left under the interstate. Once on NM 14, continue 3.5 miles through Cedar Crest to FR 299, which is marked with a sign for Cole Springs Picnic Area and Cañoncito. Turn left, then in 0.4 mile bear left again at a Y intersection. Take this rough dirt road 1.2 miles to the well-marked Cañoncito Trailhead. The last 0.5 mile of this route often requires a high-clearance vehicle.

From the trailhead, climb steeply to the right on the Cañoncito Trail, avoiding the more prominent Barts Trail straight ahead. The trail soon bears left to head upcanyon, reaching streamside near some interesting travertine terraces. After crossing the stream, watch for a sign pointing to Cañoncito Spring. Just beyond, come to a four-way intersection with the Faulty Trail. Continue straight on the Cañoncito Trail, immediately entering the Sandia Wilderness. The trail begins to climb steeply on limestone rocks, many of which are adorned with fossilized sea life.

As the trail climbs, it traverses a dry oak-scrub woodland with abundant agave and prickly pear. At mile 1.5, climb on broad switchbacks before the ascent steepens all the way to the South Crest Trail 130, reached at mile 3.2. Turn left onto the South Crest Trail and stop for a break in 200 feet at an overlook of Albuquerque and the Sandia Tramway.

Continue south on the Crest Trail, passing Barts Trail to the left at mile 3.7. Fine views to the west are found along the route. Pass Bear Shelter at mile 4.3. The trail travels through aspen groves, oak stands, and meadows as it heads toward South Sandia Peak, which is first visible at mile 5.2. Climb the peak by leaving the South Crest Trail at a small saddle and following the ridgeline. Stay right as the main trail goes left. (The main trail stays on the south flank of the peak, skirting its base to Deer Pass, 6.7 miles from the start.) Eventually pick up a faint trail on the west (right) side of the ridgeline. This trail becomes more distinct near the base of the peak, where a side trail to the left climbs straight up to the summit.

From the top, backtrack down the steep side trail to the path on the west side of South Sandia Peak. Turn left and stay on the trail near the ridgeline, now heading south. After walking this trail for 0.7 mile, cross a saddle and intersect the Embudito Trail. Bear left, descending to rejoin the South Crest Trail at Deer Pass.

Turn right onto the South Crest Trail, descending into a drainage. Pass South Sandia Spring at mile 6.9, then begin the broad switchbacks that lead down from the crest. At mile 8.5, pass South Point, the last of the viewpoints on the ridge. For the next 2 miles, descend steeply through drainages and over spur ridges. At mile 10.5, the Upper Faulty Trail angles off to the left. Continue straight on the South Crest Trail, winding down many switchbacks on a ridge above two dry drainages. At mile 11.2, intersect the Lower Faulty Trail to the left and continue straight. Soon pass a small spring, then bear right at a Y intersection. After passing a cave, continue to descend to the Canyon Estates Trailhead.

## 66 | MANZANO PEAK

**Distance: 11 miles, day hike or backpack**
**Difficulty:** difficult
**Elevation range:** 8,000 to 10,098 feet
**Elevation gain:** 2,350 feet
**Best time of year:** April to November
**Water:** carry water
**Maps:** USGS Manzano Peak; USFS Manzano Wilderness
**Managed by:** Cibola National Forest, Manzano Wilderness, Mountainair Ranger District
**Features:** long-range views, solitude

The Manzano Mountains are a southern extension of the Sandia Mountains that dominate Albuquerque's skyline. Both ranges have similar rugged west faces and sloping eastern flanks. The loop hike in Ox and Kayser Canyons is an excellent route to the summit of Manzano Peak, the highest point of the

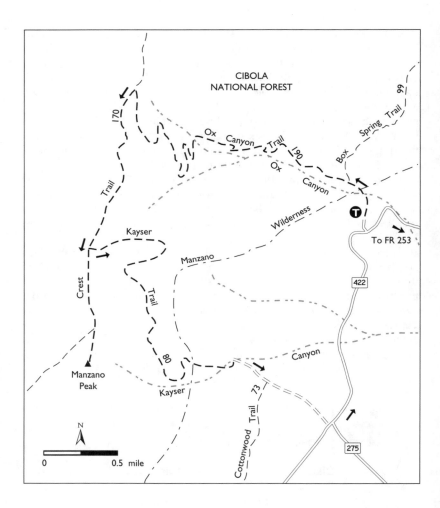

range. Like most other trails in the Manzanos, these trails are well marked and well maintained, and walking them is pure pleasure. Views from the crest reach to the isolated mountain ranges beyond the Rio Grande to the west and stretch for 100 miles across the plains to the east.

To reach the trailhead, take I-40 east from Albuquerque to exit 175 at Tijeras. Bear right onto NM 337 south, immediately continuing straight across a T intersection. Travel on NM 337 for 30 miles and turn right onto NM 55 at a another T intersection, then continue 12 miles to the village of Manzano. Bear right onto NM 131, which is signed for Manzano Mountains State Park, located 2.5 miles from the village. At the park entrance, turn right onto FR 253 heading for Red Canyon Campground. In 2.5

miles, bear left onto FR 422, an all-weather gravel road. In 2.2 miles, reach a sign for the Ox Canyon Trail 190. A short, rough road to the right leads to a small parking area.

From the trailhead, follow the signs as the Trail 190 skirts the toe of a ridge to enter Ox Canyon, then meets an old route coming up from the right. The trail turns left, heading upcanyon, and at mile 0.2 intersects the Box Spring Canyon Trail 99. Bear left to stay in Ox Canyon and begin a moderate climb through tall Douglas firs. Two short switchbacks lead past small talus slides made of banded metamorphic rock.

As the trail swings left to cross the head of Ox Canyon at mile 1.5, watch for views downcanyon out onto the plains to the east. The trail now turns in broad switchbacks as it climbs to the crest, meeting the Crest Trail 170 at mile 3.2.

Turn left onto the Crest Trail and continue climbing. The trail soon turns away from the ridgeline but continues to climb, gaining the top of the ridge at mile 3.6. Watch for cairns that mark the trail where it becomes obscure as it passes through small meadows. At mile 4.5, intersect the Kayser Trail 80 coming in from the east. Continue straight on the Crest Trail heading toward Manzano Peak. Cross a narrow ridge above Kayser Canyon, then watch for a sign pointing the way to the peak. At the sign, bear away from the main trail to reach the summit at mile 5.2. From the top, views to the

*The Manzano Mountains are capped with thick beds of limestone.*

west and north include the Manzanos, the Rio Grande Valley, and the towns of Belen and Los Lunas.

From the peak, backtrack down to and along the Crest Trail, continuing north toward the Kayser Trail. At the junction with the Kayser Trail, turn right, heading downhill across a meadow to a cairn at the edge of the forest below. From here, the trail is easy to follow through the fir forest as it drops along a ridge and skirts the head of the deep Kayser Canyon at mile 6.8. Turn down widely spaced switchbacks as the trail descends across three drainages, reaching the end of the trail on a four-wheel-drive road at mile 8.6.

Turn right and walk down the road, passing the Cottonwood Trail 73 at mile 8.9. At mile 9.5, reach FR 422 and turn left. Walk on FR 422 north for 1.5 miles to return to the Ox Canyon Trailhead.

## 67 | MANZANO CREST TRAIL

**Distance: 11.5 miles one-way, day hike or backpack**
**Difficulty:** moderate
**Elevation range:** 7,600 to 9,400 feet
**Elevation gain:** 1,800 feet
**Best time of year:** April to November
**Water:** Upper Fourth of July Spring, carry water
**Maps:** USGS Capilla Peak and Bosque Peak; USFS Manzano Wilderness
**Managed by:** Cibola National Forest, Manzano Wilderness, Mountainair Ranger District
**Features:** long hike along mountain crest, views, solitude

One-day loop hikes along the Manzano Crest are difficult to put together, so this long walk along the ridgeline makes setting up the lengthy required shuttle worthwhile. Walking north from Capilla Peak to Fourth of July Campground is a delightful one-way trip that stays on or near the crest of the Manzanos for 9 miles. Views are outstanding for much of the trip, and hikers will likely have the trail to themselves along the little-used middle portions of the route. This hike is especially rewarding in October when the bigtooth maples are blazing red and migrating raptors are commonly sighted following the ridgeline. Fossils of ancient sea life are common in the limestone that comprises the crest of the range. Few campsites are found along this route, and water is only found near the end—conditions that mandate careful planning for an overnight stay.

To set up a shuttle for this hike, from Albuquerque take I-40, NM 337, and NM 55 to Tajique. At the southern end of Tajique, turn right onto FR

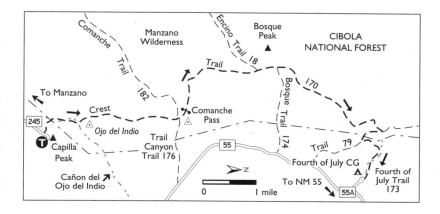

55, which is signed for Fourth of July Campground. Go 7 miles to FR 55A and turn right into the campground. Leave a vehicle at the parking area near the campground entrance. Backtrack to Tajique and turn right onto NM 55. Go south about 9 miles to the town of Manzano and turn right onto FR 245, which is signed for Capilla Peak. It is 9 miles to the trailhead near Capilla Peak Campground. The last 4 miles are steep and rough; a high-clearance vehicle is recommended, but low-slung cars frequently make the trip. Park at the sign for the Crest Trail.

Begin hiking downhill on the Crest Trail 170, entering a Douglas fir forest at the head of Cañon del Ojo del Indio. Descend steeply into the canyon on several switchbacks. After passing near the normally dry Ojo del Indio, begin a short climb through shadeless oak scrub. Pass over two low saddles before reaching the top of Comanche Ridge at mile 1.9. There are continual views into Comanche Canyon to the west as the trail passes another saddle and skirts to the west of a knoll before dropping to reach Comanche Pass at mile 3.1.

At a four-way intersection atop Comanche Pass, continue on the Crest Trail past the Comanche Trail 182 to the left and the Trail Canyon Trail 176 to the right. Begin a long climb by passing through a fenced gate, then bearing left. To the left are views of Capilla Peak and the trail just traveled. At mile 4.1, the trail begins to climb steeply, at first on switchbacks, then cutting across the shoulder of the ridge. As the trail passes a knoll to the west and begins to level, hikers soon gain the ridge and again enjoy views in all directions. Along the crest, watch for abundant fossilized shells in the limestone.

As it approaches the east slope of Bosque Peak, the trail becomes indistinct and hikers must sight from cairn to cairn to stay on the correct route. The trail passes along the east slope of Bosque Peak to intersect the faint Encino Trail 18 to the left and, a bit farther on, the Bosque Trail 174 to the right. Continue north on the Crest Trail across a huge rocky meadow where it is important to follow the cairns marking the trail and not be misled by cattle trails that crisscross the area. Begin to descend from Bosque Peak, crossing more meadows and oak scrub along the way. At mile 8.2, reach a saddle that offers views of Albuquerque to the north.

From the saddle, the trail climbs the ridgeline before skirting a low peak to the left. As the trail swings left, Fourth of July Canyon is to the right and the twin Guadalupe and Mosca Peaks are straight ahead. Continue dropping to the north, switchbacking down the east side of a ridge at mile 9.2. At mile 9.4, leave the Crest Trail and turn right onto Cerro Blanco Trail 79. Begin a long, moderate descent through a shady maple and oak forest on the slopes of Fourth of July Canyon. At mile 10, turn left onto the Fourth of July Trail 173 and round the head of several small drainages before reaching the bottom of Fourth of July Canyon. Pass the intersection with the Albuquerque Trail 78 at mile 10.5, then drop past Upper Fourth of July Spring. Continue another mile through shady maples to reach the trailhead at Fourth of July Campground.

*Looking back to Capilla Peak from the Manzano Crest Trail*
(Photo by June Fabryka-Martin)

# 68 | FOURTH OF JULY/ALBUQUERQUE LOOP

**Distance:** 5 miles, day hike
**Difficulty:** easy
**Elevation range:** 7,500 to 8,200 feet
**Elevation gain:** 800 feet
**Best time of year:** best in fall
**Water:** Upper Fourth of July Spring, carry water
**Maps:** USGS Bosque Peak and Tajique
**Managed by:** Cibola National Forest, Mountainair Ranger District
**Features:** spectacular fall colors

The short loop through Fourth of July Canyon and Cañon de la Gallina is a New Mexico classic. The dominance of bigtooth maple and Gambel oak in these drainages creates brilliant fall colors found in few other locations in the state. The bright red maples outdo the better-known aspen for adding splashes of color to the mountains. Beneath a canopy of flame-colored foliage, this easy autumn stroll is not to be missed. The colors reach their peak in late September and early October.

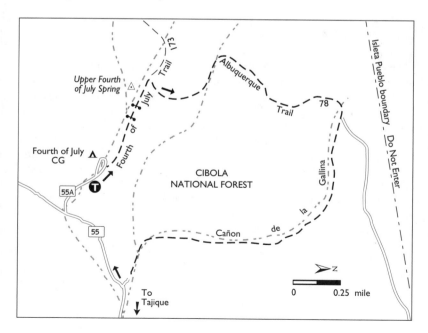

*Fossil gastropod from the limestones of the Manzano Mountains*

To reach the trailhead from I-40 at Tijeras, take NM 337 and then NM 55 about 35 miles to Tajique. At the southern end of Tajique, turn right onto FR 55, which is signed for Fourth of July Campground. Go 7 miles to FR 55A, which is past the trailhead for the Albuquerque Trail 78, and turn right into the campground. Day parking is available near the campground entrance.

The trailhead is located 0.25 mile up the campground road from the parking area. Begin hiking on the Fourth of July Trail 173 as it follows an old road up the canyon bottom. Pass through two gates as the trail climbs on gentle grades. About 0.75 mile from the start, climb more steeply through a rocky, narrow stretch of canyon, passing Upper Fourth of July Spring. Seep spring monkey flowers and horsetails grow in profusion, but keep a watchful eye open for poison ivy, which is common in this canyon. Just past the spring, meet the Albuquerque Trail 78. Turn a sharp right onto this trail and begin a steeper climb around a hill and into another small drainage.

At mile 1.2, leave the drainage bottom and climb a dry drainage to a small saddle. Drop into the head of Cañon de la Gallina, for now enjoying the maples from a distance. The trail descends to the canyon bottom and into a fine stand of maples. At mile 3.1, pass a small spring, and soon the trail widens to an old road. At mile 3.7, reach the trailhead for the Albuquerque Trail. Continue to FR 55, turn right and follow the road uphill 0.5 mile to FR 55A. Turn right to return to the Fourth of July Trailhead.

# 69 | MAGDALENA CREST TRAIL TO NORTH BALDY

**Distance: 11 miles, day hike**
**Difficulty:** difficult
**Elevation range:** 9,300 to 10,400 feet
**Elevation gain:** 1,800 feet
**Best time of year:** mid-spring to late fall
**Water:** carry water
**Maps:** USGS Magdalena and South Baldy
**Managed by:** Cibola National Forest, Magdalena Ranger
   District
**Features:** unparalleled views

The Magdalena Mountains are a small jewel of a mountain range rising out of the deserts of central New Mexico. Their highest point, South Baldy, rises to 10,783 feet. The steep mountain face and grassy summits make possible dramatic views in all directions. The best way to take in the sights is to walk the Magdalena Crest Trail from South Baldy to its lesser neighboring peak, North Baldy. The view along the entire trail takes the eye from the Jemez Mountains far to the north to the Caballo Range in the south, an incredible panorama that encompasses about a tenth of the total land area of New Mexico.

Just south of the summit is the Langmuir Lightning Observatory, located on the crest because of the frequency of summer thunderstorms in the Magdalenas. The crest is no place to be during a thunderstorm, and they are common from late June through early September. Hike the Crest Trail any time of day from April to June. In summer, start early and be off the ridge by noon, sooner if a storm threatens.

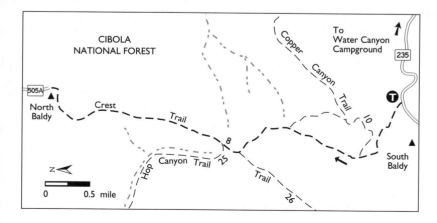

*Looking down Copper Canyon in the Magdalena Mountains*

To reach the trailhead from Socorro, take US 60 west. Drive about 16 miles to FR 235, marked with a large sign for Water Canyon Campground, and turn left. Reach the campground and the end of the paved part of the road in 5 miles. No water is available at the campground. Continue on gravel FR 235, which is rough but passable in dry weather to any vehicle, as it climbs into the mountains. The Crest Trailhead is about 0.5 mile east of the end of the road, about 8 miles from the campground.

The Crest Trail 8 starts on a saddle just east of South Baldy, on the right-hand side of the road. Begin by climbing steeply along a trail up a spur ridge of South Baldy, angling to the left from the parking area. (Do not take the more prominent double-track straight ahead.) At the ridgeline, drop into the deep forest on the other side. Descend several switchbacks before climbing to the main crest, which is reached 0.5 mile from the start. Cross the crest in a grassy meadow, then drop on a short switchback to the west side of the ridge. The trail now swings north to parallel the crest.

At mile 0.8, burst out into a broad meadow with striking views of the San Mateo Mountains to the west. Pass the junction with the Copper Canyon Trail 10 to the right. Continue north, climbing to the ridge, then dropping on the west side and crossing two talus slopes. Reach the crest again at mile 1.5, with views east into Copper Canyon, the eastern Magdalenas, and the Rio Grande Valley beyond.

As the trail drops to the next saddle, a mining road comes up from the drainage to the left. Climb a few feet to the ridgeline, then drop onto the east side of the crest, watching for rock cairns to mark the way. The trail continues on the east slope, crossing several spur ridges. At mile 2.5, reach another grassy saddle and the Mill Canyon Trail 26 coming in from the west. Just as you re-enter the woods, reach the junction with the Hop Canyon Trail 25. Bear right, staying on the crest. The trail soon becomes a bit more rough and rocky. Climb for 0.25 mile, then make a long 2-mile descent to a saddle just below North Baldy.

The final 500-foot climb to the summit is through cliffs of white rhyolite. Stay on the trail as it swings around the summit, and climb the last few yards to the top from the northeast slope. The 360-degree view from the top makes the ascent worthwhile. Each direction presents a series of overlapping mountain ranges slowly fading with distance. After taking in the sights, return by the same route.

## 70 COPPER CANYON/SOUTH BALDY LOOP

**Distance: 11 miles, day hike or backpack**
**Difficulty:** strenuous
**Elevation range:** 6,800 to 10,400
**Elevation gain:** 3,600 feet
**Best time of year:** mid-spring to late fall
**Water:** lower Water Canyon
**Maps:** USGS Magdalena and South Baldy
**Managed by:** Cibola National Forest, Magdalena Ranger District
**Features:** remote canyons, ridge-top views

This long, challenging loop leads into the heart of the Magdalena Range, climbing the steep mountain face to the crest through one canyon and descending from the crest along another. The ascent up Copper Canyon is gentle at first, but steepens as it approaches the ridgeline; Water Canyon provides a gradual drop from the high country. Campsites and water are plentiful along the middle stretch of Copper Canyon but are limited in Water Canyon.

This loop begins and ends at Water Canyon Campground. From Socorro, take US 60 west. Drive about 16 miles to FR 235, marked with a

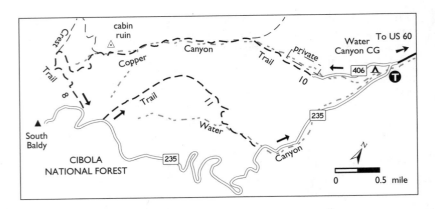

large sign for Water Canyon Campground, and turn left. Reach the campground and the end of the pavement in 5 miles. No water is available.

From the campground, walk back toward the paved road 100 yards to the junction of FR 235 and FR 406. Turn left, then immediately turn right to continue on FR 406. Walk this dirt road, crossing Copper Canyon at mile 0.9. Beyond the crossing, near a parcel of private land, a sign points the way to the Copper Canyon Trail 10. Begin walking uphill on an old road paralleling a fence that borders private property. The trail skirts a large meadow, passing the ranch house. As the canyon narrows about 1.5 miles from the start, pass a fork in the road angling sharply to the right. From this point, water is intermittently found in the canyon bottom.

After crossing the stream, the trail gently climbs to the slopes above the canyon bottom. Nice camping spots are plentiful along the stream. At mile 3.8, pass the ruins of a prospector's cabin. Water can be found in the stream near the cabin throughout the year. Just up the canyon, come to the junction of two branches of the trail leading to the crest. Take the left fork, which may be signed for Crest Trail 8 and FR 235.

The last mile to the crest is considerably steeper than the trail below. As the switchbacks grow tighter near the ridgeline, enjoy sweeping views downcanyon. Reach a meadow just below the crest and follow the faint trail over the top to the junction with the Crest Trail 8 at mile 4.8.

Turn left (south) onto Trail 8, crossing a grassy slope before re-entering the woods. At the next small meadow, the trail turns a switchback over the ridge and descends into deep forest on the east side. After a brief descent, the trail climbs again to reach a spur ridge just below the summit of South Baldy at mile 5.8. Drop to FR 235, turn left, and begin a 0.5-mile stretch on the road to meet Trail 11. At a sign on a broad saddle, turn left onto Trail 11 and begin the long descent back to the trailhead.

At the bottom of the first steep pitch is a lovely pine-covered saddle that makes a good, though waterless, campsite. Beyond the saddle, the trail drops steadily along a long spur ridge, with views through the trees back

*Steep, grassy slopes along the ridge of the Magdalena Mountains*

to the grassy slopes of the crest. After crossing the ridge, the trail winds through several drainages. The southern exposure creates an extraordinary juxtaposition of plants: on a 20-foot stretch of trail, hikers can pass yucca, scrub oak, white fir, and alligator juniper.

At mile 8.5, the trail switchbacks down to the bottom of Water Canyon. The trail is now less steep as it follows the canyon floor. A reliable water flow is reached at mile 8.8 and a few shady campsites can be found downstream. Reach FR 235 at mile 9.3. Turn left onto the road and continue down Water Canyon another 2 miles to the campground and trailhead.

# 71 | TIMBER PEAK TRAIL

**Distance: 6 miles, day hike**
**Difficulty:** moderate
**Elevation range:** 9,800 to 10,300 feet
**Elevation gain:** 1,200 feet
**Best time of year:** mid-spring to early winter
**Water:** carry water
**Map:** USGS South Baldy
**Managed by:** Cibola National Forest, Magdalena Ranger District
**Features:** long-distance views, wild ridge and canyon scenery, solitude

In a mountain range known for its sweeping views, the Timber Peak Trail offers dramatic panoramas that top all others. In addition to endless horizons, this trail includes striking views of deep canyons within the range. The attractive scenery along Timber Ridge makes even a short hike along it rewarding.

Avoid this trail on summer afternoons when thunderstorms are likely. Beyond 1.5 miles, this trail can be difficult to follow and hikers should be comfortable following an occasionally obscure trail marked with rock cairns and tree blazes.

From Socorro, take US 60 west. Drive about 16 miles to FR 235, marked with a large sign for Water Canyon Campground, and turn left. Reach the campground (no water available) and the end of the paved part of the road in 5 miles. Continue on gravel FR 235 as it climbs into the mountains. The Timber Peak Trail is 6.7 miles from the end of the pavement, and the trailhead is well marked on the left (south) side of the road. FR 235 is rough and steep but passable in dry weather to any vehicle.

From the trailhead sign, climb steeply on the grassy ridgeline to the southeast, with rock cairns marking the way. In several hundred yards, the trail crosses a dip in the crest and becomes easy to follow on the west flank of the ridge. The view extends as far as Elephant Butte Reservoir to the south. Soon the trail rises to the ridgeline and again follows the crest, with Timber Peak straight ahead. At times the trail is faint and hikers should watch for double blazes on the trees. Reach the foot of Timber Peak at mile 0.8, then enter a fir-spruce and limber pine forest.

Scratched into a steep slope, the trail contours west of Timber Peak. After crossing a talus field, the trail climbs steeply to the ridge and follows the crest on its east side. The trail dips and climbs along the ridge, passing through an open aspen stand. Along the ridge, note (and take warning from) the abundance of lightning-scarred trees.

At mile 2, the ridge takes a jog to the east. Here the trail turns left and descends to a broad saddle. Carefully locate the trail marked with cairns and blazes as it heads east across the saddle, then again turns south. As the trail becomes easier to follow, it climbs steeply up the hill on the other side. Again the trail is on the east side of the ridgeline. Follow the cairns across an open meadow, descending gradually to re-enter the trees. Enter another

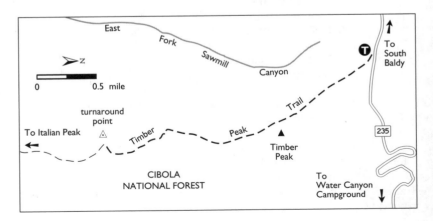

*Old blazes mark the Timber Ridge Trail.*

broad meadow at mile 2.8 and angle toward the ridgeline to enjoy the views to the west.

The meadow makes a good turnaround point. The trail continues another 2 miles along the ridge to a helipad below the summit of Italian Peak. Beyond the turnaround, the trail is difficult to follow and fails to offer the constant, dramatic views of the first section.

# 72 | POTATO CANYON

**Distance: 7 miles one-way, day hike**
**Difficulty:** moderate
**Elevation range:** 6,800 to 9,800 feet
**Elevation gain:** 3,000-foot descent
**Best time of year:** April to November
**Water:** intermittent flow in Potato Canyon, carry water
**Maps:** USGS Mount Withington; USFS Apache Kid and Withington Wildernesses
**Managed by:** Cibola National Forest, Withington Wilderness, Magdalena Ranger District
**Features:** isolated mountain range, wild country, scenic waterfall

The northern half of the long San Mateo Mountains holds one of New Mexico's least-used wilderness areas, the Withington. Because this wilderness area is so far from the normal tourist routes, just driving to it can be an adventure. This range is for experienced hikers who can follow ill-defined trails. Help is far away, so prepare carefully for any trip to the

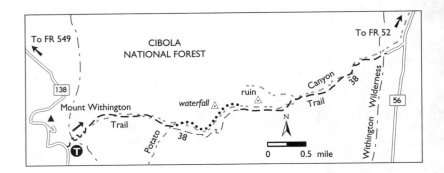

area. A topographic map and compass will help with routefinding on the little-used and difficult-to-follow upper section of this trail.

Potato Canyon, named for a rounded rock spire on a bordering ridge, holds the most accessible trail in the range. Dropping from the crest of the range near 10,000 feet, the canyon traverses all the dominant southwestern life zones from alpine forest to juniper woodlands. The walk on the brittle shales of the lower canyon is pleasantly shaded by a canopy of Arizona walnut. Because the trail is easier to follow starting from the western trailhead, this trip is described as a one-way descent from summit to valley.

To set up a shuttle from Magdalena, 27 miles west of Socorro on US 60, take NM 107 south. This dirt road is passable to all vehicles when dry. Go about 17 miles to the intersection with FR 52 and bear right. Take this rough road for 3.5 miles to FR 56 and bear left. A high-clearance vehicle will make the 3-mile journey to the trailhead a bit easier. After leaving a vehicle, return to FR 52 and turn left. In 11 rough miles, turn left on FR 549, a good dirt road. Turn left and continue 8.5 miles to FR 138. Turn left and drive about 4 miles past the Mount Withington Lookout to the trailhead. If the long drive is unappealing, even an in-and-out hike from FR 56 into the bottom of Potato Canyon is worthwhile.

Trail 38 starts on a narrow saddle just south of the summit of Mount Withington. Begin hiking downhill through the conifer forest along the crest. The trail is often very faint; hikers must watch carefully to stay on the route and make certain they do not stray from it. Frequent switchbacks cut the trail steeply down from the crest, crossing the bottom of a small canyon several times on the way. At mile 1.6, the trail reaches the bottom of a larger canyon. Bear left and follow the trail down the canyon bottom. The trail is well marked with blazes, but hikers must watch for them carefully. The route parallels the canyon bottom from here to the lower trailhead; if you lose the trail here, simply follow the streambed.

In this first stretch of canyon, the trail wanders from the streambed to the forest just above the stream. Large boulders in the canyon bottom make it easier to follow the trail. At mile 3, intersect the main branch of Potato Canyon entering from the right. Several nice campsites are located on the

*Small waterfall in Potato Canyon*
(Photo by Bob Julyan)

benches above the stream in this area. Just down the canyon, the trail turns right to climb high above the canyon floor to skirt around a narrows, but continue straight ahead in the canyon bottom. At mile 3.7, reach a lovely spot with a small waterfall.

The trail you left earlier rejoins the canyon bottom route at mile 4. Continue on the trail, passing on the left at mile 4.4 the ruins of a cabin. The canyon begins to open up as the trail passes beneath soaring cliffs of pink rock. Pass a major side canyon entering from the left at mile 5.2 and continue either on the trail or in the streambed to the wilderness boundary at mile 6.7. Here the trail widens to a road, reaching the parking area in 0.4 mile.

## 73 | VICKS PEAK

**Distance: 12 miles, backpack**
**Difficulty:** strenuous
**Elevation range:** 7,400 to 10,250 feet
**Elevation gain:** 3,100 feet
**Best time of year:** April to November
**Water:** Nave and San Mateo Springs
**Maps:** USGS Vicks Peak and Blue Mountain; USFS
   Withington and Apache Kid Wildernesses
**Managed by:** Cibola National Forest, Apache Kid Wilderness, Magdalena Ranger District
**Features:** wild country, great views, solitude

The Apache Kid Wilderness is located in the southern half of the San Mateo Mountains. Named for a renegade Apache reportedly buried there, the wilderness has almost 100 miles of primitive trails, but very few access points. The lower half of the wilderness is easily reached from Springtime

Campground, and hikers with ample time can take trips of more than 50 miles into the central range. The Apache Kid Wilderness can get hot in summer, but the usually light snowfalls in the range make it an ideal spot for a spring or late fall trip.

The journey to the summit of Vicks Peak is an excellent introduction to the range. It is a long and strenuous hike to the summit, too much for most hikers to make in one day. Start with plenty of water, and plan to replenish the supply at San Mateo and Nave Springs. Waterless campsites are located on the flat saddle at the site of Myers Cabin near the base of Vicks Peak. Plan to reach Myers Cabin the first day, then visit the peak the next morning before returning to the trailhead.

To reach Springtime Campground from Socorro, leave I-25 at exit 115, which is about 45 miles south of town. Get on NM 1 and continue south, parallel to the interstate about 10 miles to FR 225. Turn right and follow FR 225 13.5 miles to the entrance to Springtime Campground. Turn right, enter the campground, and park at the trailhead for Trail 43.

Begin hiking on the well-maintained Apache Kid Trail 43. Under ponderosa pines, the first section of trail makes a moderate climb that can be hot from late spring through the summer. The trail ascends a small drainage for 1.2 miles before bearing west and beginning a steep climb on switchbacks. At mile 2.1, reach an intersection on a saddle at the foot of a rocky knob. With the most difficult portions of the hike behind, take a long rest before turning left onto the Shipman Trail 50. (Water is found at San Mateo Spring,

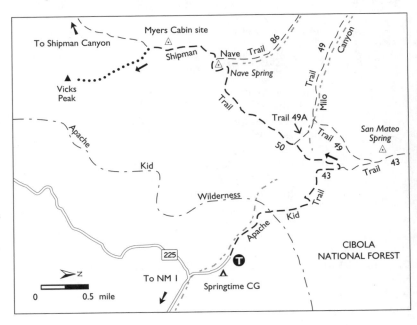

past the junction, 0.5 mile north on Trail 43.) Trail 50 is not as easy to follow as Trail 43, but numerous markers help keep hikers on the correct route.

Trail 50 stays atop a broad ridge before dropping into the head of Milo Canyon, reaching the bottom at mile 2.7. Pass the junction with Trail 49A, a branch of the Milo Trail 49, to the right. Continue straight, switchbacking up to another saddle at mile 3.3. Traversing conifer forest, the trail again drops, this time to reach Nave Spring at mile 4.3, where a small but dependable flow of water is located just down from the trail. After the spring, climb steeply to the intersection with the Nave Trail 86, then cross another saddle. Again drop into a small drainage before climbing to a broad saddle at mile 5.2. This is the site of Myers Cabin, and campsites are easily located in the open forest.

From the saddle, a faint, unmaintained path climbs the ridge to the southeast. Leave Trail 50 and angle up through the forest by the easiest route. At mile 5.7, the forest opens up near the base of an unnamed peak. Continue over the peak, then follow the ridge to the southeast to the wooded summit of Vicks Peak. The spectacular view from Vicks reaches far: east to the Capitan Range and south to the Elephant Butte and Caballo Reservoirs along the Rio Grande. Return by the same route.

*The results of a recent lightning strike on a ponderosa pine*

# 74 | BROAD CANYON

**Distance: 4 miles, day hike**
**Difficulty:** easy
**Elevation range:** 4,750 to 5,100 feet
**Elevation gain:** 650 feet
**Best time of year:** September to May
**Water:** carry water
**Maps:** USGS Sierra Alta and Souse Springs
**Managed by:** Bureau of Land Management, Las Cruces
  Field Office
**Features:** Chihuahuan Desert vegetation, narrow canyons,
  petroglyphs

At Broad Canyon the foothills are softly stroked with creosote bush and the rolling slopes are slashed with cliffs of tan volcanic rocks tilted this way and that. For those who enjoy something a bit different, it is a place of solitude and wild exploring. Both Valles and Broad Canyons are narrow defiles filled with rocky delights: swirling water-cut channels carved into the soft tuff, huge rounded boulders tumbled by flash floods, and tight, unexpected bends in the canyon floors. Much of this hike passes through private land on an easement, and hikers should stay on the described route.

Travel north on I-25 from Las Cruces about 15 miles to NM 157. Exit and go west for 2 miles to NM 185. Turn right and go another 12 miles, then

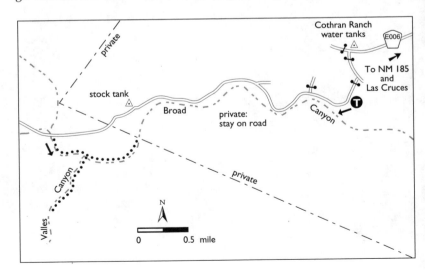

*Running water has eroded Broad Canyon down to pockets of bedrock.*

turn left onto the easy-to-miss CR E006. This road has a few rough spots but when dry is passable to all vehicles. In 7.5 miles, near the Cothran Ranch water tanks, bear left at a fork, passing through a gate. In 0.2 mile, come to another fork. This time take the right fork, pass another gate, and park in another 0.1 mile, just before the road pitches down the canyon wall.

Begin walking down the shelf road into Broad Canyon, which at this point is indeed a wide gash through the grassland hills. The road continues along the canyon bottom. At mile 1.4, the road turns away from the canyon and climbs over a low saddle, passing a stock tank halfway up. Over the saddle, descend to again meet Broad Canyon. Now turn left, leaving the road, and follow the slickrock of the canyon bottom. This is the meat of the hike, walking on scoured tuff in the deepening canyon. Boulder-hop downcanyon about 0.5 mile to where Valles Canyon enters from the right at mile 2.4. Watch for petroglyphs on the walls before exploring up Valles Canyon, a twisting, narrow watercourse full of surprises. Be alert for rattlesnakes sunning themselves on rocks, particularly in spring.

Backtrack to Broad Canyon, turning right to continue down it for a few hundred yards past a soaring wall of red tuff to a fence that marks private property. Hikers must turn around here, but they can pause to enjoy the shade of a cluster of large oaks before returning to the road by backtracking upstream. Once at the road, turn right and return to your vehicle by the same route.

# 75 | INDIAN HOLLOW

**Distance: 5-mile loop, day hike or backpack**
**Difficulty:** difficult
**Elevation range:** 5,200 to 6,800 feet
**Elevation gain:** 1,500 feet
**Best time of year:** year round
**Water:** at campground, intermittent flow in Indian Hollow
**Maps:** USGS Organ and Organ Peak
**Managed by:** Bureau of Land Management, Aguirre
  Springs Recreation Area, Las Cruces Field Office
**Features:** sheer granite cliffs, large alligator junipers,
  secluded canyon

The granite crags of the Organ Mountains are one of the most spectacular features of southern New Mexico. The east face of the range jumps abruptly from the desert floor near Las Cruces, and the ragged towers of vertically jointed granite are said to resemble the tubes of a pipe organ. Much of the Organs are under the jurisdiction of the White Sands Missile Range and are off-limits to visitors. The best access to the range is at the Aguirre Springs Recreation Area, and the primitive route into Indian Hollow is the most interesting hike. Indian Hollow, although near the

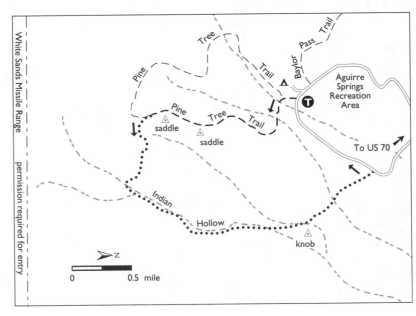

*Alligator juniper bark*

developed campground, is rugged country with confusing terrain. Few visitors make the trek into the canyon.

To reach the trailhead from the junction of I-25 and US 70 in Las Cruces, go east on US 70 toward San Augustin Pass. About 14 miles from the interstate, turn right onto the road to Aguirre Springs Recreation Area. Continue about 6 miles to the Pine Tree Trailhead and park. Note that a small fee is charged for day use in the recreation area.

Begin climbing the Pine Tree Trail in a huge amphitheater of granite with towering cliffs in three directions. This north-facing slope supports a surprisingly lush plant community dominated by huge alligator junipers. At

0.25 mile from the start, the Pine Tree Trail splits into two branches. Take the left fork and continue climbing, with views of Baylor Pass to the right. Just short of mile 1, reach a saddle and cross over to the opposite side of the ridge with views of conical Sugarloaf Peak straight ahead. Continue climbing to a second saddle at mile 1.5 where a short spur left leads to a viewpoint.

Within 200 feet of the saddle, a second, fainter trail angles off to the left. Take this lesser-used trail, which leads to Indian Hollow. Follow the light tread south, watching for rock cairns that mark the way. Continue climbing, steeply at times, skirting around the head of a side canyon. After about 0.5 mile on this faint trail, reach a spur ridge with steep canyons on either side. Drop off the east face of the ridge and descend into Indian Hollow, carefully picking a route down to the canyon bottom. Use caution on the steep slope. A trickle of water is usually found in this section of Indian Hollow, and shady and level ground makes it an interesting place for an overnight stay. Hikers can explore up two canyons heading south, but be on the watch for the boundary of the White Sands Missile Range about 0.5 mile away—do not enter without getting prior permission.

To return to the trailhead, walk north down Indian Hollow. Trails come and go along the way, but the streambed is easy to follow. After 1.25 miles, watch closely for rock cairns that mark a trail to the left that leads out of the canyon to the main road. The trail crosses several drainages before crossing a low saddle just to the south of a distinctive knob on the ridge. The trail here is faint; head generally west to reach the main road. At the road, turn left and walk uphill to return to the parking area in about 0.75 mile.

# 76 | BAYLOR PASS

**Distance: 6 miles one-way, day hike**
**Difficulty:** moderate
**Elevation range:** 4,900 to 6,380 feet
**Elevation gain:** 750 feet
**Best time of year:** year round
**Water:** at main campground only, carry water
**Maps:** USGS Organ Peak and Organ
**Managed by:** Bureau of Land Management, Aguirre Springs and Organ Mountains Recreation areas, Las Cruces Field Office
**Features:** historic pass, scenic views, easy shuttle

The National Recreation Trail over Baylor Pass roughly follows the route taken by the Confederate cavalry while engaging the Union infantry in 1862 during the Civil War. Near Las Cruces, Colonel John Baylor was attacked by

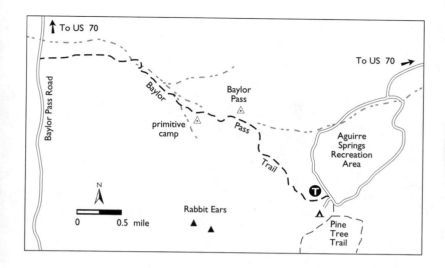

Union troops under Major Isaac Lynde. Baylor's inferior force nonetheless held its ground against the Union, and apparently the sight of blood was enough to send Lynde packing out of nearby Fort Fillmore, a supply base he considered indefensible. Legend has it that, as the Union soldiers destroyed the supplies at Fort Fillmore in preparation for their retreat, they were loath to pour out a store of good medicinal whisky, instead using it to fill their canteens. As they retreated toward San Augustin Pass, the July sun and whisky soon dehydrated the marchers. Baylor easily caught Lynde's stragglers, who readily surrendered for a drink of water. Then Baylor and several hundred mounted troops dashed across the pass that would bear his name, and surprised Lynde's main Union force at San Augustin Spring, where Lynde accepted Baylor's demand for unconditional surrender.

This hike is best done with a shuttle. Drive east on US 70 from the intersection with I-25 in Las Cruces. In about 11 miles, turn right onto Baylor Pass Road. In 0.8 mile, continue straight over a cattle guard onto a gravel road. A mile beyond, leave a vehicle at the well-marked trailhead on the left side of the road. Return to US 70, turn right, and continue 2 miles over San Augustin Pass to the road to Aguirre Springs Recreation Area. Turn right and continue about 6 miles to the Baylor Pass Trailhead. A small fee is charged for day use.

Most of the elevation gain to the pass is accomplished in the first mile as the trail winds through juniper-piñon woodland. In about a mile, pass directly beneath the lofty Rabbit Ears, twin peaks of craggy granite. Cross over a spur ridge to parallel a drainage leading to Baylor Pass. In spring, hikers will be jolted by a stiff head wind at this point. Reach the pass about 2 miles from the start and enjoy the long-distance views to the east of the city of Las Cruces, jagged volcanic peaks, and the Black Range on the far horizon.

*The ragged summits of the Organ Mountains as seen from Baylor Pass*

From Baylor Pass, the trail switchbacks down through scrub oak, white-thorn acacia, and manzanita, a striking contrast to the plants on the east side of the mountain. In the round bowl of upper Baylor Canyon, the trail is cut into decomposed granite, which makes for slippery footing. Well into the bowl at 3.3 miles, pass a waterless primitive camp shaded by a single tree.

The trail heads toward the mouth of the canyon. Just before arriving there, at a point where a short spur trail leads left to a viewpoint, the trail abruptly turns right and descends. Drop quickly over several switchbacks before crossing the canyon bottom and reaching the alluvial fan. On the open desert, drop through the last mile to the western end of the Baylor Pass Trail.

*Facing page: Blooming yucca at White Sands National Monument*

# SOUTHEASTERN MOUNTAINS

# 77 | ALKALI FLAT TRAIL

**Distance: 5 miles, day hike**
**Difficulty:** moderate
**Elevation range:** 3,900 to 4,000 feet
**Elevation gain:** 100 feet
**Best time of year:** year round, but better October through April
**Water:** carry water
**Map:** USGS Heart of the Sands
**Managed by:** National Park Service, White Sands National Monument
**Features:** world's largest gypsum dune field, endless exploring, animal tracks

A hike at White Sands is a unique experience. This huge sand pile is composed of gypsum, not the more common quartz. Gypsum sand is soft-grained and smooth, giving these dunes a different, pleasant feel to bare feet. The fine sand also makes for easy animal tracking. The gypsum weathers out of the ancient seabed rocks of surrounding mountains. It is dissolved and transported by runoff, accumulating in Lake Lucero in the western part of the monument. The gypsum precipitates out of the evaporating lake water and is deposited on the lake bottom. In this desert environment, the lake is completely dry most of the year. Strong, westerly winds then push the gypsum eastward into large dunes.

White sand is an intense solar reflector and hiking on the dunes requires some special preparation. To prevent sunburn, always use a heavy coat of sunscreen. Dark glasses are also essential: to prevent damage to the eyes,

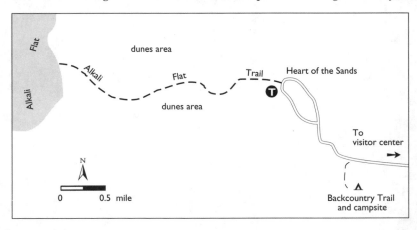

*Interdune basins at White Sands National Monument support a variety of desert vegetation.*

but also simply to make the journey more pleasant. No water is available in the dunes, so take an adequate supply. All-terrain sandals or running shoes are the best footwear for dune hiking.

Three trails are maintained by the Park Service, but hiking is possible just about anywhere in the dune field. Hikers should pick a location that strikes their fancy or follow the Alkali Flat Trail as described. Note that hikers on this trail are required to register at the trailhead and in all cases to return by sunset. Before setting out cross-country, stop and orient yourself with respect to the San Andres Mountains to the west, and the lofty Sacramento Mountains, as well as low-flying jets from Holloman Air Force Base, to the east. These are useful features by which to navigate. Use these landmarks as bearings out on the dunes. Given calm winds, hikers can easily follow their tracks back to the road.

Camping is permitted only at the lightly used backcountry campsite at the end of the 0.3-mile Backcountry Trail. A free permit is required for an overnight trip and is available at the visitor center. Note that test firing at the adjacent White Sands Missile Range occasionally requires the park to close the backcountry to camping.

To reach the trailhead from Alamogordo, take US 54/70 south and continue west on US 70 when US 54 bears left. The entrance to White Sands National Monument is about 15 miles southwest of town. Continue about 6 miles on the park road to the Heart of the Sands and the well-marked trailhead.

Begin hiking west on the Alkali Flat Trail. The trail is marked with numerous orange and white posts. Find the first post, then spot the next trail marker before moving on. Continue in this manner, walking from post to post, through the dune field. The trail traverses the dunes themselves and often crosses vegetated interdunal basins. For much of the trip, the San Andres Mountains lie straight ahead. Walking is slow in the soft sand, and distances are difficult to judge. At mile 2.1, the trail reaches the edge of Alkali Flat, the lake bed where gypsum sand is formed. The trail continues out a short distance onto the flats, which can be an unpleasant place when the wind blows. From the flats, return to the trailhead by the same route.

# 78 | DOG CANYON

**Distance: 9 miles, day hike or backpack**
**Difficulty:** strenuous
**Elevation range:** 4,400 to 7,500 feet
**Elevation gain:** 3,300 feet
**Best time of year:** September to May
**Water:** at the visitor center, and in Dog Canyon at mile 2.5
**Maps:** USGS Alamogordo South and Sacramento Peak
**Managed by:** Lincoln National Forest, Oliver Lee Memorial State Park, Sacramento Ranger District
**Features:** historic route, running water, spectacular scenery

Holding permanent running water and a steep route over the rampart of the southern Sacramento Mountains, Dog Canyon has been tramped by Mescalero Apaches, Mexican and American soldiers, and Texas ranchers. It is said that this route to the high country was a particular favorite of Apache war parties because of the ease with which they could ambush

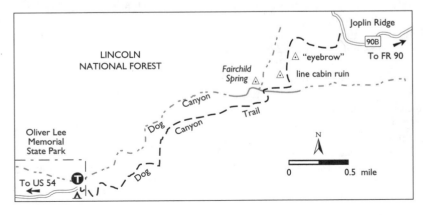

*Dog Canyon slices through hundreds of limestone beds that form nearly vertical walls.*

pursuers at the "eyebrow" section, which is perched on a narrow ledge below 800-foot walls of limestone. In 1880, the Ninth Cavalry lost several men on the eyebrow when Apaches rolled large boulders down on them from above.

The Dog Canyon Trail follows the historic route from the Tularosa Valley to Joplin Ridge. It is a steep, arduous climb with no shade or water for the first 2.5 miles; avoid Dog Canyon in midsummer. The scenery is grand every step of the way, displaying the harsh beauty of the Chihuahuan Desert. Limestone cliffs deposited on the ocean floor about 250 million years ago soar more than 3,000 feet above. Below them lies the Tularosa Valley, a huge fault-block basin with no outlet.

To reach the trailhead from Alamogordo, take US 54 south from its junction with US 70 in south Alamogordo. Drive 8 miles to Dog Canyon Road, which is signed for Oliver Lee Memorial State Park. Turn left, drive 4 miles, and stop at the entrance to pay a small fee. Continue on the main road and park at the visitor center and trailhead.

The trail immediately begins climbing through desert vegetation, including yucca, agave, ocotillo, sotol, and mesquite. The first section of trail climbs away from Dog Canyon on a steep, rocky trail. Views open along the way to include the white sand dunes on the floor of the Tularosa Valley, and in the morning sun, the striking colors of the Organ and San Andres Mountains on the other side of the basin. After a jog to the south, at mile 0.6 the trail finishes the intense climb on a broad bench that offers a bit of level walking.

The trail again approaches Dog Canyon. At mile 1.5, a side trail to Fairchild Spring angles off to the left. The climb intensifies, rising 400 feet over the next 0.5 mile to reach a lovely grassy flat. This flat has oaks, alligator junipers, cholla cacti, the unusual, fragrant ash tree, and huge boulders tumbled from the cliffs that soar above. Ideal campsites can be found near the larger trees.

From the flat, descend into Dog Canyon to reach the stream for the first time. Water is available here, dropping from the mesas above through a series of waterfalls. Shady cottonwoods offer relief from the sun, and the ruins of a line cabin are found at streamside. To prevent further damage to this sensitive area, camping is no longer permitted along the stream.

The trail continues from behind the line cabin to ascend the steepest section of the canyon, the "eyebrow," at mile 3.2. After a switchback to the left, the trail crosses a narrow ledge high above the canyon floor. Great views downcanyon open up, but hikers should keep their eyes on the trail. Climbing continually, the trail skirts around to a gap in the cliffs. Now paralleling a drainage to the left, the trail continues its steep climb to the flanks of Joplin Ridge about 4 miles from the start. Making a more moderate ascent, the trail swings east to meet the rough FR 90B descending from FR 90. Return to the trailhead by the same route.

# 79 | WILLIE WHITE CANYON

**Distance: 8 miles, day hike**
**Difficulty:** moderate
**Elevation range:** 8,200 to 9,300 feet
**Elevation gain:** 1,200 feet
**Best time of year:** May to late October
**Water:** Bluff Springs
**Map:** USGS Bluff Springs
**Managed by:** Lincoln National Forest, Sacramento Ranger District
**Features:** old railroad grades, Bluff Springs

A small logging line, the Alamogordo and Sacramento Mountain Railway began in Alamogordo and climbed 5,000 feet in 26 miles to reach Cloudcroft at the edge of the timber. The terrain required engineers to design massive trestles such as the one still standing at Mexican Canyon along US 82 just outside Cloudcroft. In the woods, canyon walls were crossed with ingenious switchbacking tracks that carried short logging trains over ridges and into uncut valleys. In 1924, rather than lay 20 miles of track in canyon bottoms, the railroad pushed tracks from the Rio Peñasco over a ridge to reach Willie White Canyon. Later, the company dropped rails into Wills Canyon, the next canyon south, on a series of precarious switchbacks. Slow-moving trains eased down a leg of track onto a short siding, then crawled backwards down the next switchback and siding, then moved forward down the next, and so on, to the bottom.

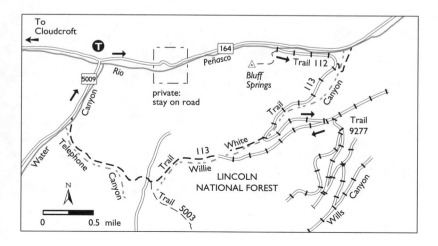

Many of the graded railbeds have been converted into hiking trails. Except for the crossing of the saddle between Willie White and Telephone Canyons, this hike is entirely on old railroad grades.

To reach the trailhead from Cloudcroft on US 82, take NM 130 south from the west end of town. In 2 miles, turn right onto NM 6563, which is signed for Sunspot. In about 8.5 miles, turn left onto FR 164, which is signed for Bluff Springs. Continue 2 miles to the intersection with FR 5009 to the right and park.

From the intersection, continue walking down FR 164 as the road follows an old railroad grade in a wide meadow bordering the Rio Peñasco. In 0.5 mile, stay on the road through a parcel of private land. At mile 1.5, come to the parking area for Bluff Springs. Turn right and explore this unusual area, climbing to the top of the bluff and perhaps to the spring 0.25 mile beyond. Return to the base of the bluff and find Trail 112 angling off to the southeast. This trail follows the old railroad grade heading into Willie White Canyon. Intersect Trail 113 in 0.5 mile from Bluff Springs and turn right, leaving the river. This trail continues on the railroad grade.

The trail soon swings southwest and heads up Willie White Canyon, passing through deep conifer forest. At mile 3.5, the trail crosses the bottom of Willie White Canyon. Here an old route continues up the canyon

*Mexican Trestle is the most dramatic remnant of the logging railroads in the Sacramento Mountains.*

floor; the trail follows the railroad grade, angling to the left and climbing gradually on the canyon wall. After heading downcanyon for 0.5 mile, Trail 113 intersects Trail 9277, remnants of another railroad grade that leads to switchbacks descending into Wills Canyon. Turn back sharply to the right to stay on Trail 113, which continues to follow a railroad grade, again heading up Willie White Canyon.

The wide trail climbs parallel to the canyon bottom, leaving the railroad grade and crossing the bottom about 5 miles from the start. Ignore the old trail along the canyon bottom and follow the new one as it climbs to the north canyon wall. At mile 5.8, reach the divide between Willie White Canyon and Telephone Canyon to the west. Here Trail 5003 goes left into Wills Canyon and a logging road follows along the crest. Continue straight and downhill on Trail 113. The trail quickly loses 700 feet over the next mile as it descends, again in lush forest, into Telephone Canyon. At the junction with Water Canyon, Trail 113 ends at FR 5009. Turn right onto the road and walk 0.75 mile back to the trailhead.

# 80 THREE RIVERS PETROGLYPH SITE

**Distance: 3 miles, day hike**
**Difficulty:** easy
**Elevation range:** 5,000 to 5,200 feet
**Elevation gain:** 200 feet
**Best time of year:** year round
**Water:** at campground
**Map:** USGS Golindrina Draw
**Managed by:** Bureau of Land Management, Las Cruces
    Field Office
**Features:** outstanding petroglyphs

Jornada-style petroglyphs are located at hundreds of sites across the desert regions of southern New Mexico. Related to the famous black-and-white Mimbres pottery style, these drawings are characterized by animal motifs, flat-headed human or godlike portraits, and complex geometric designs. A short hike along a lava cliff at the Three Rivers Petroglyph Site leads past an astounding array of hundreds of examples of this rock art. Bighorn sheep, horned lizards, fish, birds, spirals, and intertwining lines are pecked into the basalt. In a state where ancient rock art is a common feature, this is by far one of the most spectacular collections. The site and a nearby campground are carefully managed by the Bureau of Land Management, and a small fee is collected for visiting the area.

To reach the trailhead, take US 54, 30 miles north of Alamogordo or 28 miles south of Carrizozo, to FR 579. Head east, following the signs for the

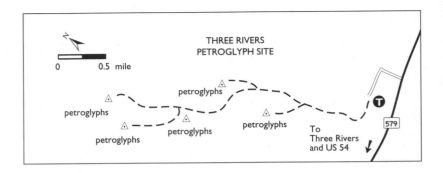

Three Rivers Petroglyph Site and Three Rivers Campground. In 4.5 miles, turn left at the entrance to the petroglyph site.

From the trailhead, follow the trail up to a low ridge, staying on the well-worn path as it climbs the basalt. At the black rocks, watch for the plentiful petroglyphs engraved on just about any flat surface. Each branch of the trail leads to more pecked artwork, so plan on taking as many side trails as possible. The trail continues past the main group of rock art to a round knoll to the north and offers dramatic views of the Sierra Blanca to the east. This makes a good turnaround point. On the return, hikers are certain to discover ancient pictures they missed on the way up.

*Geometric patterns are a common theme of the rock art at Three Rivers Petroglyph Site.*

# 81 | THREE RIVERS TRAIL

**Distance: 7 miles, day hike**
**Difficulty:** moderate
**Elevation range:** 6,800 to 8,400 feet
**Elevation gain:** 1,600 feet
**Best time of year:** April to November
**Water:** Three Rivers
**Maps:** USGS Godfrey Peak and Nogal Peak; USFS White
  Mountain Wilderness
**Managed by:** Lincoln National Forest, White Mountain
  Wilderness, Smokey Bear Ranger District
**Features:** deep, quiet canyon; running water

In contrast with the sloping east side of the range, the rugged west face of the Sierra Blanca is a formidable barrier where the mountain front jumps 4,000 feet from base to crest. Three Rivers Canyon provides a route into the range from the west, an arduous trip by any means. A day hike into the canyon is a delightfully wild experience that few people take. The craggy canyon holds flowing water throughout, and hikers quickly leave behind the desert scrub of the foothills and enter shady conifer forest. For 4 miles from the trailhead and up to the junction with the South Fork, pleasant campsites are plentiful; but hikers must resist the temptation to camp within 0.5 mile of the Three Rivers Campground.

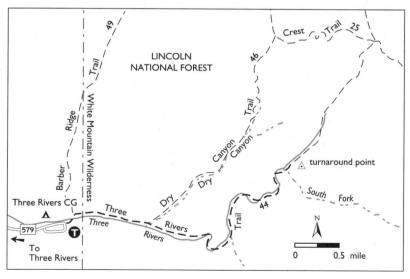

*The Three Rivers Trail lead into the rugged west side of the White Mountain Wilderness.*

Those seeking a challenge can continue past the end of the described route and follow the Three Rivers Trail to the crest—ascending 4,000 feet—and return via the difficult Dry Canyon Trail 46. Check with the Smokey Bear District Ranger Station concerning trail conditions before attempting this difficult 12-mile loop.

To reach the trailhead, take FR 579 from Three Rivers, which is located off US 54, 30 miles north of Alamogordo and 28 miles south of Carrizozo. Head east toward the Three Rivers Petroglyph Site and Three Rivers Campground. In 4.5 miles, pass the entrance to the petroglyph site, and in another mile, reach the end of the pavement. Stay on FR 579 by bearing right at mile 7.5 and left at mile 8.5, passing through private land. Continue to the campground, which is about 14 miles from US 54.

Begin hiking upcanyon on the Three Rivers Trail 44, located at the east end of the campground. Cross the stream on the main trail, avoiding the many side trails in the canyon bottom. The trail leads away from the shady trees onto the dry slopes, passing the Barber Ridge Trail 49. After passing through open stands of pine and Gambel oak, the trail swings back near the stream and enters a shady, pine and alligator juniper forest. Climb continuously along the stream, passing on the left the Dry Canyon Trail 46 at mile 0.9. Along this stretch, the stream often disappears in the rocks. It is an unusual forest with sparse understory and few wildflowers, but with abundant campsites available under the tall trees.

At mile 1.9, reach a rocky stretch of trail with tall cliffs on either side of the canyon. Bigtooth maple and little walnut (nogal) shade the stream here. After a series of bends, cross a dry side canyon and take a couple of short switchbacks to the base of a granite cliff. Beyond, the trail enters an open area that offers views of the main range. Continue another 0.5 mile to where the South Fork enters the main canyon, a convenient turnaround point.

# 82 | BIG BONITO LOOP

> **Distance: 9 miles, day hike or backpack**
> **Difficulty:** difficult
> **Elevation range:** 7,800 to 10,000 feet
> **Elevation gain:** 2,300 feet
> **Best time of year:** late April to November
> **Water:** Bonito Creek, Bonito Seep
> **Maps:** USGS Nogal Peak; USFS White Mountain Wilderness
> **Managed by:** Lincoln National Forest, White Mountain Wilderness, Smokey Bear Ranger District
> **Features:** quiet canyons, open grassland peaks, scenic views

The White Mountain Wilderness is one of the most attractive backcountry areas in New Mexico. The mountains are the highest in southern New Mexico, with rounded, gentle hills along the crest that give the range its characteristic beauty. Montane grasslands, an unusual vegetation type found in only a few areas of the state, cover much of the crest, providing the chance to walk an open ridgeline with extensive views of the range

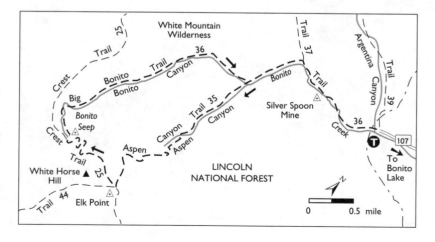

itself and of the valley and canyons below. The geology also creates a well-watered range with many springs just below the crest. Campsites are plentiful in the grasslands.

To reach the trailhead from Ruidoso on US 70, go 12 miles north on NM 48 and turn left onto NM 37. After 1.3 miles, turn left onto FR 107, which is signed for Bonito Lake. Continue on this narrow paved road past the lake and past the turnoff for the South Fork Campground, where the pavement ends on FR 107. At 7.5 miles from NM 37, continue slowly through Bonito Riding Stables and reach the trailhead in another mile.

Trail 36, the Big Bonito Trail, immediately enters the wilderness as it crosses Argentina Canyon and begins to parallel Bonito Creek, heading upstream. Bee balm, yarrow, mountain parsley, and Richardson's geranium

*The headframe of the Silver Spoon Mine along the Big Bonito Trail*

bloom here throughout the summer. The trail crosses the stream many times as it climbs steadily up the canyon floor. Pass the shaft and headframe of the Silver Spoon Mine at mile 0.75.

At mile 1, intersect the Little Bonito Trail 37. Bear left to stay on the Big Bonito Trail as the canyon turns abruptly south, offering a view of the not-too-distant crest. At mile 1.7, reach the junction with the Aspen Canyon Trail 35. The route returns to this junction later in the hike. Bear left onto the Aspen Canyon Trail and begin climbing in earnest. Beware of abundant stinging nettle close to the trail. Soon leave the forest behind and enter the grasslands, climbing several switchbacks. On the ascent, the views open to include Nogal Peak to the north and the Capitan Range to the east.

At a minor saddle near mile 3, turn right and continue climbing through a grassy bowl, gaining 500 feet to the next ridge. During the rainy season, the tread may disappear beneath a luxurious growth of alpine grass. Here the climb moderates, ascending the ridge to meet the Crest Trail 25 at mile 3.7 on a saddle between Elk Point to the east and White Horse Hill to the west.

From this high saddle, turn right and west onto the Crest Trail, skirting around the northern base of White Horse Hill. Drop quickly through several long switchbacks to Bonito Seep at mile 4.8. At the trail junction, leave the Crest Trail and head right to pick up the south end of the Big Bonito Trail and drop into a grassy canyon that parallels the flow of water coming from Bonito Seep.

Beyond the grassy bowl near the crest, the trail loses altitude. Bonito Canyon is shady and cool much of the way, often thick with Gambel oaks. The trail continues north for 1.5 miles before swinging to the east to meet the Aspen Canyon Trail again at mile 7. At the junction, bear left and backtrack to the trailhead, passing the Little Bonito Trail along the way.

# 83 | ARGENTINA PEAK

**Distance: 6 miles, day hike or backpack**
**Difficulty:** moderate
**Elevation range:** 7,800 to 9,100 feet
**Elevation gain:** 1,600 feet
**Best time of year:** late April to November
**Water:** Spring Cabin Spring, Argentina Spring
**Maps:** USGS Nogal Peak; USFS White Mountain Wilderness
**Managed by:** Lincoln National Forest, White Mountain Wilderness, Smokey Bear Ranger District
**Features:** running water, old mines, extensive views

Argentina Peak is one of the easiest destinations along the crest of the White Mountains, and the views from the trail are no less spectacular than those from other, higher locations. Cool and shady canyons lead up to and down from the grasslands along the crest, and water is available at several springs along the way. Campsites are limited along this route, but a few scenic spots are located along the crest and at Spring Cabin.

To reach the trailhead from Ruidoso on US 70, go 12 miles north on NM 48 and turn left onto NM 37. After 1.3 miles, turn left onto FR 107, which is signed for Bonito Lake. Continue on this narrow paved road past the lake and past the turnoff for the South Fork Campground, where the pavement ends on FR 107. At 7.5 miles from NM 37, continue slowly through Bonito Riding Stables and reach the trailhead in another mile.

Begin hiking on the Big Bonito Trail 36, immediately crossing the wilderness boundary. About 0.75 mile from the start, pass the impressive remains of the headframe of the Silver Spoon Mine. At mile 1, come to the junction with the Little Bonito Trail 37. Bear right and continue climbing on Trail 37 above the stream. Pass several small clearings suitable for camping along the way.

After passing a faint trail leading to Little Bonito Spring, come to the intersection with the Cut Across Trail 38, a shortcut to Argentina Canyon that bypasses the wonderful views from the crest. Continue straight, soon entering a grassy meadow with views of flat-topped Spring Point to the left. At mile 2.3, arrive at a five-way intersection. Trail 29 leads west to Spring Cabin and its spring for those who need water or a quiet campsite. Turn right onto the Crest Trail 25, climbing steeply out of the saddle. Cross a small meadow that offers nice views to the south and west. The trail skirts the eastern base of Argentina Peak, with excellent views of the ridges of the northern Sierra Blanca. The views are increasingly grand as the trail

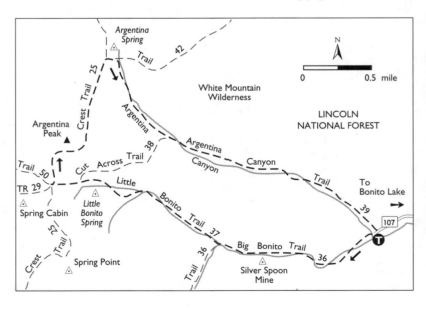

*The grasslands along the crest of Sierra Blanca*

drops from the north side of Argentina Peak and returns to the crest.
Intersect the Argentina Canyon Trail 39 at Argentina Spring at mile 3.4.
Turn right onto Trail 39, bearing right again in 0.2 mile at the intersection
with the Clear Water Trail 42. Parallel a small stream, now heading downhill, crossing the bottom of the drainage several times. Again intersect the
Cut Across Trail at mile 4.1 and continue downhill. About 2 miles from the
crest, cross the wilderness boundary and reach the trailhead.

# 84 | SOUTH FORK OF THE RIO BONITO

**Distance: 6 miles, day hike**
**Difficulty:** moderate
**Elevation range:** 7,500 to 8,400 feet
**Elevation gain:** 1,000 feet
**Best time of year:** late April to November
**Water:** at campground and along South Fork
**Maps:** USGS Nogal Peak; USFS White Mountain Wilderness
**Managed by:** Lincoln National Forest, White Mountain
    Wilderness, Smokey Bear Ranger District
**Features:** lush canyon, wild brook trout, running water

Hikers looking for something less taxing than a steep climb to the crest of
the Sierra Blanca should try the South Fork of the Rio Bonito. The lower

mile of this hike often receives heavy use on summer weekends, but above the wilderness boundary, hikers are likely to share the canyon only with elk, bear, and wild brook trout. Scenic campsites are located throughout the canyon bottom. The brook trout in the stream are voracious feeders although easily spooked in the clear water. For those out for more than a casual stroll, the South Fork Trail extends up to the crest where it joins the Bluefront Trail, creating a strenuous, 12-mile circuit with 3,000 feet of elevation gain, most of which comes in a 2-mile stretch.

To reach the trailhead, from Ruidoso on US 70, go 12 miles north on NM 48 and turn left onto NM 37. After 1.3 miles, turn left onto FR 107, which is signed for Bonito Lake. Continue on this narrow paved road past the lake 5 miles to the turnoff for South Fork Campground. Turn left and continue 0.75 mile to the trailhead at the campground.

Begin hiking at the end of the road at the South Fork Trail 19 sign. Immediately enter the deep, shady conifer forest where multiple routes lead upcanyon. As the trail climbs away from the canyon bottom, look for sections of an old wooden pipe surrounded by banded metal that was part of a water system designed to deliver water to the railroad at Carrizozo, 30 miles away. After crossing to the south bank of the stream at the base of a tall granite cliff, pass the remains of the dam that supplied water to the pipe. Cross into the White Mountain Wilderness, where the trail narrows and sees fewer users. Intersect the Bluefront Trail 33 at mile 0.8 and bear left, staying on the South Fork Trail and climbing above the stream. After passing the Peacock Trail 18 to the left, drop back down to stream level and cross the stream, where yellow thistles bloom in midsummer.

Continue up the narrowing canyon, always within earshot of the running water. The trail passes through small meadows, each offering quiet campsites. After crossing the stream several times, the trail rounds a broad

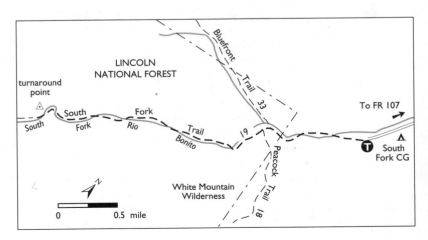

*Wild brook trout invite a bit of angling on the South Fork of the Rio Bonito.*

bend in the stream at the base of a granite ridge, a good turnaround spot about 3 miles from the start. Return to the trailhead by the same route.

# 85 | CAPITAN PEAK

**Distance: 14 miles, day hike or backpack**
**Difficulty:** strenuous
**Elevation range:** 6,100 to 10,083 feet
**Elevation gain:** 4,100 feet
**Best time of year:** late April to October
**Water:** carry water
**Maps:** USGS Arabela and Capitan Peak
**Managed by:** Lincoln National Forest, Capitan Wilderness, Smokey Bear Ranger District
**Features:** unmatched views, challenging hike

Rising 5,000 feet above the surrounding plains, the Capitan Mountains serve as a prominent landmark for travelers entering south-central New Mexico from the east or north. From the summit of the range on Capitan Peak, the expansive view takes in almost all of southeastern New Mexico from Texas to the southern Rockies. The rugged east side of the range is a little-visited wilderness area; with the exception of the fall hunting season, hikers should enjoy a day of solitude on the way to the peak.

Be prepared for a long, arduous hike. Allow 7 to 12 hours to make the 14-mile round trip to the summit and back. No water is found along the route; on a hot summer day, plan on carrying and drinking at least a gallon per person. Those seeking a less challenging trip can make the 4-mile round trip to Chimney Rock.

To reach the trailhead at the Pine Lodge Summer Home area, take NM 246 about 33 miles north and east of Capitan on US 70, or about 50 miles west of Roswell. Turn south onto FR 130, a rough dirt road that often requires a high-clearance vehicle. Continue 4 miles, passing the North Base Trailhead on the right immediately before reaching the Capitan Peak Trailhead.

Begin hiking on the Capitan Peak Trail 64. The early part of the trail parallels FR 130, passing on the edge of the summer home area. In 0.25 mile, intersect a trail from the cabins coming in from the end of the road on the right. Stay on the main trail at a small drainage and, after crossing the Capitan Wilderness boundary, begin the long, steep climb. The trail follows a ridge through a low-growing juniper forest for the next 0.25 mile before making a short, steep climb at mile 1.

At the base of the first series of switchbacks at mile 1.5, the trail turns sharply to the right. Climb a long series of switchbacks ascending a narrow ridge, with glimpses of Chimney Rock through the trees to the left. At the top of the wiggles at mile 2, the trail offers fine views of Chimney Rock. This is a good turnaround point for those seeking an easy day hike.

The trail continues to follow a narrow ridge, with another set of intense switchbacks beginning at mile 3.1. In another 0.5 mile, the trail levels a bit, now traversing Douglas fir forest. Pass a viewpoint of Sunset Peak to the east at mile 4.2.

Just past mile 5, reach a T intersection with the Summit Trail 58. Bear

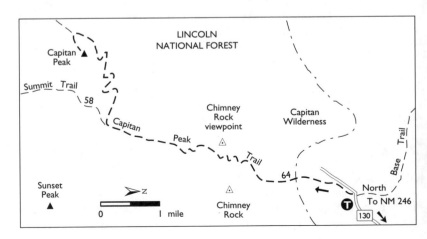

*Mushrooms can be found in conifer forests in late summer.*

right onto the Capitan Peak Trail, following the signs for Capitan Peak, which is 1.5 miles west. After a 0.5-mile traverse, the trail begins a series of broad switchbacks that lead to the summit ridge, where frequent openings in the trees offer views to the north. At mile 6.2, the trail swings below Capitan Peak. Continue climbing to a sloping meadow at mile 7, where a sign points the way to the summit. Turn left, leaving the main trail to cross the meadow, where a riot of wildflowers blooms all summer long. A few hundred yards lead to the summit and a glorious 360-degree view.

Campsites are scattered along the edge of the meadow below the peak. Return to the trailhead by the same route.

# 86 | LAST CHANCE CANYON

**Distance: 10 miles, day hike or backpack**
**Difficulty:** moderate
**Elevation range:** 4,500 to 5,200 feet
**Elevation gain:** 800 feet
**Best time of year:** fall through late spring
**Water:** White Oak Spring and along Last Chance Canyon
**Maps:** USGS Red Bluff Draw and Queen
**Managed by:** Lincoln National Forest, Guadalupe Ranger District
**Features:** large springs, high canyon walls, solitude

The story of how this canyon got its name is told so often that it just might contain a kernel of truth. Around 1881, a group of ranchers pursued Apache raiders into the Guadalupe Mountains and soon became lost amid the twisted canyons draining the southeast flank of the range. After their canteens were empty they rode from rim to rim, searching for water without

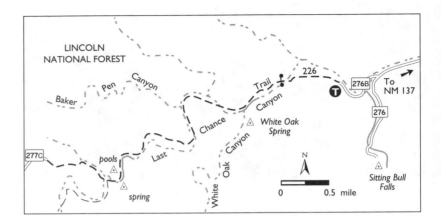

finding a spring. With their horses almost spent, they spotted the limestone walls of yet another canyon—it was their last chance. According to the legend, the abundant springs they found there saved their lives, and they named the spot Last Chance Canyon.

Just down the road from popular Sitting Bull Falls, Last Chance Canyon offers the last chance to escape the crowds at the falls and enter a lonesome limestone wilderness, one of my favorite spots in all of New Mexico. A couple of miles up the canyon is a spring and travertine wall similar to the ones in Sitting Bull Canyon, but rarely visited. With abundant water and myriad side canyons to explore, Last Chance is an excellent place for an overnight stay.

The mouth of Last Chance Canyon is located near the Sitting Bull Falls Recreation Area off NM 137. Twelve miles north of Carlsbad, turn west onto NM 137 and continue on this paved road about 24 miles to FR 276, the road to Sitting Bull Falls. Turn right and drive about 6.5 miles to FR 276B on the right. Turn and continue about 0.25 mile to the end of this rough road.

From the trailhead, walk upcanyon on Trail 226, located on the south side of the canyon bottom. The towering limestone walls of the canyon are clothed in Torrey yuccas, sotol, bear grass, and prickly pear cactus, and the canyon is very wide in its lower reaches. At mile 0.6, drop into the canyon bottom shaded by some large hackberry trees, cross the stream, and pass through a gate.

As the canyon walls squeeze in against the canyon bottom, the trail crosses limestone ledges. Small ponds of clear water stand in the canyon bottom, flowing from White Oak Spring in the side canyon entering from the south. Listen for the incongruous trill of a belted kingfisher searching for minnows in a desert canyon. Soon pass a massive gray and orange wall of travertine deposited at the mouth of White Oak Canyon. The travertine cliff has many intricate faces and includes an unusual natural bridge on its western end.

Beyond White Oak Spring, Last Chance Canyon widens. Cross to the south side of the canyon bottom before the trail swings south along a bend in the canyon. At the mouth of Baker Pen Canyon entering from the right, find several shady campsites. Near gray stair-step limestone ledges, the trail follows the rocky canyon bottom for a few yards before climbing to a bench above. Climb steeply through several switchbacks to cross a spur ridge. The trail is scratched into the slopes above the canyon floor.

The trail becomes difficult to follow as it turns south and begins to drop to some spring-fed ponds. When a route to the canyon bottom is clearly visible at mile 3.6, drop down to the stream and walk up the rock ledges near the pools of clear water. Most of the pools are only a few inches deep, but one is a wonderful swimming hole more than 6 feet deep. Flat benches along the stream offer idyllic camping spots.

Although the trail follows the north bank of the stream, it is easier and more interesting to follow the canyon bottom upstream. Continue in the streambed around a couple of bends until reaching a deep pool with intake water pipes leading to a small shed. Follow the pipe to pick up the trail again at mile 4.3, passing the ruins of a tin pumphouse with rusting machinery inside. The trail passes a large spring, then crosses the stream bottom. In a minute, reach the junction of Last Chance with a side canyon entering from the right. Cross Last Chance and follow a trail heading up this small side canyon. At a minor junction, take the fork to the right. Climb

*Flowing water supports lush vegetation in Last Chance Canyon, a striking contrast to the dry desert slopes.*
(Courtesy U.S. Forest Service)

the switchbacks leading up the south wall of the canyon until reaching the top of a knife-edge ridge. Peek over the edge to the left for another view of Last Chance Canyon. Return to the trailhead by the same route.

# 87 | SITTING BULL FALLS

**Distance: 7 miles, day hike**
**Difficulty:** moderate
**Elevation range:** 4,660 to 5,725 feet
**Elevation gain:** 1,100 feet
**Best time of year:** year round
**Water:** Sitting Bull Falls, Sitting Bull Spring
**Map:** USGS Queen
**Managed by:** Lincoln National Forest, Guadalupe Ranger
   District
**Features:** running water, unusual waterfall

Sitting Bull, a Dakota Sioux from the northern Great Plains, probably never set foot in New Mexico. But a much-repeated legend claims that cowboys chased a group of Indians that included the old chief into Sitting Bull Canyon and thereby discovered the falls. Unfortunately for the story, Sitting Bull was in Canada in 1881, the year of the reputed discovery.

An equally improbable explanation tells of early Eddy County resident Bill Jones spinning tales of the old days in the Guadalupes. His description of the falls was met with derisive comments from his brothers, who called it "pure bull." "Well, Sitting Bull," suggested one brother, "if those falls are really there, we'll name them after you!"

One can drive to the base of Sitting Bull Falls, but dropping in from the mesa above makes the trip a memorable one. This longer hike begins on NM

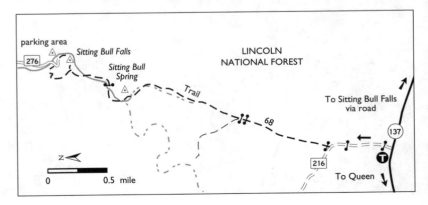

137 and drops into Sitting Bull Canyon, passing along the way the spring that ultimately trickles through matted green and red plants to create this unusual waterfall.

To reach the trailhead, turn west on NM 137 from US 285, 12 miles north of Carlsbad. In about 24 miles, continue straight when the road to Sitting Bull Falls goes right. Climb the escarpment and enter the Lincoln National Forest, passing the U.S. Forest Service's Guadalupe Work Center about 11 miles from the falls road intersection. Basic supplies and gas are available at Queen, just beyond the work center. Continue about 1 mile to a sign for Trail 68 on the right side of the road.

Begin Trail 68 by walking through a gate on a primitive road. After 0.4 mile, pass through another gate. In a few hundred yards the road, here marked FR 216, bears left. Bear right through a gate on what is now identified as Trail 68. At mile 1.5, the trail reaches two gates within 50 feet of each other. At an intersection 50 feet beyond the second gate, take the right fork. Soon the trail parallels a deep draw on the left. A low rock

*Sitting Bull Falls*

wall marks where the trail turns left to enter the draw, which soon deepens into a full-fledged canyon. Enjoy the views of the canyon below and of the plains in the distance as you descend, but watch out for loose rocks.

About 2 miles from the start, reach the bottom of the canyon and cross to the west side. The trail now meanders across the canyon bottom. As the trail swings west, pass Sitting Bull Spring on the right. From here on down, clear running water is found in the stream bottom. Descend a bit more into the bottom of a large canyon, bear right and pass through a hikers gate. Continue downstream, arriving at a trail junction 3 miles from the start. First, bear right and take the short spur trail to see the top of the falls, then return to the junction and continue down the cliff on the trail marked for FR 276. At the bottom of the hill, reach a parking lot, cross to the east side, and pick up the trail leading to the bottom of the falls. Enjoy the falls from below, then return to the trailhead by the same route.

# 88 | LONESOME RIDGE

**Distance: 12 miles, day hike or backpack**
**Difficulty:** difficult
**Elevation range:** 6,600 to 7,200 feet
**Elevation gain:** 1,400 feet
**Best time of year:** March to May, September to December
**Water:** carry water
**Maps:** USGS El Paso Gap and Gunsight Canyon
**Managed by:** Lincoln National Forest, Guadalupe Ranger District
**Features:** lonesome feeling, rugged canyon country, wildlife viewing

The smooth face of the west edge of the Guadalupe Mountains is most dramatically contrasted by the eastern rim, which is made of a series of ridges jutting like fingers from the hand of Guadalupe Ridge. Walking any of the narrow ridges presents grand views into the deeply incised canyons of the rim, a 1,000-foot section of limestone piled on top of more limestone. The Lonesome Ridge Trail leaves Guadalupe Ridge and crosses narrow saddles and ridges before ending at the head of the Golden Stairway, a steep trail that drops from the rim to private land below.

The trailhead is a long way from the nearest town, but water and supplies are available along NM 137. Guadalupe National Forest has a water

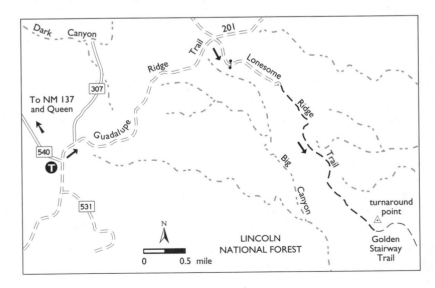

*The east face of the Guadalupe Escarpment from Lonesome Ridge*

tap for campers and hikers at its Guadalupe Work Center located about 35 miles from US 285 on NM 137. Basic supplies and gas are available at Queen, just beyond the work center. Primitive camping is permitted along NM 137 and FR 540, including a large wooded area suitable for group camping at the trailhead.

To get to the trailhead, take NM 137 west from US 285 about 12 miles north of Carlsbad. In 24 miles, pass the road to Sitting Bull Falls. Thirty-eight miles from the highway, pass the Queen store on the right. Go 3.5 miles past the store and turn left onto FR 540. This is an excellent all-weather gravel road. In 0.5 mile, bear right, and continue about 12 miles to the end of the gravel road.

Begin hiking north (left) on Trail 201, the Guadalupe Ridge Trail, which is actually a jeep road. In 0.25 mile, pass FR 307 on the left. Continue on the narrow ridge, making repeated climbs and descents, with glimpses of Big Canyon to the right and upper Dark Canyon to the left. The road surface is rocky, with sharp-edged limestone underfoot. The pine and juniper forest is occasionally broken by areas of recent fire, a common feature in the hot, dry Guadalupes. At mile 1.8, Lonesome Ridge comes into view on the right.

Three miles from the start, arrive at a four-way intersection. Take the rightmost fork onto Lonesome Ridge. At mile 3.4, views open up to the Big Canyon system. Bear left at a gate and pass through it. After the road crosses a saddle, there are excellent views in all directions. Continue on the road to just beyond mile 4.1, where the road suddenly narrows into a trail. Skirt the edge of a broad bowl of limestone, peeking over the edge for more views of Big Canyon. Cairns mark the trail as it circles the top of the ridge, then drops into a drainage heading toward the entrance to the Golden Stairway Trail. Continue about a mile farther along the very edge of Big Canyon, whose jagged cliffs offer a stunning backdrop to the trail.

Several rocky but flat areas are found on the extreme end of Lonesome Ridge, offering exposed campsites as a base for further exploration of the canyons, and from which to descend the Golden Stairway Trail. Turn around at the edge of Big Canyon at mile 5.6 or continue to the head of the Golden Stairway. The rocky descent into Big Canyon on this trail is for strong, experienced hikers only. Private land at the bottom forces those making the trip to retrace their steps along Lonesome Ridge.

# 89 | Devils Den Canyon

**Distance: 6 miles, day hike**
**Difficulty:** moderate
**Elevation range:** 6,400 to 7,200 feet
**Elevation gain:** 1,000 feet
**Best time of year:** March to May, September to December
**Water:** Devils Den Spring
**Map:** USGS El Paso Gap
**Managed by:** Lincoln National Forest, Guadalupe Ranger District
**Features:** remote, spectacular canyon

In a dry land with only a thin veneer of unfriendly vegetation, the devil gets blamed for everything. The Southwest has more devils canyons, stairways, thrones, peaks, and ridges than one can count. Devils Den Canyon is a rugged gorge slashed through the western rim of the Guadalupes, ending in a spectacular pour off along the mountain front. In the surrounding hills, a large herd of mule deer supports a small population of mountain lions. Watch for large cat prints in the soft sand.

The trailhead for the Devils Den Canyon Trail is the same as for Lonesome Ridge (Hike 88). To get to the trailhead, take NM 137 west from US 285 about 12 miles north of Carlsbad. In 24 miles, pass the road to Sitting Bull Falls. Pass the Queen store on the right in 38 miles. Go 3.5 miles past the store, and turn left onto FR 540. In 0.5 mile, bear right, and continue about 12 miles to the end of the all-weather gravel road. Note that a trailhead for a different Devils Den Trail is located on FR 540 about 2 miles north of the starting point for this hike, also off the Guadalupe Ridge Trail. This second Devils Den Trail does not connect with the trail described here.

From the end of the gravel FR 540, walk south (right) on Trail 201, the

Guadalupe Ridge Trail, which is actually a jeep road but is too rough for most vehicles beyond the first 0.25 mile. At an intersection at mile 0.3, bear right to stay on Trail 201. For the next 0.25 mile, pass through a maze of intertwined tracks heading up a rocky hill. Stay left, reaching a shallow stock tank at mile 0.6. Continue across a narrow ridge with the Big Canyon system on the left and the Devils Den Canyon on the right. At mile 1.2, in the middle of an easy climb, turn right onto an unmarked road. This road is as wide as the Guadalupe Ridge Trail at this point, but soon narrows. At another intersection in a few hundred feet, bear right, gradually dropping downhill on the rocky and rutted road surface, passing a large Texas madrone tree, recognized by its smooth red branches.

At mile 1.7, the rough roadway ends at the ruins of a cabin above Devils Den Spring. Follow the trail past the cabin, reaching a fork. Take the right branch, which drops steeply on several switchbacks to the bottom of a side canyon just down from the spring. The trail continues to the mouth of the side canyon, then swings west into Devils Den Canyon. Starting above the canyon floor, the trail soon drops to the rocky streambed. From here, walking in the canyon floor is much more interesting than taking the trail.

After passing a side canyon entering from the left, walk through a horseshoe bend. On the other side, flat ground and shady junipers invite camping for a day. At mile 2.4, a rock cairn (often made with three slabs of orange limestone) marks the trail's exit from the canyon. (A worthwhile side trip continues another 0.25 mile in the canyon bottom to a spectacular pour off

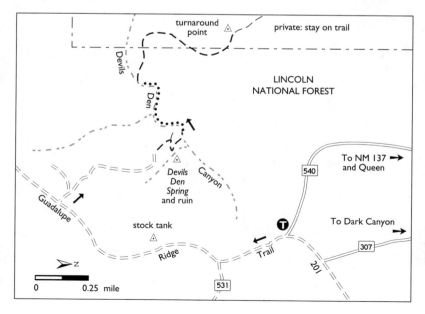

*The trail in Devils Den Canyon cuts across a sparsely vegetated slope typical of the Chihuahuan Desert.*

about 200 feet high.) Turn right and, using the trail, climb out of the canyon bottom to enter private land.

Climb the north wall of the canyon to a saddle on a narrow spur ridge, making certain to stay on the trail in this area. At mile 2.6, the pour off in the canyon is visible to the left. After rounding a turn and heading north, the trail perches on a ledge high above the floor of the canyon where views are outstanding. Follow the shelf trail until it fades away on a saddle at mile 3. Turn around and return by the same route.

# 90 | LONGVIEW SPRING

**Distance: 6 miles, day hike or backpack**
**Difficulty:** moderate
**Elevation range:** 4,550 to 6,000 feet
**Elevation gain:** 1,600 feet
**Best time of year:** fall through late spring
**Water:** Longview Spring
**Map:** USGS Grapevine Draw
**Managed by:** National Park Service, Carlsbad Caverns
    National Park
**Features:** rugged canyon, long-range views, solitude

Although spectacular, Carlsbad Caverns can leave visitors eager for an escape from the crowds. One solution is to hike one of the park's backcountry trails, such as the Yucca Canyon Trail to Longview Spring. Few make the trip to this distant corner of the park, and hikers will most likely have about ten square miles of desert mountains to themselves. Permits are not required for day hiking in the backcountry, but hikers planning an overnight stay need to stop at the Carlsbad Caverns Visitor Center for a free permit. Note that a user fee is charged to enter the park.

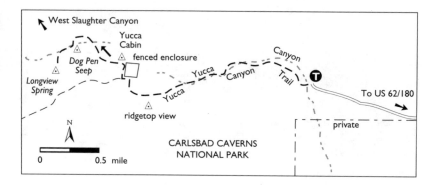

The Guadalupe Mountains are one of the world's largest biologically created structures. The entire range—and indeed a much more extensive, mostly buried, limestone structure more than 300 miles long—is a fossil reef formed at the margin of a shallow arm of the sea during the Permian period, about 250 million years ago. The reef is made from the secretions of calcareous algae and the remains of sponges, bryozoans, brachiopods, and other shelled invertebrates. Over millions of years, these plants and animals grew on the remains of their ancestors, building a pile of lime almost 2,000 feet thick.

A walk up Yucca Canyon is also a climb through the reef. Though at first glance the limestone layers appear to be homogenous, a close examination along the trail's transect of the canyon shows that each layer—ranging in thickness from a few inches to a couple hundred feet—has its own characteristics. Specific fossils are common in one layer but not the next. The texture of the limestone also changes from massive to thinly laminated layers. Some layers are tinted red and include more sand than lime, an indication of a period when the reef was exposed above sea level.

To reach the trailhead, head south on US 62/180 from the city of Carlsbad to Whites City. In another 5 miles, turn right onto paved CR 418, signed for Slaughter Canyon Cave. Follow the signs for the cave about 10 miles to a fence at the national park boundary. Turn left onto a rocky double-track heading west parallel to the fence. This road is rough, but is regularly driven by low-slung cars. Continue about 2 miles to the trailhead.

From the parking area the trail immediately drops, crosses the streambed,

*A huge pile of limestone: the Guadalupe Mountains*

and turns up Yucca Canyon. The limestone of the Capitan reef is found in every direction, forming canyon walls more than 1,500 feet high. The trail climbs steadily on the south wall of the canyon, high above the bottom. At mile 0.7, again cross the canyon bottom. The trail frequently switches between the north and south walls, and the climb is considerably steeper. The narrowing canyon supports alligator juniper and Texas madrone, which provide occasional shelter from the sun. A series of switchbacks leads high above the canyon floor, then the trail drops back to stream level. Atop the ridge at mile 1.5, the view to the south is never-ending and includes the southern portion of the Guadalupe Mountains in Texas and the rolling hills of the Pecos Valley.

Once on top of the ridge, the trail is more difficult to follow. Look for the faint tread heading north and for small cairns along the path. The trail leads to a large fenced enclosure among the piñon pine and juniper of the mesa top. Follow the south edge of the fence, then the west edge, to reach Yucca Cabin at mile 2.1, ignoring a prominent trail angling from the southwest corner of the enclosure. From the cabin, cairns mark the trail west, first along the ridge top, then dropping into a small drainage. At the bottom, pass a rock corral and muddy spot called Dog Pen Seep. The trail continues down the drainage bottom, then up on the south side of the drainage wall. Soon the trail follows a ledge high above Slaughter Canyon, swinging south. The Longview Spring is a few hundred feet farther on, about 3 miles from the start. By now it should be obvious how the spring got its name: the view into West Slaughter Canyon is spectacular. Return to the trailhead by the same route.

# 91 | RATTLESNAKE CANYON

**Distance: 6 miles, day hike or backpack**
**Difficulty:** moderate
**Elevation range:** 4,100 to 4,700 feet
**Elevation gain:** 900 feet
**Best time of year:** September to May
**Water:** carry water
**Map:** USGS Serpentine Bends
**Managed by:** National Park Service, Carlsbad Caverns National Park
**Features:** quiet desert canyon, Chihuahuan Desert vegetation

The overwhelming majority of the Chihuahuan Desert lies south of the international border in Mexico, but arms of the desert reach up the Rio Grande and Pecos River Valleys to embrace a portion of New Mexico. While monotypic stands of creosote bush cover the vast majority of this desert's area, it is the thick-leaved succulents that are its defining species. Soaptree yucca is the most common yucca in the Chihuahuan Desert and is the New Mexico state flower. Dense clusters of 3- to 4-foot-long leaves sprout like spikes from the top of the trunk. Even more spectacular is the Spanish dagger, a yucca species that can grow up to 40 feet tall. The most distinctive of the Chihuahuan Desert plants is the lechuguilla, a low-growing succulent found only in this region. The thick, sharp-pointed lechuguilla leaves grow about 12 inches tall, giving the plant its apt nickname, "shin dagger."

Rattlesnake Canyon is a short but intensely scenic trip into this world of unusual plants. The loop traverses open desert slopes and follows serpentine canyons that continually offer surprises to hikers. The moderately difficult trip can be done as a day hike, or as an overnighter which includes the opportunity for more extensive backcountry exploration. Note that campfires are not allowed in the backcountry, and a free permit is required for all overnight use.

The trailhead is located along the Scenic Loop Drive in Carlsbad Caverns National Park, reached by driving about 16 miles south of the city of Carlsbad on US 62/180 and turning west at Whites City into the park. From the visitor center, head back toward the park entrance for a few hundred feet and turn left onto the one-way, gravel loop road. Continue about 4 miles to Marker 9 on the Scenic Loop Drive and park.

Begin hiking heading west (left) and immediately begin to drop into a small drainage. The trail swings north through thick stands of creosote bush as it climbs slightly before skirting the south wall of a larger drain-

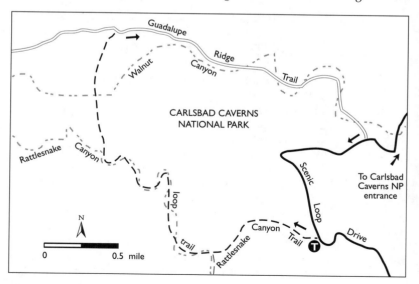

*Fossils of sea life are commonly found in the limestone of the Guadalupe Mountains.*

age. Limestone blocks along the trail hold entire cities of sea life fossil remains. Just over 0.5 mile from the start, reach a trail junction on the sandy floor of Rattlesnake Canyon. Hikers can take a spur trip on the Rattlesnake Canyon Trail by turning left and walking 2 miles to the park boundary, returning to the main trail by the same route. To continue on the described loop trip, turn right at the trail junction, traveling in the direction of Guadalupe Ridge to the north.

Follow the trail up Rattlesnake Canyon by watching for rock cairns that mark the way. Towering beds of limestone form the sometimes sheer drop, sometimes sloping canyon walls as the trail weaves through four sweeping bends of the wash. At the apex of the fourth bend, after about 1.5 miles in the canyon bottom, the trail leaves the wash to climb the slope to the right (north). Climb steeply over a low ridge, then drop into Walnut Canyon. The trail makes a gentler climb to meet the Guadalupe Ridge Trail 201 at mile 2.8. Turn right and follow this wide trail as it heads east and again drops into Walnut Canyon. The trail stays near the canyon bottom for 1.5 miles and ends at the Scenic Loop Drive. Turn right and walk with caution along the road 1 mile back to the trailhead.

# 92 | SLAUGHTER CANYON LOOP

**Distance: 13 miles, day hike or backpack**
**Difficulty:** strenuous
**Elevation range:** 4,200 to 5,850 feet
**Elevation gain:** 2,500 feet
**Best time of year:** October to April
**Water:** carry water
**Maps:** USGS Grapevine Draw and Serpentine Bends
**Managed by:** National Park Service, Carlsbad Caverns
National Park
**Features:** spectacular views, solitude, rugged canyon
scenery

The scarcity of water in the arid southeast corner of New Mexico has forced
plants to adapt to the harsh conditions with a variety of strategies. Backpackers, too, must adapt to the aridity when planning an overnight journey like a trip through the Slaughter Canyon system. Generally there is no
water available along the route. The most difficult task of such a hike is
carrying enough water for cooking, cleaning, and hydrating during 2 days
of hard work on the trail. A gallon of water for such a trip will barely suf-
fice (the rule is often a gallon of water per person per day). Carry as much
water as you can comfortably transport on the stairlike climb out of Slaugh-

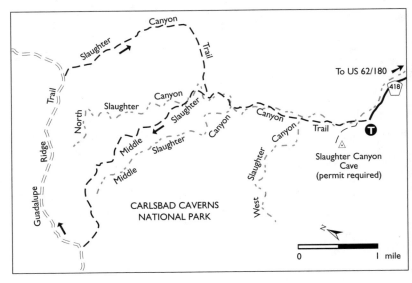

*Trails in Carlsbad Caverns National Park traverse deep limestone canyons.*

ter Canyon to Guadalupe Ridge. With almost 2,000 feet of elevation gain, hikers need plenty of fluids to stay hydrated on this trip. Consider a trip to these canyons from mid-fall through early spring when conditions are cooler and wetter.

The trip into Slaughter Canyon need not be a grueling overnighter; day hikers as well can enjoy the rugged terrain and deep canyons. For a worthwhile day hike, turn around at the junction where the loop begins 2 miles from the start. For an overnight trip, camp somewhere along the Guadalupe Ridge Trail near the middle of the loop.

Reach the trailhead by taking US 62/180 south from Whites City. Travel about 6 miles to CR 418, which is signed for Slaughter Canyon Cave. Follow the paved CR 418 for 10 miles to the end of the pavement at the park boundary, then continue 1 mile to the trailhead.

Begin hiking by taking the fainter of two trails, the one that heads right and up the wash. (Avoid the heavily used trail to the left to Slaughter Canyon Cave; a permit is required for entry into the cavern.) Follow the sign pointing to Middle Slaughter Canyon Trail. The trail heads up the wide canyon between rows of short willows, crossing low benches and sharing the route with the sandy wash. Rock cairns mark the way, but hikers must avoid side trails that lead to the left and right, away from the canyon bottom. In 1 mile, pass the broad West Slaughter Canyon coming in from the left and enjoy the striking view upcanyon. In another 0.75 mile, pass the mouth of Middle Slaughter Canyon, again to the left, and round a spur to reach a junction where the trail splits. Angle left to stay in the bottom of North Slaughter Canyon. The route continues up the wash bottom another 0.25 miles before exiting to the west and beginning the ascent of Guadalupe Ridge. This rugged, sun-exposed climb can be grueling in the heat of the day.

The trail hangs on the north slope of a spur ridge before reaching a more prominent ridgeline near mile 4.5. Continue climbing the ridge amid splendid grasslands dotted with oaks and juniper. A mile of such scenery leads to the junction with the Guadalupe Ridge Trail 201. Turn right onto the jeep road as it rolls up and down along the ridgeline. Several spur ridges in the next mile offer secluded campsites.

Walk about 2 miles along the ridge trail, enjoying the views of Bear Canyon to the left and the Slaughter Canyon system to the right. Watch for a sign for the Slaughter Canyon Trail to the right around mile 7.5. This trail segment heads southeast along a spur ridge with intricate mazes of limestone on either side. After the trail swings south, then southwest, it leaves the ridgeline about 10.5 miles from the start. Dropping over a rough slope of blocky, jagged rocks, the trail reaches the loop trail junction in the bottom of North Slaughter Canyon. Turn left and retrace your steps the last 2 miles to the trailhead.

*Facing page: Canyons of the tributaries of the Gila River*

# GILA RIVER REGION

# 93 | PUEBLO CREEK

**Distance: 8 miles, day hike or backpack**
**Difficulty:** easy
**Elevation range:** 5,800 to 6,200 feet
**Elevation gain:** 500 feet
**Best time of year:** March to November
**Water:** carry water
**Map:** USGS Saliz Pass
**Managed by:** Gila National Forest, Blue Range Wilderness, Reserve Ranger District
**Features:** minerals, isolated mountain scenery

The little-used Blue Range Wilderness abuts the Arizona–New Mexico border, part of the larger Blue Range Primitive Area. The area receives only a few hundred visitors each year, helping make this hike lovely from spring to fall. The isolated canyon of Pueblo Creek cuts through the wilderness, and the WS Mountain Trail 43 follows the canyon about 9 miles to WS Lake. Additional trails met along the way lead into Arizona. A rock outcrop on the east side of the canyon yields shiny bytownite crystals, a translucent mineral often cut into gems. The mineral is found scattered on the ground along a faint trail that leaves from the canyon bottom around mile 1.2, and lesser quantities are found along Pueblo Creek.

From Silver City, take US 180 northwest for 62 miles to the town of Glenwood. From Glenwood, continue north on US 180 about 27 miles to the junction with FR 232. Turn left and drive this good gravel road 5.6 miles to Pueblo Park Campground. The trailhead is just across the road.

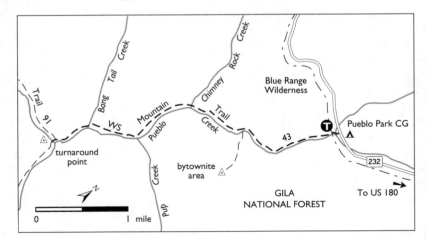

*Well-forested canyons are typical of the southwestern part of New Mexico.*

Begin hiking south on the WS Mountain Trail 43. The rugged trail follows the canyon bottom and is marked sporadically with rock cairns. Watch carefully for markers as the trail swings from bank to bank, or simply follow the floor of the canyon and pick up the trail whenever it is found. Where the canyon narrows at mile 0.4, walking is easier on the trail just above the canyon floor in the forest of ponderosa pine and alligator juniper. At mile 1.2, watch carefully for a faint trail heading up to the bytownite crystal area, or search for minerals along the main stream.

The canyon broadens near Chimney Rock Creek, which enters at mile 1.7 from the west. Water usually flows in the Pueblo Creek bottom below this point. Continue down the benches under the canopy of broad-leaved trees. Mesas of juniper and piñon pine rise higher above the canyon floor as small side streams enter from east and west, adding water to the canyon bottom. Fine campsites are located near the confluences with Pup Creek at mile 2.6 and Bang Tail Creek at mile 4. At the junction with the Tige Canyon Trail 91 at mile 4.1, turn around to return by the same route; or camp and further explore up Tige Canyon or along Bear Creek a mile farther down the WS Mountain Trail.

# 94 | WHITEWATER BALDY

**Distance: 12 miles, day hike or backpack**
**Difficulty:** difficult
**Elevation range:** 9,100 to 10,895 feet
**Elevation gain:** 1,900 feet
**Best time of year:** mid-May to November
**Water:** Bead and Hummingbird Springs
**Maps:** USGS Grouse Mountain; USFS Gila Wilderness
**Managed by:** Gila National Forest, Gila Wilderness, Glenwood Ranger District
**Features:** fine views, deep forest

The Crest Trail 182 is well used and easy to follow as it ascends a high ridge from the trailhead to Hummingbird Saddle and beyond to the summit of Mogollon Baldy, 12 miles away. A shorter trip leads to the summit of Whitewater Baldy; at 10,895 feet, it is the highest point in the Mogollon Range. Because water and campsites are readily available at Humming-

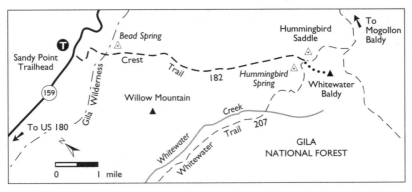

*Ladybugs covering pine branches are a common sight on mountain summits.*

bird Saddle, this hike is popular. The route leads through a deep Douglas fir forest and offers some wonderful views of the Gila River Region. The trail is exposed all along the ridge, so hikers should be prepared for severe weather. Plan to be off the summit of Whitewater Baldy during storms, which are likely most summer afternoons. Note that some snow may linger until early June on the higher sections of this trail.

To reach the trailhead, drive about 4 miles north of Glenwood on US 180 and turn right onto NM 159. Take this winding road past the town of Mogollon, and continue about 18 miles from the highway to the Sandy Point Trailhead.

Begin hiking south on the Crest Trail 182 toward Hummingbird Saddle and Mogollon Baldy. The trail begins a moderate climb through Douglas fir forest, a shady walk even in summer. Although moderate, the climbing is constant for the first 1.5 miles. Watch for occasional views north toward Mineral Creek on the ascent. As the climb levels at mile 1.6, enter the Gila Wilderness. A short spur trail to the left leads to the lush Bead Spring. Resume the ascent as the trail swings to the east of Willow Mountain before gaining the ridge at a low saddle at mile 2.5. Continue along the rolling ridgeline, climbing to a knoll above Hummingbird Saddle at mile 4.2. From the knoll, the view west is down Whitewater Creek. Drop down to Hummingbird Saddle at mile 4.9, where water from the nearby spring and plenty of fine campsites are found.

A faint, unofficial trail leads south from the saddle to the summit of Whitewater Baldy straight ahead. Follow the trail along the shoulder of the crest, climbing steeply and slowly in the thin air. On the summit, head around to the south side where the view extends far south to the Gila River canyons. Return to the trailhead by the same route.

# 95 | THE CATWALK AND BEYOND

**Distance: 5 miles, day hike**
**Difficulty:** moderate
**Elevation range:** 5,100 to 5,800
**Elevation gain:** 1,000 feet
**Best time of year:** mid-March through November
**Water:** Whitewater Creek
**Maps:** USGS Holt Mountain and Mogollon; USFS Gila Wilderness
**Managed by:** Gila National Forest, Glenwood Ranger District
**Features:** deep, narrow canyon, historic pipeline, unique trail

The Catwalk National Recreation Trail is one of the most unusual hikes to be found anywhere in the Southwest. The route follows that of a pipeline constructed to supply water to a mining mill and town located at the mouth of Whitewater Canyon. The town of Graham was founded in 1893, just after the discovery of rich ore within the canyon. Although water always flowed within the canyon, Whitewater Creek was often dry at the town-

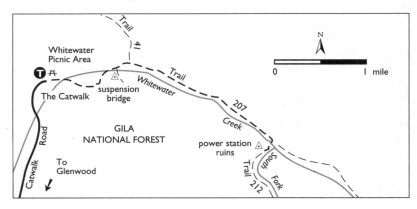

*The Catwalk is suspended above the swift waters of Whitewater Creek.*

site. The solution was to run a 4-mile-long pipe to carry water from within the canyon. As one might guess from its name, the canyon is a narrow gorge of tumbling water. The pipeline (and hence the trail) was often forced to cling to the rock walls. In the narrowest section, the pipe was suspended above the stream supported by spikes driven into the rocks. The precarious pipeline was difficult to maintain, and miners were often forced to walk the line to fix leaks. Their balancing act gave the pipeline the name "catwalk."

The gold and silver mines were worked for 20 years, and finally closed down in 1913. In 1935, the pipeline route was converted into a walking trail by the Civilian Conservation Corps. The trail maintains the unique design of the pipeline, frequently traveling above the raging water on steel grates and following the serpentine turns of the canyon, which in places is only 10 feet wide. Where the canyon widens, the route is scraped onto the cliffs high above the rapids.

From Silver City, take US 180 northwest for 62 miles to the town of Glenwood. Turn right at the signed intersection onto Catwalk Road and continue for 5 miles to the Whitewater Picnic Area. The road fords Whitewater Creek twice, the second time right at the picnic area. During spring runoff or after summer thunderstorms, these fords may be impassable. Call ahead to the Glenwood Ranger Station (see "Sources of Additional Information" in back) to check on road conditions.

The trail begins on the left (north) side of the creek at the Gila National Forest's Whitewater Picnic Area. The first mile of the trail cuts through the narrowest portion of the gorge on a series of stairs, bridges, narrow ledges, and metal grates. Because of narrow passages, hikers with backpacks will find this section of trail challenging. The roar of the water is constant. Sections of the 18-inch pipe lie scattered about, and bolts and concrete piers that once supported the pipeline are visible in many places.

About 1 mile from the start, the Catwalk Trail crosses a suspension bridge and ends on a narrow ledge. Just before the bridge, turn left at the sign marking Trail 207. The trail climbs for a short distance to intersect Trail 41 at mile 1.1. After returning to stream level, watch for sections of the pipeline that once carried water down the canyon. At mile 1.2, the route climbs and descends several steep hills on the north bank of the stream. Fishing is excellent along this stretch, particularly in the fall. Groves of tall pines offer ideal lunch spots near the water.

At mile 2.4, come to the intersection with Trail 212 where the South Fork enters Whitewater Creek. Bear right onto Trail 212, cross the stream, and look for the remains of a power generating station at the confluence. Fine campsites are found under the large trees. Return to the trailhead by the same route.

## 96 | WOOD HAUL ROAD NATIONAL RECREATION TRAIL

**Distance: 7 miles, day hike**
**Difficulty:** moderate
**Elevation range:** 6,250 to 7,350 feet
**Elevation gain:** 1,200 feet
**Best time of year:** year round
**Water:** carry water
**Map:** USGS Ft. Bayard
**Managed by:** Gila National Forest, Silver City Ranger District
**Features:** long-range views, historic road, wagon ruts

At the foot of the Pinos Altos Range, Fort Bayard was established as a frontier cavalry post in 1866. Because the post was located in open woodlands, large quantities of firewood had to be hauled down from the surrounding mountains. A steep road was built into the forest, and carefully driven wagons were used to haul the felled pines. Some sections of the road were so steep that wagon wheels had to be locked with ropes and the wagons

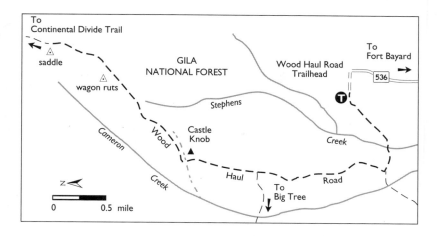

dragged down the slope. Deeply etched wagon ruts are found along the trail today. The trail passes through a state-operated elk habitat range, and hikers should watch for large herds in the woodlands.

From Central, which is located on US 180 8 miles east of Silver City, take the well-marked Fort Bayard Road north through the Fort Bayard Medical Center to FR 536. Continue north another 3.2 miles to a road marked for the Wood Haul Road Trailhead. Turn left and continue 0.2 mile to the trailhead parking area.

Begin hiking west on the trail as it passes through open juniper-piñon woodland. In 0.6 mile, the trail crosses Stephens Creek, then in a few hundred yards it turns right onto the historic wagon road heading north. Climb gradually on the wide road. At mile 1.7, bear right at a trail junction or take a 1-mile side trip to Big Tree to the left.

The trail skirts the west flank of Castle Knob before entering a drainage. At mile 2.7, bear right and begin climbing a ridge at the foot of the Pinos

*Circus beetle*

Altos Range. As the trail cuts across the slope of the ridge, watch for the deep ruts worn into the rocks by wagons heavily loaded with ponderosa pines. After the trail levels a bit, reach a saddle at mile 3.5. The trail continues another 5 miles to the Continental Divide Trail, but this saddle makes a good turnaround point.

# 97 | TURKEY CREEK HOT SPRINGS

**Distance: 10 miles, day hike or backpack**
**Difficulty:** difficult
**Elevation range:** 4,750 to 5,200 feet
**Elevation gain:** 800 feet
**Best time of year:** April to October
**Water:** Gila River, Turkey Creek
**Map:** USGS Canyon Hill
**Managed by:** Gila National Forest, Gila Wilderness,
   Wilderness Ranger District
**Features:** riparian vegetation in desert canyon, hot springs

Well-watered canyon bottoms offer some relief from the unremitting heat on the sun-blasted slopes of the Gila Wilderness. The presence of water creates a riparian environment that seems heaven-sent in the middle of the desert. The canyon of Turkey Creek is particularly inviting, offering hikers a corridor to enter the southern Diablo Range in the Gila Wilderness. Fed by springs—some of them hot—the flow in the canyon supports a tall canopy of broad-leafed trees. Most attractive is the white-trunked Arizona sycamore, which spreads its branches to create deep shade and provide welcome relief from the intense southern sun. Other portions of the canopy are formed by net-leafed hackberry, cottonwood, and western soapberry.

Scattered throughout the Gila River region are about a dozen hot

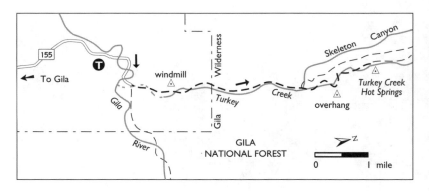

*Dozens of small pools filled with heated water line the bottom of the canyon of Turkey Creek.*

springs. Heated by radioactive decay deep within the earth, water rises to the surface through the region's extensive fault system. Hot springs are found where the heated water flows to the surface. The best of these springs is located along Turkey Creek, where water hits the surface at about 160 degrees Fahrenheit, but when mixed with creek water, cools to form delightful thermal pools. Separate soaking pools line the creek bottom for 0.25 mile, ranging in size from a private bath to a 200-foot-long pool nestled between two large rocks. Any of the pools makes a perfect reward for the sometimes difficult journey up the canyon.

As with other trips in the southwest mountains, weather plays an important role in determining the ideal hiking times. Summer temperatures can reach 100 degrees Fahrenheit. Runoff in the Gila River can block access to Turkey Creek in March and early April. Also, following summer rains, hikers must watch for flash floods in the narrow canyon bottom. The best time for a trip to the hot springs is late spring or mid- to late fall.

To reach the trailhead, drive northwest from Silver City on US 180. In 25 miles, reach the intersection with NM 211 and turn right toward the town of Gila. Continue 4 miles to the intersection with NM 153. Go straight ahead onto NM 153 as NM 211 bears left. In 4 miles, continue on the gravel FR 155. This rough road winds over a pass and drops steeply into Brushy Canyon before paralleling the Gila River. Park 9.5 miles from the end of the pavement at the end of the road. It is a good idea to check on road conditions with the Silver City Ranger District (see "Sources of Additional Information" in back) before heading out.

Begin hiking behind the dirt berm at the end of the passable road. The roadway continues to a washout where a short trail segment skirts the obstacle and rejoins the road in a few hundred feet. (When in doubt, head upstream parallel to the river.) In 0.5 mile, make the first ford of the river and continue on a wide gravel bar on the north bank. Cross the knee-deep river two more times in the next mile, with stretches of sandy road in between.

The route is a bit confusing on the other side of the third Gila River crossing. The main road angles right to stay along the river, but the trail passes near the base of the cliff to the left (north). Several routes lead across the point of land to the dry bed of Turkey Creek near an abandoned ranch with a windmill. Just beyond the windmill, a sign points to the trail. Cross the now-flowing Turkey Creek and the trail becomes easy to follow. Hikers who miss the trail should follow the dry bed of Turkey Creek north and upstream until they rejoin the trail.

Continue up the canyon of Turkey Creek under sycamores and hackberries. The stream is intermittent for the first mile, but soon flows constantly off to the right of the trail. About 3 miles from the start, the trail splits for 100 yards and the lower route along the canyon bottom eliminates the steep climb over a ridge. After the branches rejoin, watch for Skeleton Canyon coming in from the left. The trail heads up this dry canyon, climbing steeply; but to reach the hot springs, follow rock cairns that lead across Skeleton Canyon and continue hiking up the flowing Turkey Creek.

The unmaintained trail up Turkey Creek requires considerable routefinding and boulder hopping. After 0.5 mile of rough trail beyond Skeleton Canyon, pass a huge overhang on the east bank. In a few hundred yards, a deep pool forces the trail to go under a rockfall at mile 4.0. Hikers must drag their packs under a rock, then continue past some swimming holes. The route is no longer obvious, but a few trails continue upcanyon on the east bank. Green algae growing along the creek banks signal that the hot springs are just upstream. Pools, constructed of native rock, and swimming holes are found in the next 0.25 mile of canyon.

Above the springs, the canyon opens up with plenty of campsites in the oaks along the canyon floor. Slickrock terraces make this stretch attractive, and the camp spots are within a few minutes' walk of the springs. After exploring and enjoying the thermal pools, return to the trailhead by the same route.

# 98 | MIDDLE FORK/LITTLE BEAR LOOP

**Distance: 12-mile loop, backpack**
**Difficulty:** moderate
**Elevation range:** 5,800 to 6,400 feet
**Elevation gain:** 800 feet
**Best time of year:** April to October
**Water:** Middle Fork Gila River
**Maps:** USGS Woodland Park, Burnt Corral Canyon, and Little Turkey Park; USFS Gila Wilderness
**Managed by:** Gila National Forest, Gila Wilderness, Wilderness Ranger District
**Features:** wild canyon scenery, hot springs

Aldo Leopold roamed the Gila National Forest in the 1910s as a forest ranger, and the wild character of the landscape motivated him to develop the idea of preserving such areas as untouched by modern man. In 1924, 755,000 acres of the Gila was set aside as the world's first wilderness area. Although the area is not now as pristine as Leopold may have wished, the Gila has much to offer. While wild mountain scenery and abundant wildlife attract many visitors, many hikers find that the canyons of the Gila are its most appealing feature.

Of the three major headwaters of the Gila River, the Middle Fork has the best scenery and the best trout fishing. The Middle Fork Trail follows the river more than 30 miles, offering the opportunity for a 6- to 7-day trip.

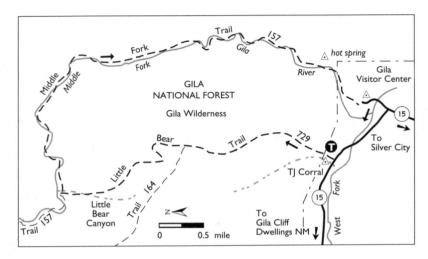

High rocky walls dominate the hike through the narrow canyon, and groves of lush riparian vegetation—sycamores, hackberries, and cottonwoods—provide relief from the open juniper woodlands that surround the gorge. Hot springs and good trout fishing in the spring and fall add to the appeal of the Middle Fork.

Hiking along the river is no easy feat. Frequent stream crossings, as many as six per mile, are tiring at low water and impossible during spring runoff and following heavy summer storms. The trail itself experiences frequent washouts and is often difficult to find. Hiking on sand and loose cobbles is apt to tire hikers faster than walking on a smooth trail. Plan on at least 6 hours of walking to complete this loop, and add more time to enjoy the many attractions of the canyon. Take advantage of numerous fine campsites found along the canyon floor. Before starting on a hike in the Middle Fork Canyon, contact the Wilderness Ranger District for current conditions. Hikers should carry a pair of running shoes or all-terrain sandals to wear on the stream crossings.

From the intersection of NM 90 and US 180 in Silver City, go east on US 180 1 mile to the junction with Pinos Altos Road, NM 15. Turn left and travel the winding and slow NM 15 through the Gila National Forest. In 22 miles, continue straight on NM 15 at the intersection with NM 35. Forty-two miles from Silver City, turn left just before reaching the Gila Visitor Center. Continue toward Gila Cliff Dwellings National Monument 1 mile to the TJ Corral Trailhead and park there.

Begin hiking on the Little Bear Trail 729. The trail ascends a sloping mesa in open juniper woodland. It is a hot route in the middle of the day, so plan an early start and carry plenty of water. In 2.2 miles, pass the junction with the Woodland Trail 164 on the left. Continue straight to cross a small pass and begin to descend into Little Bear Canyon. At the canyon bottom, bear left and

*The Little Bear Trail leads through a shady canyon to the Middle Fork of the Gila River.*

walk under tall pines—which provide welcome shade—in an interesting, narrow canyon. At mile 4.1, intersect the Middle Fork Trail 157. Campsites are found near here on the bench above the Middle Fork of the Gila River.

Continue on the described loop by turning right onto the Middle Fork Trail and walking downcanyon. The trail stays close to the river and soon makes the first of about thirty river crossings between here and the end of the trail. The trail alternates between crossing gravel bars, sand hills, and grassy meadows. As it passes through riparian areas over the next 2 miles, the trail is often difficult to follow. Hikers should find the easiest route and take their time making the knee-deep stream crossings. Soaring orange cliffs dominate the narrowest part of the canyon. Watch for raptors circling just above the rocks.

At mile 9.5, look for a small hot spring located on the left riverbank. The canyon broadens as it heads for its junction with the West Fork of the Gila. After crossing to the east bank, climb a short hill and reach the backcountry parking area at the Gila Visitor Center. Exit the parking lot and walk the entrance road out to NM 15. Turn right and walk the highway 1.2 miles to the TJ Corral Trailhead.

# 99 | WEST FORK OF THE GILA RIVER

**Distance: 14 miles, day hike or backpack**
**Difficulty:** moderate
**Elevation range:** 5,700 to 6,100 feet
**Elevation gain:** 500 feet
**Best time of year:** April to October
**Water:** carry water
**Maps:** USGS Little Turkey Park and Woodland Park; USFS
   Gila Wilderness
**Managed by:** Gila National Forest, Gila Wilderness,
   Wilderness Ranger District
**Features:** fine views, fishing, historic ruins

The abundant wildlife, gentle climate, and presence of running water in the mountains of the Gila River headwaters have led to a long history of use by Native Americans and settlers of European descent. People of the Mogollon Culture built small villages in sheltering caves in the canyon walls overlooking flats along the rivers. Later, Apaches lived a nomadic lifestyle in the canyons and on the mesas, hunting, growing crops, and enjoying the region's many hot springs. Anglo hunters and ranchers followed in the 1880s.

The West Fork of the Gila River strings little snippets of this history together like beads on a necklace. Walking up the West Fork Trail, hikers first encounter the ruins of a cabin and the grave of one of its owners. The Grudging brothers ran cattle along the West Fork, and a dispute about stolen cows ended in the murder of Bill Grudging in 1893. A bit farther up the canyon, in a cave above their former agricultural fields, sits a small pueblo used by Mogollon farmers about 900 years ago. Nat Straw Canyon reminds visitors of the colorful hunter who roamed these mountains for 40 years and whose stories were so outrageous that he earned recognition in a 1931 *Vanity Fair* piece called, "Golden Liars of the Golden West."

The trail along the West Fork of the Gila River runs 34 miles from FR

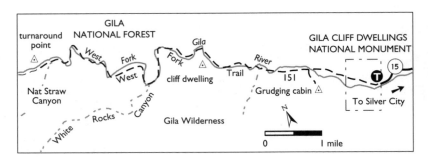

507 to Gila Cliff Dwellings National Monument and offers the opportunity for a long immersion in the backcountry. The lower miles of the trail receive the most use of any in the Gila Wilderness, but also offer the easiest access and the greatest concentration of historical features. Day hikers can wander up the trail to the Grudging Cabin or the cliff dwelling beyond. Those interested in a one- or two-night exploration of the canyon should set their sights on Nat Straw Canyon as a camp spot. The trip takes in the

*Pools along the West Fork of the Gila River*
(Photo by Bob Julyan)

features of the lower canyon, including some great swimming and fishing holes, and leaves the crowds behind.

From the intersection of NM 90 and US 180 in Silver City, go east on US 180 1 mile to the junction with Pinos Altos Road, NM 15. Turn left and travel the winding and slow NM 15 through the Gila National Forest. In 22 miles, continue straight on NM 15 at the intersection with NM 35. Forty-two miles from Silver City, turn left just before reaching the Gila Visitor Center to stay on NM 15. Continue 2 miles to Gila Cliff Dwellings National Monument, and park. The trailhead is located at the west end of the parking area.

Begin hiking on the West Fork Trail 151, heading up the canyon of the West Fork under a thin canopy of pines. The first river crossing is at mile 1.2. Once across, hikers may take a short spur trail to the left that leads up a rise to the Grudging cabin and grave. Continuing up the canyon, the trail twists through picturesque meadows with orange cliffs for a backdrop. Sycamores, hackberries, and cottonwoods provide cooling shade along the river. Make several river crossings over the next 1.5 miles of pleasant, flat walking.

As the canyon narrows 2.3 miles from the start, the river winds between towering orange walls. Watch for a small cliff dwelling in a prominent cave on the left (southwest) wall of the canyon. After another mile of traveling up the winding canyon, pass the entrance to White Rocks Canyon to the left.

Around two sweeping turns in the river, the trail traverses a narrow stretch near mile 5. A few minutes' walk after a horseshoe bend at mile 5.8 leads to a broad stretch of meadows near Nat Straw Canyon. Excellent campsites are located from the confluence upstream along a mile of flat canyon bottom, with swimming holes, brown trout lies, and shady trees nearby. From this point, hikers can explore farther up the canyon or turn around and return by the same route.

# 100 | BLACK RANGE CREST TRAIL

**Distance: 10.5 miles one-way, day hike or backpack**
**Difficulty:** moderate
**Elevation range:** 7,100 to 10,000 feet
**Elevation gain:** 2,100 feet
**Best time of year:** April to October
**Water:** carry water
**Maps:** USGS Hillsboro Peak; USFS Aldo Leopold Wilderness
**Managed by:** Gila National Forest, Aldo Leopold Wilderness, Wilderness Ranger District
**Features:** fine views

The huge Aldo Leopold Wilderness spans the crest of the Black Range from near Emory Pass to Diamond Peak 25 miles to the north. The wilderness

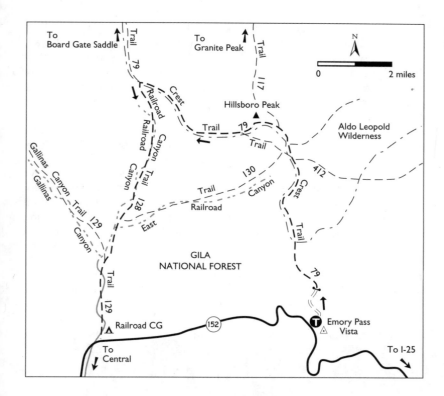

boasts an extensive network of trails that sees few hikers. The trail to Hillsboro Peak follows the southern border of the wilderness and offers fine views into the wilder reaches of the Black Range. The views along the Crest Trail and from the peak itself make this hike a New Mexico classic.

Reach the trailhead on Emory Pass via NM 152, 31 miles west of I-25 and about 33 miles east of the town of Central. Park at the Emory Pass Vista. Hikers wishing to do this hike as described should leave a second, shuttle vehicle about 5 miles to the west on NM 152 at the Gallinas Canyon Trailhead at Railroad Campground.

Begin hiking from the vista on a dirt road marked as the Crest Trail 79. Follow the road past a helipad and continue through a gate where the road becomes a trail. Begin a moderate climb that remains steady most of the way to Hillsboro Peak, passing through open conifer forest that offers frequent views to the north and east. At mile 1.9, enter the Aldo Leopold Wilderness and continue climbing on the east side of a long ridge. At mile 3, reach a small saddle before resuming the climb, now on the west side of the ridge. Watch for glimpses of Hillsboro Peak ahead.

At mile 3.6, continue straight at a four-way intersection, passing the Hillsboro Peak Bypass Trail 412 on the left. The trail swings to the south side of the peak, where snow may be found near the summit through late April. Just below the peak at mile 4.8, bear left to stay on the Crest Trail, passing Trail 117 to Granite Peak. The large, flat area of the summit of Hillsboro Peak offers many good campsites, and the views from the fire lookout tower are especially fine in all directions. Hikers with only one vehicle may choose to turn around here to return to the trailhead by the same route.

For those with a shuttle, continue west on the Crest Trail, now walking downhill and heading toward Board Gate Saddle. The Bypass Trail 412 rejoins the Crest Trail at mile 5.2. The trail stays near the crest, crossing several saddles that offer scattered campsites as well as more views to the north and west. At mile 6.8, intersect the Railroad Canyon Trail 128 at a confusing intersection. Bear left onto the trail on the west side of the drainage, heading south and downhill. The trail follows the bottom of the drainage, making frequent crossings. At mile 8.7, intersect Trail 130. (The Emory Pass Trailhead can be reached via a strenuous climb on this trail.) Continue downstream, bearing left at mile 9.6 at the intersection with the Gallinas Canyon Trail 129 to join Trail 129. Continue to follow the stream, which below this point usually has running water. Cross the stream many times in the next mile, reaching Railroad Campground at mile 10.5.

*Dipper tracks on rocks*

# SOURCES OF ADDITIONAL INFORMATION

## NATIONAL MONUMENTS AND NATIONAL PARKS

Bandelier National Monument
HCR 1, Box 1, Suite 15
Los Alamos, NM 87544
(505) 672-0343
*www.nps.gov/band/*

Carlsbad Caverns National Park
3225 National Parks Highway
Carlsbad, NM 88220
(505) 785-2232
*www.nps.gov/cave/*

Chaco Culture National Historical Park
Star Route 4, Box 6500
Bloomfield, NM 87413
(505) 786-7014
*www.nps.gov/chcu/*

El Malpais National Monument
123 East Roosevelt Avenue
Grants, NM 87020
(505) 285-4641
*www.nps.gov/elma/*

Kasha-Katuwe Tent Rocks National Monument
Albuquerque Field Office
Bureau of Land Management
435 Montaño Road
Albuquerque, NM 87107
(505) 761-8700
*www.nm.blm.gov/www/aufo/tent_rocks/tent_rocks.html*

White Sands National Monument
P.O. Box 1086
Holloman Air Force Base, NM 88330
(505) 479-6124
*www.nps.gov/whsa/*

## BUREAU OF LAND MANAGEMENT, NEW MEXICO

*www.nm.blm.gov/*

Albuquerque Field Office
435 Montaño Road NE
Albuquerque, NM 87107
(505) 761-8700
*www.nm.blm.gov/www/aufo/aufo_home*

El Malpais National Conservation Area
P.O. Box 846
Grants, NM 87020
(505) 287-7911

Farmington Field Office
1235 La Plata Highway, Suite A
Farmington, NM 87401
(505) 599-8900
*www.nm.blm.gov/www/ffo/ffo_home*

Las Cruces Field Office
1800 Marquess Street
Las Cruces, NM 88005
(505) 525-4300
*www.nm.blm.gov/www/lcfo/lcfo_home*

Taos Field Office
226 Cruz Alta Road
Taos, NM 87571
(505) 758-8851
*www.nm.blm.gov/www/tafo/
tafo_hom*e

## U.S. FOREST SERVICE, NEW MEXICO
*www.fs.fed.us/recreation/states/
nm.shtml*

## Carson National Forest
*www.fs.fed.us/r3/carson/*

Forest Supervisor
208 Cruz Alta Road
Taos, NM 87571
(505) 758-6200

Camino Real Ranger District
P.O. Box 68
Peñasco, NM 87553
(505) 587-2255

Canjilon Ranger District
P.O. Box 488
Canjilon, NM 87515
(505) 684-2489

Questa Ranger District
P.O. Box 110
Questa, NM 87556
(505) 586-0520

Tres Piedras Ranger District
P.O. Box 38
Tres Piedras, NM 87577
(505) 758-8678

## Cibola National Forest
*www.fs.fed.us/r3/cibola/*

Forest Supervisor
2113 Osuna Road NE, Suite A
Albuquerque, NM 87113-1001
(505) 346-2650

Magdalena Ranger District
P.O. Box 45
Magdalena, NM 87825
(505) 854-2281

Mount Taylor Ranger District
1800 Lobo Canyon Road
Grants, NM 87020
(505) 287-8833

Mountainair Ranger District
P.O. Box 69
Mountainair, NM 87036-0069
(505) 847-2990

Sandia Ranger District
11776 Highway 337
Tijeras, NM 87059
(505) 281-3304

## Gila National Forest
*www.fs.fed.us/r3/gila/*

Forest Supervisor
3005 East Camino del Bosque
Silver City, NM 88061
(505) 388-8201

Glenwood Ranger District
P.O. Box 8
Glenwood, NM 88039
(505) 539-2481

Luna Work Center
P.O. Box 91
Luna, NM 87824
(505) 547-2612
Reserve Ranger District
P.O. Box 170
Reserve, NM 87830
(505) 533-6232

Silver City Ranger District
3005 East Camino del Bosque
Silver City, NM 88061
(505) 538-2771

Wilderness Ranger District
HC 68, Box 50
Mimbres, NM 88049
(505) 536-2250

## Lincoln National Forest
*www.fs.fed.us/r3/lincoln/*

Forest Supervisor
1101 New York Avenue
Alamogordo, NM 88310-6992
(505) 434-7200

Guadalupe Ranger District
Federal Building, Room 159
Carlsbad, NM 88220
(505) 885-4181

Sacramento Ranger District
P.O. Box 288
Cloudcroft, NM 88317
(505) 682-2551

Smokey Bear Ranger District
901 Mechem Drive
Ruidoso, NM 88345
(505) 257-4095

## Santa Fe National Forest
*www.fs.fed.us/r3/sfe/*

Forest Supervisor
P.O. Box 1689
Santa Fe, NM 87504
(505) 438-7840

Coyote Ranger District
P.O. Box 160
Coyote, NM 87012
(505) 638-5526

Cuba Ranger District
P.O. Box 130
Cuba, NM 87013
(505) 289-3264

Española Ranger District
1710 North Riverside Drive
Española, NM 87533
(505) 753-7331

Jemez Ranger District
P.O. Box 150
Jemez Springs, NM 87025
(505) 829-3535

Pecos Ranger District
P.O. Drawer 429
Pecos, NM 87552
(505) 757-6121

## OTHER
Leave No Trace
1-800-332-4100

New Mexico Tourism Division
1-800-545-2040

Northwest New Mexico Visitor
Center
1900 E Santa Fe Avenue
Grants, NM 87020
(505) 876-2783

United States Geological Survey
Western Distribution Branch
Box 25286, Federal Center
Building 41
Denver, CO 80225

# INDEX

# ABOUT THE AUTHOR

Born and raised in the suburbs of Philadelphia, Craig Martin fell in love with the mountains of New Mexico at the age of twelve when a fellow Boy Scout shared pictures of his trip to Philmont Scout Ranch near Cimarron. He has lived in New Mexico since 1987, exploring the state on foot, bike, skis, or with a fly rod in hand.

After working as a carpenter, a naturalist for the Delaware State Parks and the National Park Service, a geology instructor, and a junior high school science teacher, Martin took over primary care of his then-infant daughter and began a career as a freelance writer. Since 1990 he has written more than three hundred publications. Most recently Martin has been a driving force in the restoration, rebuilding, and expansion of the trail system devastated by the Cerro Grande Fire around his hometown of Los Alamos, New Mexico. Martin lives in Los Alamos with his wife, June, and children, Jessica and Alex, who share his love of the outdoors.

THE MOUNTAINEERS, founded in 1906, is a nonprofit outdoor activity and conservation club, whose mission is "to explore, study, preserve, and enjoy the natural beauty of the outdoors. . . . " Based in Seattle, Washington, the club is now the third-largest such organization in the United States, with 15,000 members and five branches throughout Washington State.

The Mountaineers sponsors both classes and year-round outdoor activities in the Pacific Northwest, which include hiking, mountain climbing, ski-touring, snowshoeing, bicycling, camping, kayaking and canoeing, nature study, sailing, and adventure travel. The club's conservation division supports environmental causes through educational activities, sponsoring legislation, and presenting informational programs. All club activities are led by skilled, experienced volunteers, who are dedicated to promoting safe and responsible enjoyment and preservation of the outdoors.

If you would like to participate in these organized outdoor activities or the club's programs, consider a membership in The Mountaineers. For information and an application, write or call The Mountaineers, Club Headquarters, 300 Third Avenue West, Seattle, WA 98119; 206-284-6310.

The Mountaineers Books, an active, nonprofit publishing program of the club, produces guidebooks, instructional texts, historical works, natural history guides, and works on environmental conservation. All books produced by The Mountaineers Books fulfill the club's mission.

*Send or call for our catalog of more than 500 outdoor titles:*

The Mountaineers Books
1001 SW Klickitat Way, Suite 201
Seattle, WA 98134
800-553-4453
mbooks@mountaineersbooks.org
www.mountaineersbooks.org